Rainer Haubrich, Hans Wolfgang Hoffmann, Philipp Meuser

Berlin | The Architecture Guide

Edited by Markus Sebastian Braun

D1235650

Rainer Haubrich, Hans Wolfgang Hoffmann, Philipp Meuser

Berlin | The Architecture Guide

Edited by Markus Sebastian Braun
Photographs by Andreas Muhs

Acknowledgement

At this point, thanks go to Cornelia Dörries, Eva Maria Froschauer, Ansgar Oswald and Gernot Weckherlin for their work on this publication. Our thanks also go out to the team at the Architecture Studio in the Senate Department in Berlin, particularly Peter Jürgens, Takis Sgouros and Archimedes Siontas for the creative design of the route maps.

The Deutsche Bibliothek is registering this publication in Deutsche Nationalbibliographie; detailed bibliographical information can be found on the internet at http://dnb.ddb.de

ISBN 10: 3-938780-09-6
ISBN 13: 978-3-938780-09-1

Basics of the maps:
3D overview map with kind authorisation by the Senate Department for Urban Development, Architecture Studio

1st Edition 2006 (German first edition published in 2001 by Quadriga-Verlag)

Editor: Franziska Nauck
Translation: Fremdspracheninstitut Dresden
Design: port-d Burgold & Neumann GbR, Berlin
Typesetting: tiff.any GmbH, Berlin
Cover design: Michaela Prinz
Route text: Per von Groote

Contents

Preface

The time was ripe for a new architectural guide to Berlin. Following the turbulent years of transformation and continuous change, the city now boasts more completed buildings than cranes. The most significant of the major projects are now either finished, under construction or are the subject of a resolution for their implementation. The contours of the new Berlin are becoming more apparent by the day. Bringing this architectural landscape (the most significant and varied in the country) to the attention of a broader audience is the purpose of this architectural guide. It is now available in an English edition, updated and further improved.

The concept is a different one to that followed by most architectural guides. For the first time, the most important structures in Berlin (from the Middle Ages to the present day) are illustrated in colour. The result is a more precise image of the architecture; the book acquires a more sensual edge. The properties, some 520 in number, are ordered chronologically, not according to district. This enables a characteristic image of the individual eras to be achieved, one glance sufficient to determine how differently (or uniformly) buildings were constructed in specific historic periods. Brief introductions to each period serve as reminders of the political, economic and cultural environments pervading in the city at the time. In addition, we have studded the book with focal points, present-

ing significant ensembles such as the Museumsinsel or Potsdamer Platz, construction types such as the Berlin tenement house or detailing building techniques such as industrial prefabrication. In conclusion, there are portraits of the most influential architects and city planners of the respective eras. A further innovation is the three different forms of entry, each indicated by a small logo: demolished buildings, significant green areas and construction "flops" of the age.

A different author has taken the responsibility for each era: Rainer Haubrich for the time leading up to the 20th century, Hans Wolfgang Hoffmann for Modern and Post-Modern, Philipp Meuser for the time following the fall of the Wall. The fact that the personal preferences and judgements of the three authors are apparent from time to time is by all means intentional: it makes the book more vivid, more surprising and, hopefully, more stimulating.

We have supplemented the book concept with 10 route suggestions, making it possible to experience the interaction of the different eras of the Berlin urban landscape on foot.

If this book manages to arouse interest in the architecture of Berlin then it was worth the effort.

Markus Sebastian Braun (ed.),
Rainer Haubrich,
Hans Wolfgang Hoffmann,
Philipp Meuser

From a Trading Post to the Capital of Prussia: The Development of Berlin to 1790 (1)

Berlin is the parvenu amongst the great European capitals. The Romans never made it this far; there are no ruins to tell of earlier civilisation. There are no Romanesque churches or Gothic cathedrals. Berlin was only mentioned for the first time in a document dating from 1237. And even there the name is not "Berlin", but that of its sister town "Cölln", later incorporated into Berlin. At that time the population of the small twin settlement on the River Spree was no more than a few thousand. Berlin-Cölln established itself between the towns of Spandau and Köpenick (both at that time greater in importance) as a trading town located at the sole favourable crossing point of the river. Until the middle of the 17th century, the architecture of the town was of no more than regional significance.

It was not until the reign of the Great Elector, who returned to devastated Brandenburg from the Netherlands at the end of the Thirty Years War that Berlin began to develop into an influential, high-ranking town. The active support of immigration led to an influx of qualified migrants to the town, predominantly from France.

The first architecture of European significance was added to Berlin under the Elector Friedrich III, who crowned himself King Friedrich I in Prussia in 1701. This took the form of the Zeughaus (no. 16) and the Königliches Schloss (no. 7). Important impulses for cultural and academic circles initiated with Queen Sophie Charlotte. She managed to tempt the famous philosopher and mathematician Gottfried Wilhelm Leibniz to Berlin. On the death of Friedrich I in 1713, the town boasted a population of 60,000 – a modest figure in comparison to Paris, the capital of the "sun king" Louis XIV, who died two years later.

The westward expansion of the city begun under the first Prussian king was continued under Friedrich Wilhelm I. Based upon a rectangular street plan, Friedrichstadt included three characteristic geometric squares, each of them laid out before a city gate: the square of Pariser Platz, the octagon of Leipziger Platz and the circular form of present-day Mehringplatz (no. 333).

Architecture of European rank for the first time – Carl Friedrich Fechhelm:
View of the boulevard Unter den Linden (1755/1765).

Under Friedrich II, soon to receive the epithet "the Great", the Kingdom of Prussia developed into a major European power and its capital, Berlin, to a city in which trade and commerce, arts and science all flourished. The urban image was altered by the increase in height of the single and twin-storey houses into three and four-storey buildings, with extensions to the rear in the form of side wings making an appearance for the first time. With the Forum Fridericianum (no. 32), a new state forum was created alongside the historic city centre, the aim of which was to reflect the enlightened approach of the monarch to the concept of the state. The most significant construction of this ensemble, the Königliche Oper (no. 27) by Georg Wenzeslaus von Knobelsdorff, was also the first freestanding opera house in Germany. Independent of the Royal Court and the state administration, the Berlin Enlightenment was promoted by citizens, predominantly of Jewish origin, with an interest in academic and literary figures, such as the publisher Friedrich Nicolai, Moses Mendelssohn and Gotthold Ephraim Lessing.

In 1800, on the eve of the Napoleonic War and the great Prussian reforms, Berlin numbered 170,000 inhabitants. The borders of the built-up area stretched from Torstraße in the north to the present-day Mehringplatz in the south, from Pariser Platz in the west to the Frankfurter Tor in the east. The proportions of Berlin were manageable compared to other European cities: Paris at that time had 700,000 inhabitants, London 800,000.

Berlin was negligent in the treatment of its architectural heritage from the very beginning. A large percentage of the Renaissance and Baroque structures were pulled down in the Gründerzeit era, an era of mass industrial expansion dating from 1871, and replaced with new buildings. The destruction of the Second World War and the large-scale redevelopment of the GDR era had the consequence that the core of buildings from the founding era of Berlin can scarcely be perceived today. The few surviving Medieval, Renaissance and Baroque buildings stand in isolation, like museum exhibits in the piecemeal centre of the city.   rh

Nikolaikirche (2)
St. Nicholas Church
Started in 1230
Nikolaikirchplatz

The Nikolaikirche is the oldest stone building in the city. Construction of the church, still the most significant in Berlin, was probably begun around 1230, when Berlin received its city charter. The first version was completed in 1244. The church, a pillar basilica of stone with fortified tower, stands on a hill near the first Spree crossing at the Mühlendamm. The current triple nave structure with cross vault was erected in 1380, following a devastating fire. In 1452, the Marienkapelle, with its ornate gable, was financed by Ulrich Zeuschel. For centuries, the church had just one octagonal spire. In 1876, Hermann Blankenstein added a second tower, in brick, and two spires. The church was severely damaged towards the end of the Second World War, with the interior gutted by fire and most of the nave pillars collapsing. In the scope of the reconstruction of the Nikolaiviertel (no. 362) for the 750-year anniversary of Berlin, the church was reconstructed as a museum, a process that enabled many fittings that had been stored elsewhere to be replaced in their original position. The early history of Berlin to the end of the Thirty Years War can be traced here.

Franziskaner-Klosterkirche (3)
Franciscan Cloister Church
circa 1260
Klosterstraße 73A

Unknown to most citizens of the city and scarcely noticed, the remains of the most significant Gothic structure in Berlin stand just yards from a bustling highway. The monastery was founded by Franciscan monks in 1249. The brick construction was erected under the influence of a craftsmen's guild that worked on the Brandenburg Cathedral in the second half of the 13th century. In keeping with the building tradition of the mendicant order, the western facade had no tower. It was not until 1844 that two flanking towers were added. In 1574, it became the home of the Gymnasium Zum Grauen Kloster, the first grammar school in Berlin. The church was heavily damaged in the Second World War, with the remains of the monastery removed in 1968

during the widening of Grunerstraße. Today, the ruins of the church serve as an open-air sculpture gallery, with works including two pillar capitals from the Eosander portal of the Berlin Stadtschloss (no. 7). There are plans to move the school Zum Grauen Kloster, now situated in the western part of the city, back to this historic location. This would enable the ruins of the Franciscan church to be rebuilt and used as a function room.

ehem. Heiliggeist-Kapelle (4)
former Holy Ghost Chapel
before 1270
Spandauer Straße 1

Like the Franziskanerkirche (no. 3), the Heiliggeist-Spital, a hospital, was also located on the periphery of Berlin, directly at the walls of the city. The hospital, including the chapel, was first mentioned in 1272, and was demolished in 1825. Only the chapel remains today. The early Gothic brick construction dates largely from the late 13th century and consists of a single nave, rectangular room. The stone vault was added at the end of the 15th century. In 1905 the chapel was integrated into the new Handelshochschule, a commercial college by Cremer & Wolffenstein. Today, both of the buildings are used by the economics faculty of Humboldt University.

Marienkirche (5)
St. Mary's Church
circa 1270
Karl-Liebknecht-Straße 8

The church, a brick structure on a stone plinth, was built as the third parish church of Berlin and Cölln for the new town laid out in the mid 13th century. The oldest section is the single nave chancel, with other sections added and altered until into the 18th century. The closing section of the tower was destroyed or removed on several occasions. The current pyramidal tower roof dates back to 1790 and was created by Carl Gotthard Langhans in the mix of Gothic and Classical elements popular at that time. The interior is noteworthy for the Totentanz frieze and Andreas Schlüter's marble pulpit (see no. 18). The destruction in the Second World War of the densely built Marienviertel and its subsequent demolition means that today the church stands alone and isolated.

Stadtmauer (6)
City Wall
early 14th century
Waisenstraße

A small remnant of the Medieval Berlin wall remains parallel to Waisenstraße. This, the first city wall, was built in the middle of the 13th century, with the wall visible today dating from a renovation and reinforcement of the wall from the beginning of the 14th century. The original height of the wall was approximately 13 feet. Following the construction of the Baroque city fortifications in the 17th century further outside the original wall, sections of the city wall received the addition of residential dwellings. In this manner, the fragment in Waisenstraße was also retained. In the vicinity is a short row of bourgeois houses, the core of which is Medieval, with the facade dating from the 18th century. One of these also houses the well-known tavern "Zur letzten Instanz".

11

Berlin Palace (7)

Is there any other city in the civilised world with such a gaping void at its centre as Berlin? Where the main axes of the city floor plan converge in a giant, dull car park with a multipurpose building? Here, on the Spree Island, the Stadtschloss stood for 500 years. Despite surviving the war with only minor damage, it was demolished in 1950 on the orders of Walter Ulbricht, who saw the building as a symbol of Prussian militarism, and wished to create an area for mass parades on the spot. The sole surviving part of the castle was Portal IV of the Lustgarten front, integrated into the facade of the Staatsratsgebäude (no. 308) in 1964 – partially in the form of a copy. The GDR considered it to be worthy of saving due to the fact that Karl Liebknecht declared the Socialist Republic from here in 1918. The location of other fragments of the historic facades and the rubble from the demolition remains unclear to this day. Much of it lays in museums and depots, with other sections thought to be in undeveloped rubble tips around the city.

This was the end of a significant monument, one that represented the overall development of Prussian architecture like no other. Begun around 1450, it was continually extended and amended by the master builders of the time. The Baroque facade of Andreas Schlüter (no. 18) was created around 1700, based upon the Palazzo Madama in Rome. With the dome of Friedrich August Stüler, the castle received its final external appearance in 1850. The most famous part of the grounds was the easternmost of the two interior courtyards, named Schlüterhof in honour of its creator.

The overwhelming significance of the Stadtschloss for Berlin lay in its urban planning function. The entire westward expansion of the city hinged upon the position and architecture of this colossus, with neighbouring structures such as the Baroque Zeughaus (no. 16), the Altes Museum (no. 62) and the Bauakademie (no. 65) by Karl Friedrich Schinkel designed for their relation to the castle. The Lustgarten frontage once formed the vanishing point of the boulevard Unter den Linden, which today merely runs into empty space.

The staging of the castle backdrop in summer 1993, a private initiative on the part of the Hamburg businessman Wilhelm von Boddien, provided an impressive insight into how the powerful bulk of the castle would reunite the disparate structures at the centre of the city. Even opponents of reconstruction found themselves swayed by this argument.

When built in 1891, this was one of the biggest wells in the world: the Neptune Fountain on Schlossplatz. (Photograph from pre-war times)

After years of intense public discussion a committee of experts appointed by the Federal Government and the State of Berlin suggested that the Palast der Republik (no. 337), built by the GDR government between 1973 and 1976, should be dismantled, and that the Berliner Schloss (no. 7) should be partially be reconstructed as a building for the arts, a conference centre and a public library. The new "Humboldtforum" will be a modern building behind the reconstructed baroque facades. As of now there is no official date for the rebuilding. A temporary park is planned on the site.   rh

13

The Berlin Palace exemplified, as no other edifice did, the development of Prussian architecture.

Jagdschloss Grunewald (8)
Grunewald Hunting Palace
1542
Am Grunewaldsee
Caspar Theiß

In the mid 16th century, the Grunewald was probably still pristine forest, with Berlin both small and very far away. In this wilderness, the Elector Joachim II had Caspar Theiß build a hunting lodge, directly adjoining the lake. Today, the octagonal tower remains, along with parts of the interior fittings. The plain, white-rendered building was surrounded by a horseshoe of utility buildings. In 1701, Nering and Grünberg reworked the grounds in Baroque form. Since 1932 it has been used as a state picture gallery, with the building reopening in 1949 after the removal of war damage; the first museum in Berlin to do so.

Zitadelle Spandau (9)
Spandau Citadel
1583
Am Juliusturm

The Zitadelle Spandau is one of the best-preserved fortresses in Europe. Constructed on the site of a Slavic settlement, it represented a strategically important

defensive position at the gates of Berlin. Francesco Chiaramella da Gandino designed the fortress along northern Italian lines, with four arrow shaped bastions. Work began on construction in 1560, incorporating the Juliusturm, dating from the first half of the 13th century, and other remnants of a medieval castle. The Juliusturm is the oldest secular building in Berlin. It received its current battlements in 1838, from a design by Schinkel (see no. 44). Towards the end of the 16th century, the fortress, surrounded entirely by water, was largely complete, with more buildings added in the interior of the fortress in the 19th century. The sole martial activity involving the fortress was in 1813, during the Napoleonic occupation. Today, the building houses the Heimatmuseum Spandau, a museum of local history.

Ribbeck-Haus (10)
Ribbeck House
1624
Breite Straße 35

The sole surviving Renaissance building in Berlin, and even this building is anything but original 17th century in its current condition, not least due to the changed nature of Breite Straße, significantly widened in the GDR years. The house was created for Georg von Ribbeck, a counsellor to the Elector, by combining

two older buildings. In 1804 the four gables were replaced by a third storey – evidence of which can be seen in the different window forms. On the orders of the King, the old Renaissance dormer gable was used on the new building. The richly ornamented 17th century round arch door was also replaced with a replica in the 1960s.

Schloss Köpenick (11)
Köpenick Palace
1681
Schlossinsel
Rutger van Langevelt,
Johann Arnold Nering

Schloss Köpenick is the oldest remaining castle in the Berlin region and the most significant Baroque secular building before Andreas Schlüter (no. 18). It was built in 1677, on the southern part of an island, for Elector Friedrich, the later King Friedrich I, in Dutch Baroque style. The building replaced an older hunting lodge on the same location. The building was augmented a short time later by Johann Arnold Nering in the axis of the main building, with the addition of a castle chapel, two-storey gallery and the portal to the Schlossbrücke. The interior contains a twin oak stairway and stately vestibule with heavy, early Baroque ceiling stucco. Since 1963 the building has housed an arts and crafts museum with an important collection; today it is an outpost of the Haus am Kulturforum (see no. 311).

Schlosspark Charlottenburg (12)
Charlottenburg Palace Grounds
from 1700
Simeon Godeau, Jacques Blondel

GARDEN The Schlosspark was initiated as a regular Baroque facility along the Spree, later expanding to the northwest. It comprises a large Baroque parterre, extending the main axis of the castle, and an adjoining landscaped park with Luiseninsel, ponds, waterways and bridges. Following the Second World War, the broderie parterre between castle and carp pond was reconstructed according to French engravings from the 18th century in the form created in 1737 by Jacques Blondel, with fountain basins and lateral avenues of lime trees. The park is decorated with cast iron benches in a design by Schinkel (no. 44), together with numerous sculptures, in particular from the 19th century (some of which are copies).

15

In the Heart of Friedrichstadt – the Gendarmenmarkt (13)

The Gendarmenmarkt is often described as one of the most beautiful squares in Europe. This reputation is wholly due to three large structures on the square, as the historic structures edging the square (of which only four survive to the present day) were not prominent, with the same true of the very different buildings of recent decades. The square is home to the Schauspielhaus, built by Karl Friedrich Schinkel (no. 44). It appears almost symmetrical, flanked as it is by the Französische Dom – to the north – and the Deutsche Dom. It is a rare passer-by who notices that the Französische Dom stands slightly nearer the Schauspielhaus (no. 54) than its counterpart to the south.

The square was originally intended to be Friedrichstädtischer Markt, a market place, in the centre at the end of Friedrichstadt, laid out in rectangular form at the end of the 17th century. By decree, one church was built for the Huguenot French émigrés and one for Germans. The French church, completed in 1705 to plans by Louis Cayart, was based upon the chief church of the Huguenots in Charenton, near Paris, which was destroyed in 1685. Martin Grünberg built the German church in 1708, on a floor plan that continued that of the Parochialkirche (no. 14): a pentagon with five semi-circular cupolas.

In 1735 the soldier King Friedrich Wilhelm I had stables added to both churches for his Gens d'armes regiment – the origin of the name Gendarmenmarkt. His son Friedrich II had these removed again, instead commissioning Karl von Gontard with the construction of two, completely identical, domed tower constructions, built between 1781–85. These towers had no practical purpose, serving merely as ornamental architecture for the decoration of the square.

The present-day outer appearance of the German church dates back to a reconstruction in 1882, with the interior redesigned along modern lines following reunification, for the display of German historical exhibits. In 1905, the facades of the French church were also altered, by Otto March, in neo-Baroque style.

Exhibition architectures to adorn the square: the Deutscher Dom.

The Gendarmenmarkt was heavily damaged in the Second World War. The GDR rebuilt the three grand buildings on the square – in partially altered form. Noteworthy here is the exposed stairway on the western side of the French church, a new addition from the early 1980s. In order to divide the interior of the church into two halls, the floor was lowered and a new suspended ceiling added in approximately 13-feet height. As a consequence, the stairway had to be augmented, leading to both the new lower church as well as the upper church hall. The Baroque-style design blended effortlessly into the existing ensemble. The square was renamed Platz der Akademie in 1950, a decision reversed in 1991. The peripheral buildings opposite the Schauspielhaus allow a comparison to be made between two architectural levels: in the northeast stand three historic pre-fabricated building from the closing years of the GDR (see no. 347, 370, 374), to the southeast three commercial buildings in the Critical Reconstruction style of the 1990s: by Hilmer-Sattler (light beige), Max Dudler (dark grey) and Josef Paul Kleihues (brown). rh

17

One of the most beautiful squares of Europe: the Gendarmenmarkt.

Parochialkirche (14)
Parochial Church
1703
Klosterstraße 66–67
Johann Arnold Nering, Martin Grünberg

This church, designed by Johann Arnold Nering along Italian lines, possesses a form unique in the Berlin region: a square floor plan with four semi-circular cupolas. Following the death of Nering, Martin Grünberg executed the plan in a simpler form. On the Klosterstraße side, he added a porch with entrance hall and church tower, open at the top. The original plan was for this to incorporate bells intended for the collapsed Münzturm (no. 17) of Andreas Schlüter (no. 18), although these had to be recast due to a

Counsellor Rademacher, the Palais takes its name from Minister of State von Podewils, who purchased it in 1732. The front-facing house with a side wing received the addition of a further wing in 1880. The centreline of the facade is highlighted by a projection with Ionic double pillars, triangular gable and balcony. Following damage in the Second World War, the Palais was reconstructed in the years to 1954 with a modern interior, with a subsequent restoration in 1970 following a fire. In the GDR, the building served as Haus der Jungen Talente, literally, the house of young talent.

Zeughaus (16)
Arsenal
1706
Unter den Linden 2

In a letter, Karl Friedrich Schinkel (no. 44) wrote that Berlin only possessed two colossal structures – the Stadtschloss (no. 7) and the Zeughaus. Following the demolishing of the Stadtschloss, the Zeughaus advanced to become the most significant Baroque building in the city. Plans for the construction of an arsenal date back to the Great Elector. Under the reign of his son, Friedrich III, Johann Arnold Nering began construction in 1695 (shortly before his death) probably using plans by François Blondel. The difficult construction continued under various project leaders: Martin Grünberg, Andreas Schlüter (no. 18), Jean de Bodt.

poor tone. The church was burned out in 1944, with the upper section of the tower collapsing, together with the tower roof. After being provisionally repaired, the church was rebuilt in 1991, although with a simplified interior.

Palais Podewil (15)
Podewil Mansion
1704
Klosterstraße 68-70
Jean de Bodt

The Palais Podewil is one of the most significant private buildings dating from the early 18th century in Berlin, an example of the classically influenced Berliner Baroque. Originally commissioned by Court

18

The Frenchman designed the central projection and completed the building, which draws influences from the French Classicism of the 17th century. The decoration of the building is the work of a number of different sculptors. The heads of dying warriors by Andreas Schlüter are some of the most significant works of Baroque sculpture. In 1730, three-quarter staircases were added in two corners of the courtyard. In 1877, Friedrich Hitzig converted the building into a pantheon with armoury museum. After the Second World War, the building was reconstructed along original lines by Otto Häsler as the Museum für Deutsche Geschichte, the museum of German history, a process that involved the replacement of a number of parapet sculptures with replicas. After reunification the building became the Deutsches Historisches Museum. It was converted by I. M. Pei and also received an extension (see no. 498).

Münzturm (17)
Coin Tower
1706
Andreas Schlüter

FLOP In 1702, on the orders of the King, Schlüter began to encase the water tower at the northwest corner of the Stadtschloss (no. 7), and to raise the height. With two artistic freestanding columns, the Münzturm was to reach 298 feet in height, a new symbol of the royal residence. Two years later (with two thirds of the building completed) the tower began to lean. Schlüter tried unsuccessfully to stabilise the structure by adding new extensions. In 1706, an investigative commission declared that the building was damaged irreparably, with the foundations inadequate. It was decided to demolish the building completely. Schlüter lost his position as director of castle construction.

19

Andreas Schlüter
* 1659 in Danzig (?), † 1714 in St. Petersburg (18)

"If we remove Schlüter from the history of Berlin, little remains to elevate the city amongst the ranks of great art metropolises on this planet."   Max Osborn 1909

Andreas Schlüter is the most important architect in Berlin, prior to Knobelsdorff and Schinkel (no. 44). He was the first master builder, raising architecture to the highest of artistic levels in the royal seat. He also elevated the standard of building and craftsmanship in Berlin to a level that was previously unknown, and that was to endure for a considerable time.

The son of a sculptor, Schlüter was educated in Danzig, the place of his birth. The first evidence of his activity can be found in Warsaw, where he worked from 1689-93, on objects including the gable relief of the Krasinski-Palais. It was here that Schlüter learned the functions of a construction site, under the leadership of the court artist Tilman van Gameren. It appears that his work in Poland was not yet that of an architect. In 1694, the Brandenburg Elector Friedrich III, later King Friedrich I, in Prussia, called him to Berlin to work as a sculptor. There was no mention of architecture at this point, with Johann Arnold Nering in charge of the construction matters of the city at that time. On his return from a study trip in 1696, Schlüter was commissioned with the design of keystones on the windows and doors of the Zeughaus (no. 16), which had been designed by Nering. In addition, he also received a commission for a bronze rider statue of the Great Elector, which was to become his greatest work as a sculptor. It was created for a prominent location on the Lange Brücke between Schlossplatz and the present day Nikolaiviertel (no. 362). Today it stands in the forecourt of Schloss Charlottenburg (no. 19), with a copy in the cupola hall of the Bodemuseum (no. 131).

In 1698, Schlüter succeeded Nering as architect for the construction of the Zeughaus. He also created the famous masks of the dying warriors in the courtyard, together with the trophies on the roof balustrade. In the same year, he was assigned with the task of converting the Elector's Renaissance castle on the Spree Island into a royal palace. Friedrich I appointed him director of castle construction for this purpose. The castle (no. 7), with the Schlüterhof that was later named after him, is his chief work. It was damaged in the war and demolished in 1950 on the orders of Walter Ulbricht. The Staatsratsgebäude of 1964 (no. 308), erected on Schlossplatz by the GDR government, incorporated a portal of the castle with sculpted ornamentation in the facade.

Schlüter fell from favour after the Münzturm (no. 17) that he had designed on the northwest corner of the castle collapsed. It was to have been the royal trademark of the royal residence. In 1704, two thirds of the construction were already completed when the tower began to tilt, threatening to collapse. Schlüter attempted to save the tower with the addition of supports and iron rings, covered by a second, more complex design. Despite these efforts, in 1706, he was forced to pre-empt the threatened collapse by demolishing part of the tower. He was released from the service of the court in 1707. Schlüter never really recovered

from this ignominy. The misfortune not only affected his artistic pride; it also pulled him down into a severe nervous crisis. To the King he remained a bad memory: "Schlüter, the rogue who built the tower so rottenly".

In 1710, Schlüter left the Akademie der Wissenschaften, the academy of sciences in Berlin. His final building in Berlin was the Landhaus Kameke, built in 1711–12. It was damaged in the Second World War and later demolished (see no. 21).

Schlüter's second proposal for the Münzturm, 1704.

Following the death of Friedrich I, whose ornate tin coffin Schlüter had modelled and prepared for casting, Schlüter left Berlin in 1713, heading for St Petersburg, where he pitched himself headlong into his work. He died one year after his arrival, before he was able to begin the implementation of his grandiose plans. The exact date of his death (like that of his birth) is unknown; no authentic image of him exists. Only Schlüter's sculptures remain, telling the tale of the genius of this extraordinary artist to the present day. rh

21

Schloss Charlottenburg (19)
Charlottenburg Palace
early 18th century
Spandauer Damm 20/22
Johann Arnold Nering,
Johann Friedrich Eosander

Schloss Charlottenburg, following the demolition of the Stadtschloss (no. 7) is the most significant remaining Baroque structure in Berlin, on a par with the Zeughaus (no. 16). The historic core of the modern-day district of Charlottenburg was created from a medieval settlement by the name of Lietzow. To the west of this, directly on the Spree, Elector Friedrich III ordered the construction of a summer residence for his wife, Sophie Charlotte. In 1695, work began on the construction of a castle built on eleven axes, to plans by Johann Arnold Nering. In the course of the following centuries, the residence received repeated additions and conversions, without limiting the unified overall effect (see no. 28). The first expansion to a three-winged structure followed the King's coronation in 1701, and was realised by Johann Friedrich Eosander. He was later to add the 157-feet high dome. A number of streets

and lines of sight in the surrounding area were focused upon this. Following the Second World War, the heavily damaged castle was initially to be demolished. Thanks to the efforts of the later director of castles and gardens, Margarethe Kühn, a decision was taken to rebuild instead, work on which began in 1956, with the project largely completed in 1962. The Rococo, Classical and Biedermeier interior was also recreated to a significant degree, including the so-called Eosander-kapelle, containing a lavishly carved pulpit. This process included a much-lauded attempt to replace the lost ceiling paintings with abstract forms of the original colours.

Nicolai-Haus (20)
Nicolai House
1710
Brüderstraße 13

Only two Baroque houses survive in Brüderstraße, originally part of Cölln. The Nicolai-Haus is of even more cultural-historical significance than house no. 10. It was named after the publisher and writer Friedrich Nicolai, who purchased it in 1788, making it an important meet-

enced in the preceding years, Schlüter demonstrates here that his architectural creativity was unbroken. This was his last construction in Berlin. Where both sides of the low building were replaced by large town houses at the end of the 19th century, the Landhaus Kameke remained until the Second World War. It was severely damaged in 1943, with the ruins demolished after the war.

ing point for the Berlin society of the day. Built in 1674 on two medieval plots, the house received its current form in around 1710. It is a simple, early Baroque rendered building, divided primarily by pilaster strips. The interior contains many original fixtures. The rear-facing transverse and side wings surrounding a courtyard are a typical housing style of Berlin.

Landhaus Kameke (21)
Kameke Country House
1712
Dorotheenstraße 27
Andreas Schlüter

DEMOLITION Following a period without significant assignments, Schlüter constructed a suburban country house for Minister of State Ernst Bogislav van Kameke in Dorotheenstadt, near the Spree. The style took the form of the Lustgarten buildings popular at that time. Despite the failures that he had experi-

Opernpalais
(ehem. Prinzessinnenpalais) (22)
Opera Palace
(former the Princesses Palace)
1733
Unter den Linden 5, Oberwallstraße
Friedrich Wilhelm Diterichs

The former Prinzessinnenpalais was destroyed in the war. Following the demolition of the ruins, Richard Paulick rebuilt it as the Operncafé, with the exterior true to the original and the interior in keeping with the more modern usage. The terrace is also a creation of the post-war era. The stairway, with its wrought ironwork, was once located in Schloss Buch. Combining a number of residential houses created the original construction. The central projection in the Oberwallstraße running along the side is richly ornamented. In 1810 Heinrich Gentz added a central structure to the Unter den Linden side, connected to the Kronprinzenpalais (no. 76) via a bridge construction.

23

**Berlin-Museum
(ehem. Kammergericht)** (24)
former Superior Court of Justice
1735
Lindenstraße 14
Philipp Gerlach

This is the only remaining Baroque palace in Friedrichstadt – even if only externally. Erected as an academic building in the line of sight of Markgrafenstraße, the three-winged building, later used as a superior court of justice, was converted several times in the 19th century, most significantly by Hermann Friedrich Waesemann in 1858. The building was severely damaged in the Second World War

Sophienkirche (23)
Sophien Church
1734
Große Hamburger Straße 29–31
Johann Friedrich Grael

The centre of Berlin is not overrun with picturesque perspectives. One of the most attractive is the view from Große Hamburger Straße to the tower of the Sophienkirche, framed by two neo-Baroque residential buildings. The tower was superimposed on the church of 1712 in 1734. The church was built on the orders of Queen Sophie Luise, third wife of Friedrich I, as a parish church for the Spandau suburbs. The motif is reminiscent of the collapsed Münzturm (no. 17) of Andreas Schlüter (no. 18). A compact tower shaft is followed by two slimmer floors housing the bells, enclosed by a copper cupola. It is the only Baroque tower in Berlin to survive the course of the centuries. The interior of the church was redesigned in neo-Baroque style in 1892. The residential houses in Große Hamburger Straße, also neo-Baroque, were built in 1905, with their symmetrical position taking the church as reference point. To the rear, Sophienstraße is one of the best-preserved and most picturesque streets of old Berlin.

and rebuilt in the years up to 1969 as the Berlin-Museum. The end of the 1990s saw a further reconstruction, by Daniel Libeskind, in connection with the construction of the neighbouring Jewish Museum (no. 428), which is joined to the Baroque building below ground level.

Alt-Berliner Handwerker Hof (25)
Old Berlin Craftsmen's Yard
1735
Große Hamburger Straße 17

In comparison to the Nicolai-Haus at Brüderstraße 13 (no. 20), this address is the petit bourgeois variant of the urbanisation of Berlin. Built from 1725 as a farmhouse to Schloss Monbijou, the increase in importance of the trade along the road to Hamburg in the following century was such that the two gabled buildings were joined together in 1827, with the height of the building also raised. 55 years later, the timber-framed front received a Classical facade of ren-

dered brickwork. Evidence of the continued working character of the building is provided by the central gateway, a feature that (where at all evident) is usually eccentrically designed in more prestigious buildings; as well as the open steps in place of the normal stairway. The garden house was demolished in the post-war period; the front wing and stables continue to house a variety of enterprises to this day.

Pfarrhäuser (26)
Vicarages
1739
Taubenstraße 3

From here it is possible to catch a glimpse of how Friedrichstadt must have looked around the middle of the 18th century (Pariser Platz was also surrounded by this style of building at one time). In the present day commercial district, the vicarages are the sole survivors of the first construction period. The architects are unknown. The ensemble was erected to a

unified plan and consisted originally of three buildings, connected at the rear via a courtyard with greenery. The building in Glinkastraße, inhabited by theologian and philosopher Friedrich Schleiermacher from 1809–16, was destroyed in the Second World War.

Staatsoper Unter den Linden (27)
State Opera Unter den Linden
1743
Unter den Linden 7
Georg Wenzeslaus von Knobelsdorff

The Staatsoper Unter den Linden was the first freestanding theatre construction in Germany to stand outside a castle grounds. It was also the first building of significance erected by Friedrich II and also represented the starting point for the ensemble of the Forum Fridericianum (no. 32). The oldest opera house in the country has been converted and augmented on numerous occasions. The original appearance was the main facade alone, created by Knobelsdorff in Palladi-

25

an Classical style. By 1787, Carl Gotthard Langhans had already begun the first reconstruction work in the interior. Following a fire in 1843, the interior was redesigned by Karl Ferdinand Langhans in late Classical style, augmented by a fourth tier. In 1926, the building received its first drawing floor – and a somewhat clumsy one at that. Following the Second World War, the building received a new form both interior and exterior, along historic lines. The work was completed between 1952 and 1955 to plans by Richard Paulick, and involved reconstruction of the drawing floor and side extensions in keeping with the historic facade of Knobelsdorff, auditorium and Apollo room received a completely new appearance, following the example of the Friedrich Rococo in Berlin and Potsdam. Cloakrooms and interval rooms were moved to the basement. In the vicinity, Paulick also constructed a new administration building in the style of Knobelsdorff's architecture (no. 280).

Neuer Flügel
Schloss Charlottenburg (28)
New Wing of
Charlottenburg Palace
1746
Schlosspark Charlottenburg
Georg Wenzeslaus von Knobelsdorff

Knobelsdorff added a new eastern wing to Schloss Charlottenburg (no. 19) for Friedrich II, also known as the Knobelsdorff wing. The 460-feet long structure is raised in the middle by a pavilion. Tuscan double columns frame five high French doors. The castle wing was reconstructed on the exterior, as well as in the interior, with the Rococo interior of the Goldene Galerie.

Magnushaus (29)
Magnus House
1754
Am Kupfergraben 7
Georg Wenzeslaus von Knobelsdorff

The name of this stately Baroque building comes from the physicist Gustav Magnus, who worked here from 1842–70, establishing the first institute of physics in Germany on the site (later to become the Deutsche Physikalische Gesellschaft, the German Physical Society). The well-proportioned rendered building was proba-

bly designed by Knobelsdorff and rests upon a cuboid cellar level, with the three central axes accentuated by Corinthian colossal pillars. In 1822, a two-storey extension was added on Dorotheenstraße, together with a courtyard wing. The interior boasts an elegant stairway with wrought iron Rococo banisters. Today, the building is home to the Max Planck Library.

Knoblauchhaus (30)
Knoblauch House
1760
Poststraße 23

The Knoblauchhaus is one of the few remaining buildings of the Nikolaiviertel (no. 362). The three freestanding facades lend it a dominant position within the quarter. The facades were redesigned around 1800 in early Classical form, with broad frieze and foliage bordering as window overhangs. The first floor includes a distinctive bay window. The extensive Knoblauch family lived here for the best part of 170 years, the most famous member of the family being the architect Eduard Knoblauch (1801-65). Amongst other buildings, he constructed the synagogue in Oranienburger Straße. Today, the former living area with its sumptuous interior is part of the Stadtmuseum. A wine tavern is located in the cellar.

Ephraimpalais (31)
Ephraim Mansion
1766
Poststraße 16/Mühlendamm
Friedrich Wilhelm Diterichs

This building, once known as the "most beautiful corner in Berlin", was absent from the urban landscape for over fifty years of the past century. In 1935, it was torn down to make way for the widened Mühlendamm. In 1985, in conjunction with the rebuilding of the Nikolaiviertel (no. 362), work began on the reconstruction of the Ephraimpalais – although a few yards away from the original location. This project included the return of components of the building stored in the western part of the city. The original building was erected by Friedrich Wilhelm Diterichs for the court jeweller and minter Veitel Heine Ephraim. In 1892, Hermann Blankenstein extended the house by three axes on the Mühlendamm. Noteworthy details are the intricate wrought iron balcony railings and the groups of putti. Behind the rounded corners of the building are oval festival

rooms, and behind them the oval stairway. One of these rooms had a Baroque ceiling fitted, originally from the Wartenbergsche Palais and designed by Andreas Schlüter. Today, the Ephraimpalais is used primarily for alternating exhibitions on Berlin urban and art history.

The State Concept of Frederick the Great in Bricks and Mortar – the Forum Fridericianum (32)

The Forum Fridericianum is one of the most significant building ensembles in Berlin. Work began on the prestigious project directly after the coronation of Friedrich II. The King wished to express his concept of the state as a tightly knit unit of monarchy, art and science in the form of a construction project on Unter den Linden. The King himself drew up the plans for an opera house, academy building and royal palace, with the plans further developed by his favoured architect, Georg Wenzeslaus von Knobelsdorff. Of the original plans, only the opera house actually came to fruit, built by Knobelsdorff in Palladian style between 1741–43 (see no. 27). Today, the group of buildings presents less of a uniform appearance than was originally intended by Friedrich II and Knobelsdorff.

St.-Hedwigs-Kathedrale (no. 33) was built in 1747 for the Catholic community, at an angle to the Forum. Its purpose was for Friedrich II to establish a symbol of religious freedom. One year later, on the site of the planned royal palace to the north of Unter den Linden Johann Boumann began construction of a palace for Prince Heinrich. The plans for this were provided by Friedrich II and Knobelsdorff. In 1810 the building became the Friedrich-Wilhelm-Universität, the present-day Humboldt University. The rear wing of the university building was added by the counsellor for construction Ludwig Hoffmann (no. 141) between 1913 and 1919, with the pattern of the Baroque facade simply further extended.

Where once the academy was to stand, the Königliche Bibliothek (no. 171) was built, to plans of Friedrich II, with construction beginning in 1755. The King based his idea upon a fifty-year old plan by Fischer von Erlach for the Vienna Hofburg. An unfortunate choice, as the sweeping construction bears no relation to the opera house and does not go with the more severe form of the rectangular Forum.

Following heavy damage in the Second World War, the entire Forum was reconstructed in the GDR era, largely true to original, as least as far as the exterior is

The former Royal Library.

concerned. The interior of the Hedwigs-Kathedrale, the Alte Bibliothek and the Humboldt-University were redesigned in modern style.

In 1995, in the centre of present-day Bebelplatz, the Israeli artist Micha Ullman created a memorial in memory of the book burnings of the National

The main building of Humboldt University.

Socialists on this spot in 1933. A glass plate offers a view into an underground room, illuminated at night, with empty bookshelves. Around the monument, an underground car park has been built beneath the square, which was once a green space. The planning of the car park drew heavy criticism from a number of artists.   rh

29

Close relationship of royalty, art and science at the boulevard Unter den Linden.

St.-Hedwigs-Kathedrale (33)
St Hedwig's Cathedral
1773
Bebelplatz
Johann Boumann

This is a symbolic structure of tolerance: with the construction of St.-Hedwigs-Kathedrale, Friedrich II erected the first Roman Catholic church in Protestant Brandenburg. Situated on the prominent Forum Fridericianum (no. 32), it was the second building to be completed, after the Staatsoper (no. 27). Friedrich II provided his own sketches of ideas, modelled along the lines of the Roman Pantheon. The reliefs in the frieze and between the portal columns were added at the end of the 19th century. The church was gutted by fire in 1943. In the reconstruction of 1952, Hans Schwippert replaced the original dome with one made from reinforced concrete, plainer and somewhat lower than the original. The entrance to the crypt was widened with a stairway. The

interior is modern in style; the colossal columns were retained, but without the original Corinthian capital. Today, the building is a cathedral of the diocese of Berlin.

Wohnhaus (34)
Residential Building
circa 1785
Neue Schönhauser Straße 8
Georg Christian Unger

Neue Schönhauser Straße was built after 1750 on the site of the former ramparts. The late Baroque three-storey residential house is richly decorated in the so-called 'Zopfstil', a late rococo style. It was built during the expansion of the city in the late phase of the regency of Friedrich II. An unusual feature is the round arched windows on the ground floor with garland decoration and female busts. To the side of the passage is a round wooden staircase with carved banister. The master builder is thought to have been Georg Christian Unger.

Schloss Bellevue (35)
Bellevue Palace
1786
Spreeweg 1
Philipp Daniel Boumann

Prince Ferdinand of Prussia, the younger brother of Friedrich II, had this triple-winged building erected in the middle of the Tiergarten hunting grounds (no. 60). It is the first royal Prussian castle to be built in Classical style, taking its cue from Schloss Wörlitz, by Erdmannsdorff. In the second half of the 19th century, the building changed ownership on a regular basis. In 1939, Paul Baumgarten senior converted the Schloss into a Reichsgästehaus, a guesthouse for the government. In the process, the side entrances were converted into round arched windows, with a new portal replacing them in the central projection. Following damage in the war, the building was reconstructed in 1959 with a more simplified interior as the Berlin office of the Federal President. Only the Ovale Saal of Carl Gotthard Langhans remained in its original condition. Following the relocation of the German government and parliament to Berlin, the castle is the sole official residence of the Head of State (see no. 420).

Mohrenkolonnaden (36)
Mohren Colonnades
1787
Mohrenstraße 37b und 40/41
Carl Gotthard Langhans

Today, there are very few indications remaining that, until the beginning of the 20th century, the old city of Berlin was surrounded by a moat dating from Ba-

roque times. The moat was gradually filled in; the bridges disappeared. They were once decorated with colonnades at four points. The Mohrenkolonnaden are the only ones remaining on their original location. The decorative sculpture work depicts reliefs of ancient deities, with the frames showing river gods from the four corners of the earth.

Belvedere (37)
The Belvedere
1790
Schlossgarten Charlottenburg
Carl Gotthard Langhans

This gem stands at the northeastern periphery of the Schlossgarten, on what was originally an island. Nine years prior to the construction of his Classical Brandenburg Gate, Carl Gotthard Langhans designed the intricate Belvedere as a teahouse with balconies. The shape of the building is basically an oval, with rectangular structures added on all four sides. The building was heavily damaged in the war and the exterior was reconstructed using engravings as a guide. The interior was lost completely. Today, in its place, each floor consists of a large, open-plan room, which are used for the presentation of an important collection of porcelain. The three boys bearing a flower basket on the roof are a free interpretation of the original sculpture.

31

From Prussian Residence to Capital of the German Empire 1790–1871 (38)

The first indication of a new era in Berlin was a lively intellectual movement. In the famous salons of the city, the leading heads of the burgeoning middle class met to debate the ideas of the Enlightenment, art and literature. In 1791, as the starting signal for a new architectural age, Carl Gotthard Langhans erected his neo-Greek Brandenburger Tor (no. 40) between the Baroque palaces on Pariser Platz. With its references to the ancient world, Classicism stood for the ideal of a free civic society.

The military defeat at the hand of Napoleon, which heralded the collapse of Prussian absolutism, provided a new impetus for this breakthrough. A small group of reformers grouped around Freiherr vom Stein introduced a phase of political and intellectual renewal. One of the more durable reforms was the new Städteordnung, the municipal self-administration, of 1808, which heralded the self-government of the Prussian state. In 1810, Wilhelm von Humboldt founded the Friedrich-Wilhelm-Universität (today's Humboldt University), with lectures held, amongst others, by Fichte,

Hegel, Schleiermacher and Ranke. The school system was improved; after 1850 there were scarcely any children of school age that were not being taught.

The political constitution of Prussia, on the other hand, failed to fulfil the expectations of the citizens. However, one of the contradictory aspects of Berlin is that, in the time of political repression and social problems, science and education, arts and culture experienced one of their most glorious ages.

The outstanding architect of this time was Karl Friedrich Schinkel (no. 44). He not only left his mark on the face of the city with outstanding buildings such as the Neue Wache (no. 52), the Schauspielhaus (no. 54) and the Altes Museum (no. 62), as chief Prussian civil servant in the field of construction he also controlled and improved all other significant construction projects in the city, and throughout Prussia. Schinkel handed Berlin architecture of a European radiance, of a type that it was only to replicate again at the beginning of the 20th century. The works of his numerous pupils, such as Stüler, Strack or Persius (the so-

Architecture of European vibrancy – Friedrich Gilly: proposal for a monument to Friedrich II at Leipziger Platz (1797).

called Schinkel school) led to his influence remaining tangible in the architecture of Berlin up to the establishment of the German Reich in 1871. The numerous churches, municipal buildings and residential houses of the Schinkel school are characterised by cuboid structures, harmonious proportions, restrained ornamentation and careful details. The archetype of Schinkel's Bauakademie (no. 65) can be seen on the facades of many buildings.

In the layout of the new city districts, a decisive role was played by the garden architect Peter Josef Lenné. The Royal director of gardens was handed responsibility for all urban planning in 1840. The principle result of his work was an overall plan for decorative and peripheral elements, which foresaw, amongst other projects, a semi-circular boulevard for the north and east of the city, as well as a broad axis to the south of the centre, broken up by squares. A large proportion of these plans were subsequently incorporated into the 1862 development plan of James Hobrecht (no. 74). In the so-called "Hobrecht plan", the pattern of streets was laid out upon which the dense Berlin of tenement houses was to grow over the following 50 years, a pattern that continues to characterise the inner city areas to this day.

Where liberal ideas were suppressed in the political field, the commercial and industrial policies of Prussia followed the principle of free trade. The highest priority here was the establishment of a competitive industrial base in keeping with the European industrialised nations, the most modern of which was Great Britain.

In the 1830s, an economic dynamism gathered pace that, in just a few decades, was to turn the royal capital city of Prussia into the pre-eminent German industrial metropolis. 1837 saw the opening of the first railway line in Prussia, between Berlin and Potsdam. Berlin expanded beyond the city walls, which had been removed by the second half of the 19th century. Following the war with Napoleon, Berlin numbered a mere 160,000 inhabitants, by the eve of the establishment of the German Reich in 1871 the city already boasted a population of 800,000.   rh

Anatomisches Theater (39)
Anatomical Theatre
1790
Luisenstraße 56
Carl Gotthard Langhans

Situated in one of the many courtyards to the rear of the Charité (no. 178) is an architectural jewel by the architect Langhans, who was also responsible for the Brandenburger Tor (no. 40). Built for the Tierärztliche Hochschule, the veterinary college in Berlin (no. 70), founded in 1790, the building occupies an almost square floor plan and is one of the few remaining examples of the strict style of early Berlin Classicism. The heart of the building is the circular auditorium with its steeply rising rows of seats (much in the form of an amphitheatre) which is still in its original state. It is topped by a flat timber dome with a rounded drum.

Brandenburger Tor (40)
Brandenburg Gate
1791
Pariser Platz
Carl Gotthard Langhans

It is the symbol of Berlin and the most famous structure in the city, known around the world. The gate towards the town of Brandenburg is the sole survivor amongst the original 15 Berlin city gates. When Carl Gotthard Langhans designed a new gate for Pariser Platz, the square was surrounded by two-storey Baroque palaces with mansard roofs. The gate formed a stark contrast to these. The design was a significant one, even when compared to others throughout Europe. With it, Langhans placed the powerful forms of ancient Greece in the Baroque city for the first time. The inspiration

came from the Propylaion on the Athens Acropolis, although Langhans managed to achieve an entirely new creation of his own. The quadriga of Johann Gottfried Schadow crowning the gate was tilted

through 180 degrees on a number of occasions, with Napoleon even removing it to Paris for a time. The current quadriga is a complete cast replica of the original, which no longer exists. The original colour of the gate is uncertain. There was an extensive public discussion regarding the possible painting in the scope of the latest renovation work.

ehem. Schlosstheater
Charlottenburg (41)
former Palace Theatre
Charlottenburg
1791
Schlosspark Charlottenburg
Carl Gotthard Langhans

As with the Belvedere, Langhans' theatre building for Schloss Charlottenburg (no.

21) combined Baroque with elements of early Classicism. The city and garden sides were designed in the same style, with the unusual composition of the central projection a point of note. The building was destroyed in the war, with the exterior later rebuilt; the original interior was lost. Today the building is home to the Museum für Vor- und Frühgeschichte, a museum of prehistory and early history.

Wohnhaus (42)
Residential Building
1794
Auguststraße 69

The broad, two-storey rendered building dates from the year 1794, but was altered in 1840 and 1860. Noteworthy is the accentuated window above the portal, in the passage is an attractively winding timber stairway with an oval window, the courtyard to the rear is also charming. Following restoration, the names of former owners can be seen above the gateway arch: Süssmann & Wiesenthal.

Jungfernbrücke (43)
Bridge Jungfernbrücke
1798
Friedrichsgracht

The Jungfernbrücke, today almost hidden amongst modern buildings, is the last example of a type of Dutch bridge that was once very common in Berlin and the Brandenburg Marches. The first bridge to be built at this point was erected in the last quarter of the 17th century. It served to connect Cölln to Friedrichswerder and the Leipziger Tor. The bridge that stands on the site today was built in 1798. The apertures for the River Spree, of varying widths, are made from red sandstone, with the central aperture a bascule bridge. Although the various components have been renewed, the mechanism remains essentially unaltered to this day.

Karl Friedrich Schinkel
*1781 in Neuruppin, †1841 in Berlin (44)

"True vitality only exists where new things are created."

Karl Friedrich Schinkel

Karl Friedrich Schinkel is the most significant German architect of the 19th century. He owes this position to his enormous creative energy, his extensive versatility (not only as architect and civil servant but also as painter, stage designer and furniture designer) and to the remarkable scope of his work. In his larger buildings and his written works, Schinkel returned time and again to the basic questions of architecture, answering these in his own manner. This is a further reason why Schinkel's works have remained vivid and fruitful like those of scarcely any other master builder.

His legacy is so universal that even today he is still quoted by the most varied of architects working in Berlin. The avant-garde point to perhaps the most famous of Schinkel's quotes: "True vitality only exists where new things are created." More traditional master builders appreciate more the tectonic linkage of his historically-rooted structures and his tal-

Strictly utilitarian buildings – proposal for a department store on Unter den Linden.

ent for the picturesque. Born and raised in Neuruppin, Brandenburg, Karl Friedrich Schinkel moved to Berlin with his mother, who was widowed young. In Berlin he studied under Friedrich Gilly, also spending time in his family home. Gilly's individual style, with its hints at the architecture of the French Revolution, had a great influence upon Schinkel's own designs.

His debut work was the Pomonatempel with Ionic porticus, erected in 1800 on the Pfingstberg in Potsdam. It has recently been restored. From 1803 to 1805, he travelled through Italy, France and Germany. Due to a lack of large commissions, Schinkel painted panoramas and dioramas, as well as romantic landscape paintings. An intensive interest in theatre sets followed; his most famous design is the starry sky for the appearance of the Queen of the Night in The Magic Flute.

In 1810, Schinkel was recommended by Wilhelm von Humboldt for an administrative position at the Prussian construction office, becoming privy construction counsellor in 1815 and director of the Prussian construction office in 1830. With this appointment, he was responsible for all large construction projects from the Rhineland to East Prussia, often intervening in their implementation.

Schinkel's main works were built in Berlin between 1816 and 1830: the Neue Wache (no. 52), the Schauspielhaus (no. 54), and the building that Schinkel himself considered his best: the Altes Museum (no. 62). Influenced by Gilly's drawings of the Marienburg, Schinkel also designed neo-Gothic structures such as

the Kreuzbergdenkmal memorial or the Friedrichwerdersche Kirche (no. 61).

Although Schinkel never constructed in a truly revolutionary style, in his later works he erected buildings that were oriented strongly towards their intended purpose, moving away from the classical lines of the ancient world, for example in the plans for a store on the Unter den Linden, which was never realised. He also incorporated the state-of-the-art construction techniques of the time into his buildings. Many of the later principles of Modernism can be seen here. However, a complete casting-off of the familiar forms was not the intention of Schinkel. On his voyage to England he noted, on seeing the modern, completely unornamented factory buildings: "It makes a terribly eerie impression, monstrous buildings constructed by workmen alone, without architecture and for the most basic of requirements."

His talent for painting can be seen primarily in two smaller buildings in Potsdam, Schloss Charlottenhof and the Roman Baths. Numerous imaginative projects from his final years were never realised, but exercised a great influence on his pupils: a royal castle on the Acropolis in Athens and Castle Orianda in the Crimea, with the richly ornamented ancient Greek building forms dominating once more.

Schinkels' most significant later work was the red brick cube of the Bauakademie (no. 65), a groundbreaking building in which he lived in an apartment with office. It was here that he died on 9th October 1841. rh

Wohnhaus (45)
Residential Building
circa 1800
Gipsstraße 11

The early Classical bourgeois house was constructed around 1800 and reconstructed in 1840. A broad meander frieze runs along the portal and flanking windows of the two-storey rendered building. The stucco ornamentation on two windows on the courtyard side of the building depicts Baroque forms.

Wohnhaus (46)
Residential Building
circa 1800
Schustehrusstraße 13

The core of this building dates back to 1712, with the present form added in around 1800. Following partial demolition, it was rebuilt in 1994. It is the oldest existing residential house in Charlot-

tenburg. As a twin parlour house with central hall, it corresponds to the Normalhaus design of Eosander von Göthe.

Ermelerhaus (47)
Ermeler House
1804
Märkisches Ufer 10
Friedrich Wilhelm Diterichs

The interconnected, canal-like construction is deceptive: this is not a historic grouping, it was created in the 1960s, where historically significant buildings from destroyed areas of Berlin were moved to this location. The Ermelerhaus, built in 1760, presumably by Friedrich Wilhelm Diterichs, originally stood at Breite Straße 11. In 1804, the facade was

redesigned in Classical style; the frieze above the portal contains a reference to the tobacco trading of the owner of the time Neumann. In 1824, the building was purchased by Wilhelm Ermeler, after whom it is named. In 1953, the building was restored (still on the original location) before being relocated to the Märkische Ufer in the course of the widening of Breite Straße in 1968. Original features in the interior are the gilded wrought iron stairway, the festival room on the first floor and the Rosenzimmer room. There is an internal connection to house no. 12, which originally stood on the other bank. The facade was reconstructed in the style of the era around 1740.

40

Herrenhaus   (48)
Stately Mansion
1804
Wrangelstraße 2
Heinrich Gentz

With its simplified and compact ancient world form, the stately house is one of the few well-preserved examples of early Classical architecture in Berlin. A farmhouse is known to have existed on the site of the former manor since the 18th century. In 1803, Heinrich Gentz took charge of a skeleton building, probably begun by David Gilly, and completed it to his own plans. The two floors are divided by a meander frieze; on the garden side is a central projection with Doric columns. The building received its current name, Wrangelschlößchen, after it was home to General Field Marshall Wrangel, who lived here around 1853. The numerous conversions were reversed in the course of a restoration in 1995, during which interior decoration from the late 19th century was discovered. The effect of the building is restricted by those surrounding it.

Schadowhaus   (49)
Schadow House
1805
Schadowstraße 10/11

The prominent Berlin sculptor Johann Gottfried Schadow had a two-storey Classical residential house built on this site,

the architect of which remains unknown. Following Schadow's death in 1850, his son added a further floor to the house with side wings. The facade is characterised by block rendering. The reliefs on the ground floor are by Schadow; those on the left depicting the history of art in ancient times, those on the tight patrons of the arts from ancient times to the Renaissance. The portrait relief of Schadow on the main floor is by Hermann Schievelbein and was created a year after the death of the sculptor. In the hallway plaster mouldings of Schadow reliefs can be seen. The neglected building is in urgent need of renovation.

Acropolis of the Arts: Museum Island (50)

When, in 1824, Karl Friedrich Schinkel (no. 44) began work on his Museum am Lustgarten (no. 62) no one could have guessed that the following hundred years would witness the growth of a museum complex (unique of its kind in the world) on the island in the Spree to the rear of it. The impetus for this came from Crown Prince Friedrich Wilhelm (later King Friedrich Wilhelm IV) with his 1835 vision of a "Refuge of the arts and sciences". The first to arrive was Stüler's Neues Museum (no. 77). He also designed the raised temple of the Nationalgalerie (no. 89). Von Ihne built the Bodemuseum (no. 131) on the northern tip of the island, and finally, in 1930, the three wings of the Pergamonmuseum (no. 153) were completed, to plans by Messel. After being damaged in the war, the buildings were reconstructed in the GDR era – with the exception of the ruins of the Neues Museum. Since 1999, the buildings have been part of the Unesco World Heritage.

Within the scope of the "Museumsinsel master plan" the five buildings are to be restored over the next 10 to 12 years and linked at the foundation levels using an "architectural promenade". Inaccessible for so many decades, the open areas of the island are to be open to all visitors in future, including those without tickets for the museums. The colonnade cornice around the Alte Nationalgalerie is to be enclosed, the gardens restored to the approximate status of 1900, the Monbijoubrücke at the Bodemuseum (no. 131) is to be extended and an additional footway added to the rear of the Pergamonmuseum.

In addition to the connecting promenade, a subject of much debate is the new central entrance building, which the British architect David Chipperfield is to erect between Neues Museum and Kupfergraben. The intention is to use this to accommodate a large portion of the infrastructure, such as cloakrooms, museum shop and cafeteria, as well as an auditorium and areas for alternating exhibitions. It is the first time in over 70 years that the group of buildings on the Museumsinsel is to be augmented by a new building.

The work on the Alte Nationalgalerie has already been completed by the architect HG Merz. The completion of the reconstruction of the Bodemuseum by Heinz Tesar followed in autumn 2005. David Chipperfield is working on the Neues Museum and its new entrance building, Hilmer-Sattler-Albrecht are commissioned to renovate the Altes Museum. A new, vertical development in the courtyards means that it will be possible to remove the disruptive glass wall between the columns on the front. The reconstruction of the Pergamonmuseum by Oswald Mathias Ungers could be completed by 2015. This will enclose the courtyard with the addition of a new, largely glazed link for ancient architectural fragments, thereby enabling a circular tour to be made of the main floor. rh

In the Alte Nationalgalerie.

"Sanctuary of the Arts and Sciences", to be open to every visitor: Museumsinsel.

Neue Wache   (52)
New Guard House
1818
Unter den Linden 4
Karl Friedrich Schinkel

The Neue Wache stands at the beginning of a row of Classical monumental buildings by Schinkel, forming the image of the "Athens of the Spree". The structure stands alone between the monumental forms of the Zeughaus (Deutsches Historisches Museum/no. 16) and the Humboldt University. The cubic form, reminiscent of a Roman Castrum, has sandstone vestibule, corner towers, cornice and architrave, with the facade elements behind in brick. In place of the Classical triglyph and metope frieze, the columns of the vestibule are decorated with metal Victorias. The Neue Wache was dedicated in 1818 as a "Monument to the Victims of the Anti-Napoleonic Wars". Over the course of the 20th century, this dedication was reformulated three times. In 1931 Heinrich Tessenow converted the central atrium into a "Memorial to the Fallen of the World War", enclosing it with the exception of a small fanlight. From 1960, the GDR government used the monument to honour the victims of fascism and militarism. Since 1993, the Neue Wache has honoured a more comprehensive memory as "Central Memorial of the Federal Republic of Germany for

Mausoleum   (51)
Mausoleum
1812
Schlosspark Charlottenburg
Heinrich Gentz

The Mausoleum is the final work of the Berlin early Classicist Heinrich Gentz, constructed as a tomb for Queen Luise, who died whilst still young. According to the instructions of Friedrich Wilhelm III, it was originally to have been a Doric temple with block rendering and a sandstone portico. This portico was moved to the Pfaueninsel in 1828, under the supervision of Karl Friedrich Schinkel (no. 44) and faced in polished, grey granite in the same manner as the Mausoleum. Schinkel also designed the first annexe to the tomb of Friedrich Wilhelm III, completed in 1840. In 1891, a further extension was made for the sarcophagus of Wilhelm I and his wife.

44

the Victims of War and Tyranny". This formulation is just as controversial as the enlarged sculpture by Käthe Kollwitz placed in its interior, a grieving mother with her dead son.

Kreuzberg-Denkmal (53)
Kreuzberg Memorial
1821
Viktoriapark
Karl Friedrich Schinkel

As a young man, Karl Friedrich Schinkel (no. 44) painted architectural visions and designs in a romantically interpreted Gothic style, at the time of the wars of liberation seen as a particularly "German"

approach. The monument to the wars of liberation against Napoleon is an echo of those romantic projects, it was erected by Schinkel on a raised area to the south of the city at the request of Friedrich Wilhelm III. The memorial, with its similarity to a Gothic tower, stands on a cross-shaped floor plan and is crowned with an iron cross designed by Schinkel. This is the origin of the name Kreuzberg, literally "cross hill". The Classical figure decoration is by the sculptors Rauch, Tieck and Wichmann.

ehem. Schauspielhaus
(Konzerthaus) (54)
former Theatre
(Concert Hall)
1821
Gendarmenmarkt
Karl Friedrich Schinkel

The Schauspielhaus was erected on the site of Carl Gotthard Langhans' theatre, which was destroyed by fire in 1817. Schinkel incorporated the six Ionic columns and the foundation of the previous building into the new structure. With great skill, he designed a clearly structured, cubic composition. In the centre is the main building, with a small chamber music hall to the left and administrative rooms to the right. The facades are constructed in a manner novel at that time, a system of two-storey pillars in the shape of a grid with windows between them. Initially they were only rendered, with the sandstone covering added in 1884. Christian Friedrich Tieck designed the sumptuous sculpture decorations. Premieres at the Schauspielhaus included Carl Maria von Weber's opera "Der Freischütz", together with legendary performances with Gustaf Gründgens. In the Second World War the building was heavily damaged and gutted by fire. During the GDR era, the building was restored to its original condition externally, with the theatre room in the interior replaced by a large concert hall based upon the historic chamber music hall of Schinkel, although this only possessed a fifth of the volume. Few visitors recognise the great hall as a contemporary addition. The new chamber music hall had its proportions altered and was designed along Classical lines.

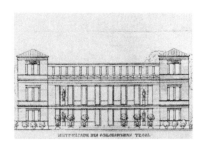

Schloss Tegel (55)
Tegel Palace
1824
Adelheidallee 17–21
Karl Friedrich Schinkel

The original 16th century building was owned by the Humboldt family from 1766. Although Schinkel integrated the old structure into the new, prestigious castle, it continues to be visible. From the southern Renaissance tower, Schinkel developed three further towers, thus establishing a symmetry. The plain elements of the layout, together with the reliefs, are based upon structures from the ancient world, as is the interior, with its numerous statue niches.

Schlossbrücke (56)
Palace Bridge
1824
Unter den Linden
Karl Friedrich Schinkel

Schinkel's (no. 44) bridge replaced the older Hundebrücke, upon which the Electors and Kings assembled their hounds before heading off to hunt in the nearby Tiergarten (no. 60). Following an 1818 plan, the structure was erected as a new link between Schloss (no. 7) and Lustgarten (no. 448) on the one side and the boulevard Unter den Linden on the other side. The rhythm of the three stone bridge pillars is accentuated by a pedestal of red granite on the balustrade. Cast iron railings stand in between, with richly ornate sea horses and dolphins. The Carrara marble figures were added after Schinkel's death, between 1847 and 1857, and were created by sculptors from the school of Christian Daniel Rauch. Young heroes are depicted as a monument to the wars of liberation, accompanied by goddesses of victory.

Schinkel-Pavillon (57)
Schinkel Pavilion
1825
Schlossgarten Charlottenburg
Karl Friedrich Schinkel

This building was erected as private quarters for Friedrich Wilhelm III, under the name "Neuer Pavillon", the new pavilion. It was modelled on the Villa Reale del Chiatamone in Naples, where the King had stayed on a visit. The structure stands on an almost square floor plan at the eastern end of Schloss Charlottenburg (no. 19), laid out on the Baroque axis system. The rooms are arranged around a central stairway; a gallery on iron trusses surrounds the upper floor. The building was heavily damaged in 1943, with almost all of the furnishings lost. As the building was well documented, it proved possible to rebuild the exterior and interior walls in the years up to 1966, with the pavilion accessible again since 1970. Today, it houses an important collection of art and artefacts from the Schinkel era.

Classical form. He added to the tower and redesigned the interior. Heavily damaged in the war, by 1956 the church had been rebuilt, with the original exterior recreated with the exception of the final section of the tower. The modern interior added at that time was removed in 1987 and replaced with the Schinkel version.

Maxim-Gorki-Theater
(ehem. Singakademie)   (59)
Maxim Gorki Theatre
(former Musical Society)
1827
Am Festungsgraben 2
Karl Theodor Ottmer

Luisenkirche   (58)
Luisen Church
1716
Gierkeplatz
Philipp Gerlach,
1826 Karl Friedrich Schinkel

The two-storey parish church was built on the floor plan of a Greek cross. In the 1820s, it was renewed by Schinkel in

The oldest concert hall building in Berlin, it was built at the wish of Karl Friedrich Zelter, who founded the Singakademie choir in 1791. Ottmer used plans drawn up a number of years previously by Karl Friedrich Schinkel (no. 44), who had failed to receive the commission. Following bomb damage, the interior was modernised in 1952 for the Maxim Gorki Theater. The original facade, with pilasters and doors framed with edicules remains in place to this day.

47

Tiergarten (60)
Animal Garden
circa 1830
Peter Joseph Lenné

GARDEN From the 16th century onwards, the area before the gates of the city, rich in game, served as a hunting area for the rulers of the day. The area is first mentioned as "Thiergarten" in a deed of 1527. The creation of the Lietzenburger Chaussee in 1698, leading to the Schloss in Charlottenburg (no. 19), was the first route to transect the area. Further routes were to follow, crossing at the Großer Stern (no. 245). Over the course of the centuries, the area has been altered and added to on many occasions, as well as being opened to the general public, under Friedrich II. The current form is based largely on designs of the prominent landscape architect Peter Joseph Lenné, from the 1830s. Following the bomb damage of the war years and the deforestation in the privation of the postwar years, the replanting since 1949 has been performed in accordance with the plans of Lenné. Most of the historic statues were lost in the war years or replaced by copies at a later date. Today, the Tiergarten is the largest green area in the city centre. Considerable damage continues to be caused on an annual basis as a result of the Love Parade.

Friedrichwerdersche Kirche (61)
Friedrichwerder church
1830
Werderscher Markt
Karl Friedrich Schinkel

For the reconstruction of this church on the site of an earlier Baroque structure, Schinkel completed two alternative drafts: a Roman temple and a Gothic-inspired church. Crown Prince Friedrich Wilhelm, later King Friedrich Wilhelm IV, decided on the latter version. The building, surrounded closely by other buildings until the Second World War, displays a peculiar mixture of cubic towers and plane side frontage on the one side and Gothic elements on the other. It is the first of Schinkel's buildings to have a facade in roughly-hewn bricks. Inside the church, a simple plaster was used for reasons of expense, painted in the form of sandstone blocks in the form of a trompe-l'oeil. Heavily damaged in the war, the building was reconstructed by the GDR government in the 1980s. This involved the reversal of later alterations

made by Stüler, with the realisation of details by Schinkel that had originally failed to be implemented. At the same time, the usage of the building was changed, becoming a museum for 19th century sculpture. Significant defects in the reconstruction led to a further restoration after reunification, completed in 2000. In a number of years time, the effect of the historic Werdersche Markt will also be recreated with the dense rebuilding of the adjoining plots, currently standing empty.

Altes Museum (62)
Old Museum
1830
Am Lustgarten
Karl Friedrich Schinkel

At the time of its creation, the Altes Museum was the only museum in Germany. At the same time, with the Madrid Prado (1787) and the British Museum in London (1753), it was only the third museum anywhere in Europe. The rectangular, broad, two-storey structure with its four wings is connected through a staircase almost 98 feet in width. The stairway is one of the most remarkable of Schinkel's creations. 18 ionic columns underscore the monumental nature of the current entrance building to the Museumsinsel (no. 50). The heart of the Altes Museum is the rotunda, some 75 feet in height, in which 20 Corinthian columns support a gallery structure. This design has a parallel with the Pantheon in Rome, which is also lit with zenital lighting and the cupola of which is also decorated with panels.

Elisabethkirche (63)
St. Elisabeth Church
1834
Invalidenstraße 3
Karl Friedrich Schinkel

This temple-like building was built in combination with three further churches planned by Schinkel for the northern suburbs of Berlin (see no. 64). The Elisabethkirche was gutted by fire in 1945. For decades it was no more than a ruin, until action groups recently successfully lobbied for its restoration. The church is a single-nave, rectangular rendered structure with apse and tympanum, together with a pillared portico, also gabled. Both

gables are decorated with acroters. The interior once housed two-storey timber galleries, with a corresponding double row of rectangular windows on the side fronts, with sandstone crossbars. A cast zinc font remains of the original fittings. In future, private organisers will be able to use the church for exhibitions, concerts and other events.

Nazarethkirche (64)
Nazareth church
1835
Leopoldplatz
Karl Friedrich Schinkel

Schinkel designed four new church buildings (see no. 63) for the northern suburbs
that had been created as a consequence
of the expansion of the city. The most
prominent site, in the centre of a square,
was occupied by the Nazarethkirche.
Like the other three churches, it is a single nave hall design without tower, with
semi-circular apse and galleries. In the
design, Schinkel referred back to the
Romanesque forms of upper Italy, with
three round arch portals and a rosette
window decorating the enclosed front of
the church. In the 1880s, the church
received the addition of an apse, with a
suspended ceiling added in 1906, still in
place to this day. In 1981, a fundamental
restoration was carried out, with the il-
lustrations on the panelled ceiling and
walls recreated.

Bauakademie (65)
Academy of Architecture
1836
Schinkelplatz
Karl Friedrich Schinkel

DEMOLITION Situated in a prominent,
central position with numerous visual
links to the Lustgarten, Schloss and

Werdersche Markt, Schinkel's Bauakademie is the most modern of his buildings:
a cube-shaped brick building with four
equal facades without a central intona-
tion. The eight respective axes formed
the interior pattern of the design from
segmented arches, a feature that he had
noted on his voyage to England. The function of the sparse decor of violet bricks
and beige terracotta stripes was to refine
the building, making it appear less bulky.
Terracotta tablets beneath the windows
depict the history of architecture. The serial construction of the Bauakademie
makes it an early forerunner of modern
raster structures. The interior of the
building was reconstructed on a number
of occasions. Following partial destruction in the Second World War, work had
begun on its reconstruction. Despite this,
the Bauakademie was demolished in
1961 to make way for the new Foreign

Ministry of the GDR on Schinkelplatz
(see no. 317). Following the demolition of
this building, the site is vacant once
more. There is broad agreement on the
reconstruction of the Bauakademie.
Since early 2001, the northeast corner of
the building has stood on the rebuilt
Schinkelplatz, reconstructed by appren-

tices. It has not yet been decided to what extent a new construction should adhere to the historic original. One possible use of the new building is as a museum of architecture.

Altes Palais (66)
Old Palace
1837
Unter den Linden 9
Carl Ferdinand Langhans

As with so many other buildings in Berlin, only the facade of the Altes Palais is original. But what a facade! Distinctive features are the high, broad surfaces of the main storey and the richly ornamented mezzanine above it. Frieze-like, small window openings interchange with allegoric figures and coats of arms, with a radiant blue serving to further vitalise the pattern. Two mighty eagles occupy the corners. In 1943, the building was burnt out, with the magnificent interior lost. A side veranda, linking to the rolling form of the library on Bebelplatz, was also lost. In 1963, the front facades were rebuilt, with all rear sections torn down and replaced by a modern building, used by institutes of the Humboldt University. There is an internal connection to the adjoining building, the reconstruction of a 1721 Baroque house from Rathausstraße, with an altered entrance.

Hollmannsche
Wilhelminen-Amalien-Stiftung (67)
Hollmannsche Wilhelmine Amalie
Foundation
from 1839
Koppenplatz 11

This plain, rendered building is an example of the continuity of noble Classicism in the architecture of Berlin. The original building was supplemented by a tower-like extension in 1850, with the new sections of the building on Koppenplatz from 1869 and 1873 adapting to the same style. Beneath the entrance is an inscription with a reference to the original use of the building. Following the death of Wilhelmine Amalie Hollmann, her husband established a foundation for the widows and daughters of senior civil servants. During the GDR years, the building was used as a home for senior citizens.

Kunsthof (68)
Art Courtyard
1840
Oranienburger Straße 27

The late Classical construction is a completely preserved example of the Berlin mixture of residential and commercial usage in a courtyard system. Construction was begun in 1840. During the GDR era, the ensemble was in danger of collapse, before being saved with a significant financial contribution from the heritage conservation office and private investors, with a subsequent comprehensive modernisation. In 1989, the Kunsthof Gesellschaft drew up new usage concepts for artistic and creative trades. The courtyard is distinguished from others by its choice of colour and cloud like rendering, a contrast to the clinical appearance assumed by its neighbours following renovation. The Café Silberstein took up the tradition of a restaurant of the same name dating from 1910. The courtyard houses galleries and shops.

Wohnhäuser (69)
Residential Buildings
1840
Schumannstraße 14-17

The street was named after the soap boiler Schumann, who had houses erected

here from 1823 onwards. The district was long characterised by barracks and parade grounds, later also by theatres (see no. 142). The Biedermeier houses of no. 14−17 represent the remnants of a formerly complete row of houses, and were constructed in the course of the development of Friedrich-Wilhelm-Stadt between 1830 and 1840. The three-storey rendered buildings have large passages and side wings to the courtyards. House no. 16 boasts a generous timber stairway.

Tierärztliche Hochschule (70)
Veterinary College
1840
Luisenstraße 56
Ludwig Hesse

When the afternoon sun shines upon this building, one has the feeling of being transported to Italy. One reason for this is the attractive patina of the ochre-coloured rendering. The house is a prime example of the Classicism of Schinkel's

successors in Berlin. The imposing three-winged construction with its side passage gateways forms a courtyard to the street. An eye-catching element is the sturdy central projection with large rounded arch for the main entrance and halls in the first floor. The reserved decor consists of a Classical group of figures in the triangular gable, relief busts of renowned veterinarians and acroters on the gables of the side wings.

Wohnhäuser (71)
Residential Buildings
circa 1840
Marienstraße

Marienstraße is the best-preserved street with original buildings in the centre of

Berlin. Like the adjoining streets, it was built around 1825 on the site of former gardens and was part of a planned expansion of the city, Friedrich-Wilhelm Stadt. Most of the three-storey rendered buildings were constructed between 1830 and 1840. Stairways from this era can still be found in building nos. 11, 12, 14, 21 and 27. The facades were restored for the first time in 1970, and almost all of the houses have been completely renovated in recent years.

St.-Jacobi-Kirche (72)
St. Jacob's Church
1845
Oranienstraße 132–134
Friedrich August Stüler

Somewhat lost in the centre of a group of new buildings stands a picturesque church construction from the Schinkel school. Stüler designed a brick basilica along the example of early Christian and Italian models. It is framed by two con-

structions added at a later date, the vicarage and the parsonage. Following destruction in the Second World War, the church was rebuilt in 1957 with a new, simple interior, without galleries. In 1982, Gerhard Spangenberg added two further vicarage buildings at the rear, weaving them sensitively into the existing material and symmetry of the church complex.

St.-Matthäus-Kirche (73)
St. Matthew's Church
1846
Matthäikirchplatz
Friedrich August Stüler

The Matthäi-Kirche stands rather forlornly in the midst of the spacious, postwar Kulturforum (no. 311); the sole surviving building of a once elegant district. Albert Speer wished to tear down parts of the historic quarter as early as the 1930s, in order to erect a section of the "north-south axis" of his Germania plan (see no. 225). The Matthäi-Kirche originally stood at the centre of a rectangular square, the outline of which can still be seen today in the current layout of the streets. It was constructed in Byzantine style with round arched windows and a horizontal brick pattern. The triple nave complex can be seen from the three gables and apses. Heavily damaged in the war, the exterior was reconstructed in 1960, with the interior redesigned in an extremely plain, modern form.

53

James Hobrecht
* 1825 in Memel, † 1902 in Berlin (74)

"How much of the earnings from the services required by the better-off trickle down to the poorer inhabitants of the tenements!"

James Hobrecht, 1868

James Hobrecht created what continues to be the core of the German capital to this day: the urban development plan that, during the Kaiser era, turned Berlin into the "largest tenement city in Europe" (see no. 113), together with a sewer - system that was to establish itself as the most resilient network in the city.

Following a significant period in which the "tenement" model was held to be an example of inhuman construction, Hobrecht's work is now generally acclaimed. Attempts are now even underway to rebuild the Gründerzeit city.

James Hobrecht (the first name came from English ancestors) was born in 1825 in the eastern part of East Prussia, the second of five children. He broke off his studies in agriculture, working initially as a surveyor, moving to the Prussian capital in 1847, in order to pursue his studies at the Bauakademie (no. 65). One year later, the revolution broke out. As a National Liberal fighting on the side of the rebels, Hobrecht remained a child of the 1848 revolution for the rest of his days: marked by his experience that seemingly immovable circumstances can be brought into motion, and that freedom and self-determination of the people are no longer abstract formulations.

It is against this background that the development plan of 1862 should be seen, conceived by Hobrecht as the government's master builder on behalf of the Berlin Chief of Police. The fact that the population of the city had doubled in scarcely 25 years led to him extending the municipal area by five and half times its size. Legislation was more supportive of the public sphere than that of the property owners, who nonetheless maintained their grip on state power due to the linkage of suffrage with property ownership. Hobrecht developed a street plan interspersed at relatively regular intervals by squares. The streets were 72 feet wide or more, and laid out as decoratively as the garden artist Peter Joseph Lenné (see no. 60) had previously decreed.

A minimum of rules enabled a maximum of urban growth: with the entry into force of the development plan scarcely a decade passed before the population of Berlin had doubled again. Hobrecht favoured tenement buildings due to their "recommendable mixed habitation" of rich and poor – the richer inhabitants in the piano nobile at the front of the complex, poorer citizens in the roof and cellar apartments, as well as to the rear. This cohabitation of the different social classes did not last long, however. In addition, living in such close proximity soon endangered the health of the population: over one thousand inhabitants died each year from typhus alone, one of the principal reasons for this lying in the fact that excrement was collected in cess pits, which became breeding grounds for infection. After Hobrecht had pressed for hygiene to become a primary concern for some years, in the 1860s, as construction counsellor of Stettin he was able to plan and construct the sewage systems of the city, together with the waterworks. With

this reference, and the support of the doctor and politician Rudolf Virchow, in 1872 he received the commission to construct a similar system for Berlin. Four years later the sewage system was inaugurated, with completion in 1907. In contrast to systems such as that in use in London, the sewage was not channelled into the rivers from which drinking water was drawn, but employed as fertiliser on fields. With this concept, Hobrecht became a leading and recognised urban engineer for more than 30 German towns and cities. He also developed similar plans for Moscow, Cairo and Tokyo.

In 1885, Hobrecht was appointed construction counsellor for civil and underground engineering. During the 12-year occupancy of this position, he had the Spree regulated within the municipal district of Berlin, thus hindering flooding and water logging of the ground. In addition, 28 bridges were constructed, with at least six of these designed by Hobrecht himself. The effects of his municipal activity are still tangible in the urban landscape today.

On his retirement in 1897, Hobrecht was honoured by the city with the elevation of the privy construction counsellor to the position of alderman of Berlin. He remained an esteemed figure in his field, associated intrinsically to construction in the capital as a member of the Königlichen Akademie des Bauwesens, the royal construction academy, and Berliner Architektenvereins, Berlin's architectural association, until his death in 1902. hwh

Hygiene becomes a sovereign task: Hobrecht's sewerage plan.

ehem. Hamburger Bahnhof (75)
former Hamburger Railway Station
1847
Invalidenstraße 50–51
Friedrich Neuhaus

The oldest existing railway station in Berlin and one of the oldest anywhere in Germany, it was in use for a mere 37 years. An elegant, Classical complex with characteristic double tower facade, in which trains could originally drive right into the courtyard of the building, before being rotated on a turntable. In the 1990s, the station was converted into a museum of contemporary art (no. 391) by Josef Paul Kleihues (no. 356).

Kronprinzenpalais (76)
Crown Prince Palace
1857
Unter den Linden 3
Johann Heinrich Strack

From the outside, it is impossible to recognise that the current Kronprinzenpalais is a complete reconstruction. The structure was originally a two-storey affair, with a mansard roof. In 1857 this was replaced by an additional floor, the facade was redesigned in late Classical style and a pergola was added on the left hand side. Heavily damaged in the Second World War, the ruins were later torn

down completely. It was not until 1968 that work began on the external reconstruction, as part of the general reapprai-

sal of Prussian heritage. The reconstruction work was headed by Richard Paulick, who also designed the new room layout of the interior, in Classical style. In 1990, the Unification Treaty was signed at this location.

Neues Museum (77)
New Museum
1859
Bodestraße 4
Friedrich August Stüler

The Altes Museum (no. 62) by Karl Friedrich Schinkel (no. 44) was originally planned to stand alone. However, whilst still Crown Prince, the later King Friedrich Wilhelm IV worked on the idea of developing the entire northern tip of the Spree Island as an area for arts and sciences. The first element of this plan was

the Neues Museum. The centrepiece was an imposing stairway, as high as the building itself, in the centre of the rectangular building, decorated with a cycle of paintings by Kaulbach, depicting the history of mankind. Stüler grouped the rooms of the respective north and south wings around a courtyard. While Stüler maintained the elegant, reserved Classicism of the Schinkel school for the exterior, the interior was lavishly decorated with motifs from the Ancient World. These are reminiscent of Schinkel's later plans for a royal castle in the Crimea, which were never realised. The Neues Museum suffered severe damage in the war, with the northwest wing completely demolished. While the GDR government

rebuilt and renovated the other structures on the Museumsinsel, the Neues Museum remained a ruin until the fall of the Wall. The British architect David Chipperfield plans to have the building reconstructed by 2007.

ehem. Garde du Corps Kasernen   (78)
former Garde du Corps Barracks
1859
Schloßstraße 1 – 1 A und 70
Friedrich August Stüler

These buildings were erected in late Classical style as a counterpart to Schloss Charlottenburg (no. 19) and to accentuate Schloßstraße. They are crowned by small rounded temples, through which light falls into the courtyards. From 1967 until 2005, the eastern side of the complex was home to the Egyptian collection of the Staatliche Museen, with the bust of Queen Nofretete. The western barracks had housed the antiquities collection since 1958. In 1996, the architects Hilmer-Sattler-Albrecht converted this building for the Sammlung Berggruen collection. Heinz Berggruen was forced to leave the city in 1936, at the age of 21, and went on to become an important art dealer and collector in Paris. Today, the upper floor of the building is the Berlin apartment of the Berggruens.

ehem. Jüdisches Krankenhaus (79)
former Jewish hospital
1860
Auguststraße 14–16
Eduard Knoblauch

Amazing what effect a rendered facade can have! This late Classical building, today flanked by two brick-built structures, has a most unusual layout: a mighty round arch doorway, connecting the two lower floors, and above it a piano nobile with elegant decorative elements, topped off by a richly ornamented cornice fascia. The doorway of the rear building is also decorated with noteworthy ornamentation. Originally erected as a hospital for the Jewish community, the complex soon became one of the most modern medical establishments in Germany. After the First World War, a children's home was added to the rear building. In 1938, the building was closed down by the Nazis, who subsequently used it to house elderly people from the district prior to their deportation.

Villa von der Heydt (80)
Villa von der Heydt
1861
Von-der-Heydt-Straße 18
Hermann Ende, G. A. Linke

Not much remains of the once-rich villa landscape in the southern Tiergarten district. Even the Villa von der Heydt, a rendered building in late Classical style with Ionic porticus and imposing cornice, is only retained in original style on the exterior. Following destruction in the war, the house was rebuilt in 1967 as the official seat of the president of the Stiftung Preußischer Kulturbesitz, the Prussian cultural foundation. The plain interior, inspired by Classical images, was designed by Nany Wiegand-Hoffmann.

Palais am Festungsgraben (81)
Mansion at the Moat
1863
Am Festungsgraben 1
Heinrich Bürde, Hermann v. d. Hude

Somewhat concealed behind the Neue Wache (see no. 52) stands this elegant Classical building. The core of the building dates from the middle of the 18th century, and the building was home to the Prussian Minister of Finance from 1787. The house was converted and extended in 1863 by v. d. Hude to plans by Bürde. The interior conceals a number of treasures, most significant of which are the twin stairway and a hall on the ground floor, which was added in 1934 from the former Weydingerhaus, possibly originating from the hand of Karl Friedrich Schinkel (no. 44).

Neue Synagoge (82)
New Synagogue
1866
Oranienburger Straße 30
Eduard Knoblauch, Friedrich August Stüler

This building was once the largest synagogue in Berlin and remains the most attractive to this day. It was erected in Oriental style as part of the development lining the street and is crowned by an imposing dome, flanked by two smaller cupolas and visible over a significant distance. The grand facade with terracotta on the main portals is divided horizontally by coloured bricks. An imposing cast iron stairway is located inside the building. During the "Night of Broken Glass", the rear of the building, in particular, was heavily damaged, and later demolished. The front of the building was rebuilt in 1988-91 with financial support from the Federal Republic of Germany. The height

of the original nave is indicated today by a glazed roof. In 1991, the dome was also reconstructed. Today, the rooms are used by the Jewish community in Berlin. A museum and the dome are open to visitors.

Berliner Rathaus   (83)
Berlin City Hall
1869
Rathausstraße 15
Hermann Friedrich Waesemann

This building continues to be referred to as the Rotes Rathaus, the red city hall, to this day. A name that refers to the colour of the bricks, not, as many suspect, to the political circumstances of the GDR era. The new building was erected on the site of the Altes Rathaus in a round arch style based upon that of the Italian early Renaissance, on an almost rectangular floor plan. It has three courtyards and a 318-feet high tower, in the style of Flemish belfries, which, when approached from the west, stands precisely in the axis to the Unter den Linden. The brick structure is decorated with architectural sculpture in sandstone and terracotta. The balustrade of the main floor balcony boasts a long terracotta frieze, the Steinerne Chro-

nik or stone chronicle, depicting scenes from the history of Berlin from its foundation to the establishment of the Reich in 1871. Behind the main portal, steep steps lead up to the Festsaal, the festival hall. In 1945, the building was heavily damaged by bombs; the interior was partly redesigned in the reconstruction. Since 1991, the Rotes Rathaus has been the seat of the ruling Mayor of Berlin.

Thomaskirche   (84)
St. Thomas' Church
1869
Mariannenplatz
Friedrich Adler

The little-known Thomaskirche is the most significant church structure of the Schinkel school (see no. 44). Adler combined stylistic elements of the Bauakademie and Romanesque churches in Cologne and Italy. From an urban planning viewpoint, the church forms the conclusion of the axis Mariannenplatz – Mariannenstraße. Characteristic features are the highly-visible double tower facade and drum cupola. In the interior of the church, cast iron struts were employed for the first time in church con-

Wohnhäuser (85)
Residential Buildings
um 1870
Neue Schönhauser Straße 12-15

In Neue Schönhauser Straße, a reanimated area since the fall of the Wall, stand a number of residential houses from the middle of the 19th century, a number of them with well-preserved front steps (nos. 12 and 14). The courtyard of house no. 15 would not look out of place in a village scene, with two timber galleries reminiscent of the old towns of other central European metropolises. No. 13, the former Volkskaffeehaus, is one of the earlier works of Alfred Messel, from the year 1891.

Siegessäule (86)
Victory Column
1873
Großer Stern
Johann Heinrich Strack

struction. The reconstruction in the years up to 1963 enabled the exterior to be recreated in original form, whereas, inside, the pulpit was moved forward and the side galleries removed.

The Siegessäule originally stood in front of the Reichstag (no. 106) in the centre of Königsplatz (now Platz der Republik). It

danten, the town commander. In 1873, the Baroque mansard roof was replaced by an additional storey and the facade redesigned in Renaissance style with a distinctive block rendering. Undamaged in the Second World War, the building was torn down in the early 1960s to make way for the GDR Foreign Ministry, itself pulled down in 1995 (no. 317). Behind the facade of the Kommandantenhaus, rebuilt on original lines, the Bertelsmann Group has erected its Berlin office, as meeting venue for the corporation (no. 508). The Cologne architect Thomas van den Valentyn was commissioned with the design of the interior. This was the first historic building to be reconstructed in Berlin following reunification.

was erected here in 1866-73 as a monument to the victorious Franco-German war. At the top of the column stands Viktoria, goddess of victory, by Friedrich Drake, in the Berlin vernacular Goldelse. The shaft of the column is decorated with golden cannon, with martial scenes depicted on the plinth in relief form. In the course of the Germania plans of Hitler's master builder, Albert Speer (no. 225), the column was moved to the current position on modern-day Straße des 17. Juni, and increased in height with the addition of a column drum. Today, it forms the central point of the Tiergarten, visible from a great distance, forming an interesting contrast to the trees of the park over the course of the seasons. The traffic island upon which it stands can be reached using a pedestrian underpass, for the entrance of which Speer designed four neo-Classical temples in 1938. A narrow spiral staircase leads up to an observation platform.

Kommandantenhaus (87)
Commander's House
1873
Unter den Linden 1

DEMOLITION In 1653, this superb site opposite the Zeughaus (no. 16) was chosen as the location for the private house of Johann Gregor Memhardt, architect to the Elector. From 1799, the building was the seat of the Berliner Stadtkomman-

Landesvertretung von Sachsen-Anhalt
(ehem. Palais Bülow) (88)
State Representative for Saxony-Anhalt
(former Bülow Palace)
1874
Luisenstraße 18

With its core a bourgeois building of 1828, the facade received a new decorative appearance with late Classical orna-

mentation in 1874, with frieze and reliefs. In 1946, the famous East Berlin artists' club "Die Möwe" moved into the building. The ground floor is in a different form today. The interior retains a cast iron staircase with marble fittings from 1874, together with richly decorated rooms. Following many years in which it stood empty, and numerous changes of ownership, today the building is the state representative for Saxony-Anhalt.

Alte Nationalgalerie (89)
Old National Gallery
1876
Bodestraße 3
Friedrich August Stüler,
Johann Heinrich Strack

This was how the romantic Prussian King Friedrich Wilhelm IV imagined the Museumsinsel (no. 50): like an emperor's forum in ancient Rome, with mighty, elevated temples and spacious squares sprinkled with colonnades. And it is in this style that Stüler's Nationalgalerie continues to stand majestically on the Museumsinsel. Stüler drew inspiration for his design from a memorial temple by Friedrich Gilly, designed for Friedrich II and never realised. The original plan was for the structure to house an auditorium and lecture rooms for the university. During the construction period, the intended purpose of the building was altered. The collection of contemporary German painting was to be housed there, after having been donated to the state in 1861 by Consul Wagener. As a consequence, the building had to adapted to meet the requirements of an art gallery. To ensure an adequate source of light for the exhibition rooms, the original full columns were amended as semi columns and the north facade was converted into a semicircle. The imposing open staircase added appears to serve the sole purpose of framing the statue of Friedrich Wilhelm IV. It has no true function, as the building is entered through the round arched doorway on the ground floor. The red sandstone building with its temple form stands perched on a 39 feet-high plinth. Between 1911–13, the order of the rooms in the interior was partially altered by Justi. In the GDR era, the interior of the museum was reconstructed, with a number of alterations. The most recent renovation, by the Stuttgart architect HG Merz involved the building being fitted (almost invisibly) with the latest technology. The interior, dating from a variety of eras, was not reconstructed in a uniform new style, but augmented carefully in the style of the age. The Alte Nationalgalerie is the first building to have its reconstruction completed in the scope of the master plan of the Museumsinsel.

63

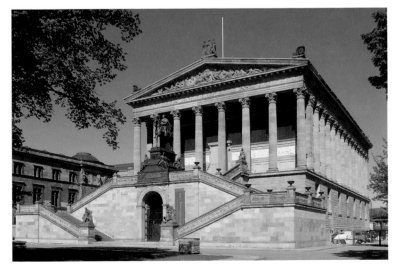

From Capital of the Empire to European Metropolis 1871–1918 (90)

With the founding of the German Reich in 1871, Berlin took the final step to becoming the political, economic and cultural centre of Germany. The metropolis attracted migrants from throughout Germany like no other city. In the last four decades of the 19th century, the number of inhabitants quadrupled from 500,000 to two million. The reparation payments from France, defeated in the Franco-Prussian War, led to a general economic upswing. A characteristic aspect of this era, often referred to as "Wilhelminian", after the Kaisers Wilhelm I and Wilhelm I, was that Germany, although economically the most advanced nation in Europe, had the most regressive political constitution.

A consequence of this period of upheaval was a fundamental alteration of the visage of the city. Within the space of just a few decades, the historic city centre and Tiergarten (no. 60) were surrounded by an enormous ring of tenement districts (no. 113), with numerous churches, schools, hospitals, public baths and public parks. In 1873, work began on a new sewer network, to plans by the construction counsellor James Hobrecht (no. 74),

supported by the doctor and politician Rudolf Virchow. This sewer system is still in functional use today. At the turn of the century the "world's largest tenement district" was both one of the healthiest and cleanest major cities in Europe. The architecture of the municipal buildings was influenced heavily around the turn of the century by Ludwig Hoffmann (no. 141), who was construction counsellor in Berlin for a period of almost 30 years.

The middle classes were attracted primarily to the "Neuer Westen", the centre of which became established in the neo-Romanesque district around the Kaiser-Wilhelm-Gedächtniskirche (no. 107). The Kurfürstendamm (no. 145) was laid out to a width of 177 feet, and was soon flanked on either side by ostentatious residential buildings. Wilmersdorf and Schöneberg also saw breathtaking growth in new street networks, interspersed with decorative squares (see Viktoria-Luise-Platz no. 120). The centre of the city saw the addition of two poorly-situated Wilhelminian state buildings, the Reichstag building (no. 106) and the Berliner Dom.

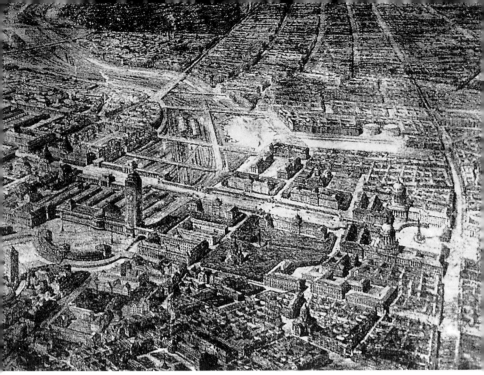

A world metropolis as envisioned at the beginning of the 20th century: Bruno Schmitz's entry for the Greater Berlin Competition (1910).

The drive for the decorative saw a blooming of the city. Every unused space, every green area was decorated with sculptures from the school of Berliner Realismus. The most famous sculptor of the time was Reinhold Begas, whose works included the Kaiser-Wilhelm-Denkmal memorial at the Schlossfreiheit, demolished after the war along with the Berlin Stadtschloss (no. 7).

The first lines for the over ground and underground urban railways were built. Before the gates of the former city walls, a ring of railway stations, port facilities, city canals, slaughterhouses and giant factories grew. In 1882, the first electric arc lamps were fitted in Leipziger Straße and on Potsdamer Platz, three years later the first large municipal power station entered into operation.

In 1910, the capital held an urban planning competition (no. 157), covering a much larger area than the municipal area, which by 1920 had reached the borders that it occupies today. This was the first attempt to plan the Greater Berlin area. No other European metropolis had investigated this theme at such an early stage.

At the same time, in Berlin in the early years of the 20th century (similarly to the beginning of the 19th century), a new architectural form of European influence took shape: Alfred Messel designed his large department stores (of which no single example remains today (see no. 126, 137)) and Peter Behrens built the famous turbine hall for AEG (no. 151).

These novelties are often described as a "preliminary stage" for the Modernist era of the 1920s. For the Berlin architectural historian Julius Posener, in contrast, this evaluation is an inadequate one. He notes that, "this era ... has its own colour and its own value", and, moreover, "that the years up to 1918 were the decisive ones".   rh

Volkspark Friedrichshain (91)
Friedrichshain Public Park
1876
Am Friedrichshain/Friedenstraße/
Landsberger Allee
Gustav Meyer

GARDEN The original park dates back to a resolution of 1840, for the creation of an eastern counterpart to the Tiergarten (no. 60). This became the first public park in the east of Berlin. The park was expanded significantly in the time up to 1876 by the same architect. In 1913, Ludwig Hoffmann (no. 141) created the popular Märchenbrunnen fountain. The travertine neo-Baroque feature was heavily damaged in the war and rebuilt later. The anti-aircraft bunker that stood in the park from the early 1940s was demolished after the war and buried in a larger and smaller mound together with stone rubble from the demolished Berliner Stadtschloss (no. 7). The park was subjected to numerous alterations in the GDR era; in the early 1970s a section was converted into sports and games areas.

Wasserspeicher (92)
Water Reservoir
1877
Knaackstraße 23
Henry Gill, Wilhelm Vollhering

The first networked water supply facility for a German municipality was built from 1852 on the (then pristine) Windmühlen-

berg. In the years up to 1856, on behalf of the Prussian state, the British Berlin Waterworks Co., with Henry Gill, built a minaret-like riser pipe tower and an open basin for 105,930 cubic feet of water, which was covered with vaulted rings in 1889. From 1875, with the area now an established urban district, the facility was extended with the addition of a bulky neo-Gothic water tower with a cone roof. Beneath the elevated tank Wilhelm Vollhering added five apartment floors with conical rooms. Where the apartments continue to be inhabited, the engineering fittings were closed down between 1914 and 1952. Today, the underground tank has a temporary use as a space for artists.

ehem. Haupttelegrafenamt (93)
former Central Telegraph Office
1878
Jägerstraße 42–44
Carl Schwatlo

The oldest surviving postal complex in Berlin was built as a central telegraph office, along the lines of a Venetian palace of the high Renaissance. The deep, richly decorated sandstone facade has a horizontal structural layout. Above the rusticated ground floor are two main floors with Ionic and Corinthian domed columns, with pairs of putti between the windows of the attic storey. The facade facing Oberwallstraße was rebuilt after reunification. In 1902, an extension was added to fit in exactly with the existing building. Today, the complex is used as the Berlin office of Deutsche Telekom.

ehem. Institutsgebäude (94)
former institute building
1878
Dorotheenstraße 94–96
Paul Spieker

The uniform architectural design of the original, late Classical three-storey building has its roots in the traditions of the Schinkel school (see no. 44). This comprehensive building complex was erected for a number of scientific institutes of the Humboldt University. The facades are clad in yellow brick and broken up by horizontal strips of coloured stone. Profile and terracotta stone were used for the cornices, surrounds and balustrades. Inside, a cast iron stairway dates back to the

time of construction, together with the largely original auditorium with surrounding gallery and skylight. The wing on Reichstagufer was destroyed in the war, with the site now home to the new Berlin studios of the ARD broadcasting company, amongst other tenants.

Anhalter Bahnhof (95)
Anhalter Railway Station
1880
Askanischer Platz 6–7
Franz Schwechten

DEMOLITION A remnant of a portico is all that remains of Schwechten's once imposing Anhalter Bahnhof. This fragment enables an idea to be conveyed of the rich sculptural ornamentation of the structure. The open area behind provides an idea of the scale of the former departure hall. It was 558 feet long and 203 feet

67

wide, covered by an audacious iron and glass roof construction. Having survived the war intact, this "mother cavern of railways" (Walter Benjamin) was blown up in 1959.

Postfuhramt (96)
Postal Transportation Authority
1881
Oranienburger Straße 35/36
Carl Schwatlo, Wilhelm Tuckermann

In 1875, on the site of the former Postillonhaus, work began on one of the most complex administrative buildings of its time. The imposing building with extensive courtyard area housed various branches of the postal authority, including a fleet of vehicles with over 200 horses over two storeys. An eye-catching element of the structure is the corner of Oranienburger and Tucholskystraße with its monumental rounded alcove, capped by an octagonal drum, flanked by two smaller octagonal cupolas. The striped facade is faced with bricks and coloured terracotta in Italian Renaissance styles. A striking element is the quality of the ornamental and figurative reliefs.

Martin-Gropius-Bau
(ehem. Kunstgewerbemuseum) (97)
Martin Gropius Building
(former Museum of Arts and Crafts)
1881
Stresemannstr. 110
Martin Gropius, Heino Schmieden

This splendid, significant building of the Schinkel school (see no. 14) almost disappeared from the urban landscape. It stood in the way of a new road in the 1960s and a committee of experts decided that it was not worthy of preservation. The intervention of Walter Gropius (the great nephew of the builder, flown in for the occasion) saved the building. The exterior was reconstructed in 1981 by Winnetou Kampmann and designated for the staging of alternating, large-scale exhibitions. Since then, visitors have accessed

the building via the rear entrance as the main doorway was unusable, due to the Wall running directly in front of it (no. 301). A renewed renovation with café and the recreation of the former entrance situation was performed by Hilmer-Sattler-Albrecht, with completion in 1999. The building was originally erected as an arts and crafts museum, closely based upon Schinkel's Bauakademie (no. 65). The facade decoration refers to the various departments of the museum and the artistic goals of the arts and crafts school. The interior boasts an impressive courtyard.

Stadtbahnviadukt (98)
City Train Viaduct
1882
between Savignyplatz and Ostbahnhof
Ernst Dircksen

The growing importance of the railways led to a requirement for a capable rail connection through the inner city. In 1871, August Orth realised the idea of the "detached central railway stations". Eight railway termini for long-distance transport, together with the S-Bahn ring under construction at that time were to be connected with the construction of a Nord-Süd-Tunnel (no. 252) and an east-west embankment. In the historic centre, in particular, the problem emerged as to how the line was to traverse the densely built-up area, without the necessity of demolishing too many buildings. The

continental innovation lay in the form of a space-saving viaduct, erected on the filled-in Baroque fortified moat, and whose 757 arches continue to provide the rail company with good rental income to this day. The fact that these structures continue to be the home of workshops, flea markets, dance halls and exhibition areas makes the S-Bahn an incomparably urban form of transportation.

Bahnhof Hackescher Markt (99)
Station at Hackescher Markt
1882
Neue Promenade, Am Zwirngraben
Johannes Vollmer

The railway station was built in association with the construction of the Stadt-

69

bahnviadukt (no. 98), which commenced in 1878 and ran through the inner city on the foundations of the former Baroque fortified moat. It is preserved in original condition, in contrast to the railway stations of Alexanderplatz (no. 418) and Friedrichstraße, built at the time, but altered on numerous occasions through the course of their history. The roof of the 328-feet long, 52-feet wide platform hall is borne by flat iron arches. The facade of the station, in particular in the direction of the Neue Promenade, is richly faced with brick and terracotta panels, with the encrusted ornamentation reminiscent of Italian structures.

Ackerhalle (100)
Covered Market Ackerhalle
1888
Invalidenstraße 158
Hermann Blankenstein

At the end of the 19th century, it was planned to replace the standard open-air weekly markets with two large central covered market halls and 13 covered market halls. Of these, only the Ackerhalle remains standing today. Its spine is formed by a slightly raised "nave", 39 feet in width, running parallel to Invalidenstraße, joined on both sides by two 20 feet wide "aisles". These are separated from one another by means of cast iron props. The facade is faced with brick in Renaissance style and is still in original condition. On Ackerstraße, a portal alcove in the form of a victory arch marks the main entrance. After additions from 1970 had restricted the spatial impression for a considerable time, the interior was restored to its original form in a heritage reconstruction in 1991.

**Bundesministerium
für Verkehr und Bau** (101)
*Federal Ministry of Transport
and Construction*
1888
Invalidenstraße 42–44
Hermann Blankenstein

The present-day Federal Ministry was originally built as Geologische Landesanstalt (see no. 439) and was the westernmost section of a building complex for the natural history museum and institute of Humboldt University. It was built in Renaissance style, with accents of French Classicism. Two twin buildings stand directly on Invalidenstraße. Between them is the Museum für Naturkunde, the natural history museum, set back, with a subsequent forecourt. The Landesanstalt was erected in the form of a four-winged complex around a large atrium with surrounding pillared arcades. In the foyer is a bench with eagle motif and two lions lying on the stair strings.

**Deutscher Beamtenbund
(ehem. Pschorr- Brauerei/
ehem. Haus der Demokratie)** (102)
*Civil Servants Association
(former Pschorr Brewery/former House
of Democracy)*
1889
Friedrichstraße 165
Karl von Großheim, Heinrich Joseph Kayser

This prestigious corner building was erected much in the typology of a public bar. Originally, the complex stretched to Französische Straße, from where it took supplies of goods and raw materials. On Behrenstraße, the former Pschorr-Brauerei presents a solid construction, combining decorative elements of neo-Baroque (upper floors) and neo-Renaissance (ground floor). With its rough rustic brickwork and deep pointing, the two-storey base is illustrative of the typically heavy, solidity of a Berlin commercial building of this era. The heavy profiling of the sandstone facade continues into the cornice beneath the guttering, as well as in the opulent decorative elements beneath the segment gables of the implied central projection. The building boasts a colourful past. In the GDR era, the building was the local seat of the ruling SED party, after reunification it was used by a number of initiatives and associations as Haus der Demokratie. Since 2001 it has been home to the Deutschen Beamtenbund.

Kulturbrauerei
(ehem. Schultheiß-Brauerei) (103)
Culture Brewery
(former Schultheiß Brewery)
1891
Schönhauser Allee 36–39,
Sredzkistraße 1–17, Knaackstraße 75–97
Franz Schwechten

Water quality and soil conditions, which enabled deep cellars to be constructed, were the reasons why numerous breweries were established on Prenzlauer Berg in the mid 19th century. From 1886, Schultheiß presided over the construc-

tion of the largest lager beer factory in the world. Franz Schwechten, architect of the Anhalter Bahnhof (no. 95) and the Kaiser-Wilhelm-Gedächniskirche (see no. 107), constructed power supply room, magazine, boiler and brewing house, fermenting cellar, cellars, despatch and a public bar in brick. A tower on the corner of Sredzkistraße and Schönhauser Allee makes the complex recognisable from afar. The typical, neo Romanesque round arched style was an effective marketing ploy: the castle-like appearance signalled a good lager beer. Following the (relatively late) relocation of production in the post-war period, the complex was converted into a "Kulturbrauerei", a multicultural centre for the district, which, following reunification, was equipped with gastronomy, a theatre, supermarket and multiplex cinema.

»Wintergarten-Ensemble« (104)
Building Ensemble Winter Garden
1892
Fasanenstraße 23–25
Becker & Schlüter, L. Mertens,
Hans Grisebach

In elegant Fasanenstraße, there are two buildings bearing witness to the original development of this area with detached villas. Today, the picturesque ensemble is named after the conservatory of house no. 23, built by Becker & Schlüter in 1889 in the form of an Italian Renaissance palazzo. Today, it is used as a house of literature, with café and bookshop. House no. 24 was erected in 1871 by a master builder Mertens in textbook late Classical style, and later extended. Today, it houses the Käthe-Kollwitz-Museum. In

1892, the adjacent residential house, no. 25, was built by Hans Grisebach; today it is an art gallery. In the 1970s, it was planned to demolish the war-damaged building in favour of broadening the street, but the house was saved thanks to an action group and private sponsors.

Komische Oper (105)
Opera House Komische Oper
1892
Behrenstraße 54–57
Ferdinand Fellner

The original building was erected in 1892 as Theater Unter den Linden, later renamed Metropol-Theater. It was once linked using the Kleine Lindenpassage to Unter den Linden and boasted an ornately decorated historic entrance facade. Following damage in the Second World War, the main front on Behrenstraße was recreated in extremely plain form, with the stage area extended and an adminis-

tration building added on Unter den Linden. The two-level auditorium in Viennese late Baroque style and the central stairway remain in an almost unaltered condition.

Reichstagsgebäude (106)
Parliament Building
1894
Platz der Republik 1
Paul Wallot

The Reichstag has one of the longest planning histories of any building in Berlin. Following the establishment of the German Reich in 1871, a new parliament building was planned as a symbol of the newfound national unity. However, even the search for a suitable plot proved extremely difficult. A site on the other side of the current Platz der Republik was too far for the parliamentarians, and the site occupied by the Reichstag today was already occupied by a Palais, whose owner was most unwilling to sell. An initial competition in 1872 resulted in no decision being made, the second (only open to German architects) was won by the Frankfurt architect Paul Wallot. Where the other designs were characterised by an academic historism, Wallot employed elements from the Italian high Renaissance and motifs from the ancient world to create a "synthetic Reich style" (Tilmann Buddensieg). With the steel and

glass dome, Wallot also indicated a grasp of the contemporary technical options at his disposal. Kaiser Wilhelm II followed the process of construction with a critical eye, and not only because of this dome, which represented competition to the dome of the Schloss. The cube shaped building was considered unfortunately sited, due to having its "back" to the city centre, and comprised two inner court-yards. The compact corner towers, rising above the building, give it a bulky appearance. The two-storey main front is divided up by column porticos and colossal order with three quarter columns, with the remainder of the facade over three storeys. It was not until 1916 that Peter Behrens' inscription "Dem deutschen Volke", literally "for the German people", was added. The Reichstag was heavily damaged in the Second World War, with the dome, which threatened to collapse, later demolished. In the 1960s, the structure was reconstructed by Paul Baumgarten as a building for meetings of parliamentary parties and committees of the German Bundestag, with almost all of the remaining historic interior destroyed and replaced with extremely plain, modern elements. The majority of the rich sculpture work on the exterior was also removed. After the fall of the Wall, there was a new, fundamental reconstruction of the building, including a new dome, by Sir Norman Foster (no. 452). Opposite the rear side of the Reichstag stands the former house of the Reichstag president, dating from 1904 and also erected by Paul Wallot. Today this is the seat of the Parlamentarische Gesellschaft, an association of parliamentarians.

Kaiser-Wilhelm-Gedächtniskirche (107)
Emperor Wilhelm Memorial Church
1895
Breitscheidplatz
Franz Schwechten

During the period of division of the city, the damaged spire of the Kaiser-Wilhelm-Gedächtniskirche was the symbol of West Berlin. The preservation of the church ruin had previously been the subject of

an intense public debate. The Gedächtniskirche was built in a Rheinish late Romanesque style as part of a square development, which was also in late Romanesque style – that included the famous Romanische Café – of which nothing remains today. Following heavy damage in the Second World War and partial demolition in the 1950s, today only the mosaics of the entrance hall indicate an impression of the former interior. In 1963, Egon Eiermann added a tower and a church room, one of the best-executed ecclesiastical rooms of the post war period (see no. 302).

Oberbaumbrücke (108)
Oberbaum Bridge
1895
Warschauer Straße/Mühlenstraße
Otto Stahn

On the site of a timber bridge dating from 1724, the planned elevated railway required the construction of a new bridge. The seven-arched reinforced concrete

construction is faced with granite and brickwork. Alongside the tracks, structural elements were added in brick Gothic style. Two towers similar to the Mitteltorturm in Prenzlau recall the former function as a toll bridge. In the 1990s, the bridge was extensively renovated; in 1994 a steel bridge by Santiago Calatrava (see no. 394) was added for the centre section.

Geschäftshäuser (109)
Commercial Buildings
1895
Rosenstraße 1, 16–19
Otto March, Kayser & von Großheim

Despite their historic appearance, these commercial buildings were an example of early Modern design, oriented on the factory structures of the time. The complex, which originally comprised seven courtyards, was erected for leasing. Of the five original buildings, three remain today. An area for shops was planned behind the pedimental windows of the ground floor, with the floors above broken up by vertical pillars, with large, three-sided windows and painted metal balustrades between them. The courtyards are faced with brickwork.

AEG-Apparatefabrik (110)
AEG Apparatus Factory
1895
Ackerstraße 71–76
Franz Schwechten

Along with the Anhalter Bahnhof and Moabit power station, this factory building is one of the most significant technical structures erected by Schwechten. However, he was only responsible for the design of the facade, with the floor plan

provided by the AEG engineering department. This is an indication of how important the image was to the company at this early stage. The facade structure, with pedimental arches, pilasters and terracotta reliefs, is a direct successor to Schinkel's Bauakademie (no. 65). The wing facing on to the rear Hussitenstraße was damaged in the war and removed, with the exception of the ground floor.

Theater des Westens (111)
Theatre of the West
1896
Kantstraße 12
Bernhard Sehring

As with Kaufhaus des Westens (no. 143), the name of this theatre does not refer to the era of the divided city, but to the period of frantic westward expansion in the city at the end of the 19th century. The Theater des Westens was erected as a stage for light theatrical works, in an opulent mixture of styles: the main building is in French Renaissance and Art Nouveau style, the stage area Medieval, with timber framework. The theatre was rebuilt in the 1950s in simplified form and served as a location for the Deutsche Oper until it moved into its own building (no. 304). During the renovation of 1978, the theatre was refitted with its original, elaborate neo-Baroque fittings. In 1987, the roof lanterns and the crowning middle section were reconstructed, in the late

1990s the former entrance on the left side front, including a historic Schankterrasse – a wine terrace.

Museum für Kommunikation
(ehem. Postmuseum) (112)
Museum of Communication
(former Post Museum)
1897
Mauerstraße 69–75, Leipziger Straße 16–18
Hake, Techow, Ahrens

In 1871, the post office became an institution of the Reich. In the same year, work began on the construction of the Kaiserlichen Generalpostamt, the Imperial general post office, in Leipziger Straße. An extension towards Mauerstraße soon proved necessary (including for the then Postmuseum); work which was completed in 1897. The heart of the structure is a bright courtyard with adjoining stairway. The rounded corner building in Wilhelminian style is prestigiously designed on the exterior and was originally crowned by two towers. The administrative wing clearly indicates the lines of the Italian Renaissance. The original building was lost in the war, with the corner building rebuilt in the early 1960s as postal ministry and museum of the GDR, with the interior constructed in modern style. Following renovation and conversion to a Museum für Kommunikation in 1990, the atrium obtained its original form once more. The group of giants, bearing the atlas with theatrical gestures, has also returned to the roof cornice of the corner building. Its size and architectural splendour makes the central courtyard a popular location for large parties and galas in the city.

The Berlin Tenement House (113)

In spite of the destruction wrought by war and demolition, the visage of a large portion of inner-city Berlin remains heavily influenced by one type of building: the Berlin apartment block.

The origins of the building lie in the 18th century, where landowners began to develop rear courtyards for residential purposes. Over the course of time, side wings were added on. The later construction of apartment blocks adopted the pattern of erecting a front building with side wings and cross buildings. As the apartment block represented almost the sole form of housing in the 19th century, the result was the mixture of varied social classes in front and rear house that was so typical for the city.

The overwhelming majority of Berlin apartment blocks were constructed during the period of breakneck growth experienced by the city in the last two decades of the 19th century. Their form was greatly influenced by the Hobrecht Plan (1862, see no. 74), which specified the street plans and the minimum size of the courtyards. By 1887, these were only required to be 17.40 x 17.40 feet in size. This was sufficient for the wagons of the fire brigade to be able to turn around. As a consequence, Berlin had the highest population density of all European metropolises. Living conditions in the overcrowded, often squalid apartment blocks were soon subjected to heavy criticism from contemporary sources. The urban hostility of the Modernist movement has many of its roots here. It was not until 1925 that side and cross wings were forbidden in the new building ordinance.

In layout and comfort, apartments varied from district to district. Where working class districts had more courtyards behind one another and extremely small apartments, in Charlottenburg or Wilmersdorf, large middle class houses were erected with green courtyards and apartments with more than a dozen rooms (see no. 145). The height of the floors also varied. The older apartment blocks exhibit strictly patterned facades, whereas road fronts were later vitalised with balconies and bay windows. Depending on taste, they were decorated in Gothic, Renaissance, Baroque or a mixture of styles.

Following the Second World War, one of the primary objectives of the urban planners was to replace the much-criticised apartment blocks with modern, new apartments. In the course of the Kahlschlagsanierung, the process of razing entire areas, in the 1960s and 1970s entire districts were torn down. This ignored the fact that many inhabitants actually liked living in their old apartments and only wished for modernised kitchens, bathrooms and heating (see IBA no. 355). Older apartments renovated in this fashion remain among the most popular forms of housing amongst all sectors of the population to this today. The century-old floor plans have proved their extreme flexibility over the course of the years.

One of the saddest chapters in the construction history of Berlin is the "de-stucco-ing" of the tenement houses. In the 1960s and 1970s, in both East and West, around three quarters of all old housing stock buildings had their facade stucco hacked off – with the perpetrators both housing associations and private owners. Reasons included a belief that a "simplified" facade would be cheaper to maintain, as well as ideological reasons: the stucco was a relict of an abominable era. The architect of the Philharmonie (no. 307), Hans Scharoun (no. 281), formulated it thus: "The stucco on the walls is the stucco in our heads." No other city treated its historic substance with such a degree of harshness.   rh

The vastly predominant form of living in the 19th century: the tenement house.

Wohnanlage (114)
Residential Complex
1898
Proskauer Straße 14/15/17
Alfred Messel

This groundbreaking complex of over 100 apartments (1 to 2 rooms) and six shops was built by Messel for the Berliner Spar- und Bauverein, a building society. It was awarded a prize at the Paris World's Fair of 1900. The five-storey, U-shaped structure encloses a large courtyard with a four-storey garden house. With this complex, Messel avoided the typically restricted courtyard planning of the time. On the site of the poorly-lit Berliner Zimmer rooms in the corners of the building he placed the stairways. All

apartments have closed hallways and indoor toilets. The courtyard served as a children's play area. The facades of the individual buildings are designed in a varied, yet uniform manner. The five shops and two restaurants were initially organised and run by the association. Following their destruction in the Second World War, a few of the houses (often highly simplified) were rebuilt in 1950.

Geschäftshaus (115)
Commercial Building
1898
Gertraudenstraße 10–12
Max Jacob, Otto Roensch
Gertraudenbrücke
1895
Otto Stahn

Seldom noticed, today these two witnesses of the old Gertraudenstraße stand on

the busy 1960s roadway. The new bridge built to carry the traffic of the widened Gertraudenstraße means that today the old Gertraudenbrücke is only used by pedestrians. On the northern side stands a bronze statue of St Gertrud with a travelling journeyman. On the street front of

the commercial building, built by Jacob and Roensch, the former route of Gertraudenstraße can still be seen. Following a resolution of the Senate in the scope of the "Planwerk Innenstadt" (no. 491), the Gertraudenstraße is to be reduced to its former width and guided back over the historic bridge.

Elisabethhof (116)
Elisabeth Industrial Yard
1898
Erkelenzdamm 59–61
Kurt Berndt

The Elisabethhof, one of the largest industrial yards in Kreuzberg, is one of the few remaining examples of the mix of residential and commercial usage in a restricted space – necessitated by the limited amount of space in the city. The front building, with its triple-gated entrance and residential area is a conventional rendered building; behind it, three elongated courtyards harbour four industrial sections. These are combined brickwork and steel girder structures, with large window areas, sparsely decorated with ceramic panels and decorative stone.

**Abgeordnetenhaus von Berlin
(ehem. Preußischer Landtag)   (117)**
*Berlin Parliament
(former Prussian Legislative Assembly)
1898
Niederkirchnerstraße 5
Friedrich Schulze*

The new construction for the Preußischer Landtag was supposed to relieve the temporary lodgement of the two chambers in Leipziger Straße and on Dönhoffplatz. Built on the south side of the plot, the Landtag took an almost square, cubic shape, in the form of the Italian high Renaissance. The manor house was later added on the north side, connected to the Landtag. Following reunification the building was converted for use by the Berlin House of Representatives, which had met in Rathaus Schöneberg during the cold-war era of division. This conversion included the restoration of the imposing stair hallway and the redesign of the plenary hall in modern form.

Elefantentor Zoologischer Garten (118)
*Elephant Gate at the Zoological Garden
1899
Budapester Straße 30 A / 36
Zaar & Vahl*

A little-known reconstruction: the Elefantentor was completely destroyed in the Second World War. In the mid 1980s it was back again – as a copy. Shortly after this the Löwentor, the lion gate, the other entrance to the zoological gardens on Hardenbergplatz, was also reconstructed, after having also been destroyed in the war. As with the Elefantentor, the de-

sign of the 19th century animal houses in the interior of the complex also reflected the country of origin of the animals within. Examples remaining include the antelope house (1872) or the soliped house, with its Persian tower (1910). In 1913, the architects of the two gates also designed the aquarium in Budapester Straße. In 1929, Franz Hessel posed the interesting question of "whether the Indian elephant is interested in the mosaic dragons decorating the doors of his palace? Does the zebra love its African homestead?" The Berlin zoological gardens are the oldest in Germany, having been established in 1844.

Riehmers Hofgarten (119)
Riehmer's Garden Courtyard
1899
Yorckstraße 83–86; Großbeerenstraße,
56/57 A; Hagelberger Straße 9–12
Wilhelm Riehmer, Otto Mrosk

In 1881 Wilhelm Riehmer erected a complex for medium-income customers unable to afford a villa. The idea was such a new one that a suitable term for it did not emerge until 1912. The master builder connected the purchased plots via a private road. The public was kept at bay using a wrought iron gate. In contrast to standard apartment blocks, the 20 or so individual buildings are not arranged in closed groups, but were orientated on an interior space, towards which they displayed the same eclectically ornamented facades as faced the outside. This represented nothing less than the invention of the large garden courtyard, which continues to represent the tower block ideal to this day.

Viktoria-Luise-Platz (120)
Viktoria-Luise Square
1899
Fritz Encke

Although only half of the original buildings surrounding the square remain, Viktoria-Luise-Platz is one of the most attractive squares in Berlin. It lies in a district that is typical of the middle class residential housing districts that sprouted up around the turn of the century at such a blistering pace. Within the composed network of streets, six axes gravitate in a star shape towards the square, which is almost oval in form. The semi-circular arcade on the western side of the square corresponds to the U-Bahn entrance on the eastern side. Following a simplification of the square in 1957, the historic image was recreated in 1980, with a central water basin, fountains and areas of lawns and flowerbeds.

ehem. Berliner Handelsgesellschaft (121)
former Berlin Trading Company
1900
Behrenstraße 32/33
Alfred Messel

Before the Second World War, Behrenstraße was the most important banking street in Berlin. Messel designed a three-storey monumental structure for the Berliner Handelsgesellschaft, with colossal columns and pilasters in sandstone on a sturdy rusticated plinth. The main entrance was set to one side, covered by ledges crowned with balconies. Although Messel had previously explored new architectural paths with his commercial buildings, this building was largely built on the Classical lines of the bank buildings of its day.

ehem. Marstall (122)
former Royal Stables
1900
Schlossplatz 7 / Breite Str. 36
Ernst von Ihne

With the design of the neo-Baroque new stables on Schlossplatz, Ernst von Ihne took motifs from plans for new stables drawn up by Broebes and de Bodt at the end of the 17th century. The lower two storeys take the form of a rusticated plinth, with the upper two combined into a colossal order. A baluster parapet concludes the building. The interior contains remnants of the old stables from 1669, which are integrated into the new structure.

Wohn- und Geschäftshaus
Friedrichstraße 166 (123)
Residential and Commercial Building
at Friedrichstraße 166
1900
Friedrichstraße 166

This three-storey, red sandstone building is neo-Gothic in style, oriented on the Berlin style of commercial buildings. The two lower floors are separated from the remainder of the facade through a fascia, above which the apertures develop into either a large display window or a row of three, clover-arched windows. The high proportion of glass in the facade is an idiosyncratic interpretation of the residential and commercial building typology of Alfred Messel, who, a number of years previously, had provided a significant impetus to the contemporary architectural debate with the glazed pillar

81

front of the Wertheim department store on Leipziger Platz. As the building was built on the exact floor plan of its predecessor, today it is one of the narrowest buildings in Friedrichstraße, with a width of just 39 feet.

Deutscher Sparkassen- und Giroverband (ehem. Privat- und Commerzbank)   (124)
German Savings and Giro Association (former Private and Commercial bank)
1901
Behrenstraße 46, Charlottenstraße 47, Rosmarinstr. 10
Wilhelm Martens

Since 1998, this building has been used as the Berlin headquarters of the Deutscher Sparkassen- und Giroverband. The building was built in a number of stages from 1872 onwards, largely to plans by Wilhelm Martens. A significant alteration was made in 1950. The size and monumental nature of the building has left its mark on the buildings surrounding it. An original feature is its connection using a bridge over Französische Straße. The basket handle arch is supported by semi-figured Atlases, representing the four seasons.

Haus Springer   (125)
Springer House
1901
Am Großen Wannsee 39
Alfred Messel

This residential house shows clear indications of the influence of English country house architecture. Despite this, here Messel developed a new expression of

simplicity and clarity, later continued in the structures of Hermann Muthesius. Externally, the plinth dominates, with its rough natural stone; the gables are faced with shingles. The individually designed rooms are grouped freely around a hallway, which can also be seen from the exterior in the form of bay windows, ledges and set-offs. The garden is closely linked to the interior and can also be easily reached from there.

Bauteil Wertheim-Kaufhaus   (126)
Section of the Wertheim Department Store
1903
Sophienstraße 12–15, Rosenthaler Straße 28–31
Alfred Messel

Not one of Alfred Messel's celebrated department stores survives today. They were either destroyed in the war or demolished later (no. 137). Only one section of the comparatively small building in Rosenthaler Straße has been preserved in its original condition. The facade, in Dorla sandstone, bears the pillar system typical of Messel, a form that he devel-

oped from Gothic buttresses. Basket handle arches conclude the plinth, with an intricate, frame-like raster structure above.

Tropenhaus Botanischer Garten (127)
Tropical House of the Botanical Gardens
1903
Unter den Eichen 5–10, Königin-Luise-Platz
Alfred Koerner

The first botanical garden was created in 1573 on the site of the present day Lustgarten (no. 448), at the heart of the city. In the 17th century, it migrated to the site currently occupied by the Kleistpark in the district of Schöneberg. At the end of the 19th century, the new site was finally developed in Lichterfelde, in the south west of the city. A number of glasshouses were erected for the more sensitive plants. The most impressive of these is the Große Tropenhaus or large tropical house, with a surface area of 1,937 square feet and a ridge height of 82 feet. The angle of the steel girders, beginning above a plinth height of around 16 feet,

gives the building the impression of a single, mighty glass roof of monumental elegance.

Löwenpalais (128)
Lion Mansion
1904
Königsallee 30 / 32
Bernhard Sehring, conversion: BASD

The Löwenpalais is one of the largest and most ostentatious examples of the requirement of private house builders to display their opulence in the later years of the Gründerzeit era. It was built as a country house for the Imperial cellar master Habel and his family. The street

front is elongated in form, with the ends falling lower to both sides, decorated lavishly with groups of figures, with the terrace guarded by two lions. As with other Gründerzeit structures, the rear side of the building is completely without decoration. After 1930, the Löwenpalais was divided into luxury apartments, inhabited by residents such as prominent actors until into the post-war era. Today, the building is home to an arts foundation, which organises exhibitions and provides opportunities for visual artists to work.

with Art Nouveau elements. The wing in Grunerstraße was demolished in 1968 in order to broaden the street. The remaining tracts were reconstructed in simplified form following heavy damage in the Second World War. In 1983, the staircase hall in Littenstraße was redecorated in a colour approaching that of the original.

ehem. Hotel Splendid (130)
former Hotel Splendid
1904
Dorotheenstraße 37
Gronau & Graul

Gerichtsgebäude (129)
Courthouse
1904
Littenstraße 12–17
Paul Thoemer, Rudolf Mönnich,
Otto Schmalz

The most imposing of the court buildings in Berlin, on its completion it was the second largest building in the city, after the Stadtschloss. It is the structural expression of the awareness of power of the state courts following the judicial reform at the end of the 19th century. In its original form, the 656-feet long building enclosed five courtyards. The fantastic staircase halls combine high Baroque architecture

FLOP Some passers-by will make an involuntary detour around the former Hotel Splendid. The reason is that the two brave Atlas figures on both sides of the portal appear to be struggling to maintain their grip on the overloaded facade of misconstrued southern German Baroque and Art Nouveau. They already hang much too low above the pavement. Where formerly a coat of arms of the ruler was sufficient, the central projection of this building has no less than three cartouches for the builder of this "ghost house". It becomes immediately apparent why the late Historism era was subjected to so much contemporary criticism.

Bodemuseum (131)
Bode Museum
1904
Am Kupfergraben
Ernst von Ihne

This building was built in new Baroque style as the Kaiser-Friedrich-Museum on the initiative of Wilhelm von Bode, to house the collection of paintings and sculptures. With its rolling facade and cupola, the building is a dramatic presence on the northern tip of the Museumsinsel (no. 50). Built on a triangular floor plan, it encloses five courtyards. The sandstone facades are concisely divided by a Corinthian colossal order and gabled projections. At the main entrance, open arcades lead into an atrium, connecting the splendid dome hall with gallery and symmetrical open stairways. At the centre stands a copy of the statue of the Great Elector by Andreas Schlüter (no. 18). The central connecting axis continues into the so-called basilica, designed in the manner of a Florentine Renaissance church, and the smaller stairway (also domed) at the other end of the museum. Architectural fragments from Italy and the Netherlands are incorporated into the exhibition rooms. The building was being restored and converted by Heinz Tesar as part of the master plan for the Museumsinsel.

Bundesrat (ehem. Preußisches Herrenhaus) (132)
Federal Council of Germany
(former Prussian House of Lords)
1904
Leipziger Straße 3/4
Friedrich Schulze

This former Prussian manor house is part of an extended building complex running to the south of the Preußischer Landtag, the Prussian legislative assembly (which is the present-day Berlin House of Representatives). It stands on the site of the former Imperial porcelain factory. With its three wings and neo-Renaissance style, light, sandstone facade, the new building forms a large forecourt to the street. Two plinth floors with rustication are followed by two upper storeys with parapet balustrades, connected via colossal pilaster. The facade is broken up by a central projection with six columns and a tri-

85

angular gable. The plenary room was destroyed in the Second World War. Following the repair of the damage, the building was used by the Akademie der Wissenschaften, the Federal academy of sciences, in the GDR era. After reunification, the building was converted into the seat of the Bundesrat by Peter Schweger.

ehem. Warenhaus Jandorf (133)
former Jandorf Department Store
1904
Brunnenstraße 19–21
Lachmann & Zauber

The facade of this department store remains in original condition, conveying, albeit modestly, an impression of the magnificent department store architecture of Berlin after the turn of the century. It was erected after the Wertheim department store in Leipziger Straße (no. 137), constructed by Messel. The five-storey building has a vertically-or-

dered limestone facade and minimal Art Nouveau decor. It is rounded off at the corner, a feature accentuated by a copper-plated tower. The stairway and courtyard received their first alterations as early as 1926. Until 1990, the building was home to the central institute of fashion of the GDR.

ehem. Landesversicherungsanstalt (134)
former Regional Insurance Office
1904
Am Köllnischen Park 3
Alfred Messel

The Landesversicherungsanstalt was built at the same time as the Märkisches Museum opposite (no. 146). However, in contrast to Ludwig Hoffmann with his museum, Alfred Messel distanced himself from the historicizing style of the age. With no plinth, the brick-faced colossal pilasters begin almost at pavement level, and the absence of a classical framework enables them to stretch up to the eaves. The windows in between appear to have been hung in place. The main entrance and gable area serve to highlight the central axis of the building, the limestone decorative elements of which are based on the Baroque. The original tower cover was lost. Today, the building is the official home of the Senatsverwaltung für Stadtentwicklung, the Senate department for urban development.

Automaten-Restaurant (135)
Automatic Restaurant
1905
Friedrichstraße 167/168
Bruno Schmitz

This steel skeleton construction was the first secular building for the painter and architect, familiar as the constructor of the Leipzig Battle of Nations Monument. The barrel-vaulted hall on the ground

namental sculpture work, largely the work of the Breslau stonemason Christian Behrens, lends an animated air to the exterior of the building.

Berliner Dom (136)
Berlin Cathedral
1905
Lustgarten
Julius von Raschdorff

With the Reichstag (no. 106), this is the second worst-situated public building of the Wilhelminian era. With its dimensions, it destroyed the existing balance between the Stadtschloss (no. 7), Altes Museum (no. 62) opposite and the Classical cathedral in between. The latter, a church building converted by Schinkel (no. 44), was demolished to create room for the Berliner Dom, which the Kaiser intended to become the foremost church in the Protestant world. The mighty church of the Hohenzollern was both court church and place of burial, it takes its style from Roman Baroque. It is held to be the most significant ecclesiastical structure from the late Gründerzeit era in Germany. On the south side stands the church for christenings and weddings, with the memorial church that complet-

floor, clad with marble, housed vending machines for food and drink – an extremely modern facility in the early years of the 20th century. In contrast to this somewhat progressive usage, Schmitz turned to figurative motifs for the design of the facade, aspects that he had already applied to numerous monuments in his capacity as a leading proponent of German Historism. Consequently, the porches of the three display windows on the ground floor are supported by three naked figures and accentuated in the middle by a stylised man's head. The or-

ed the complex to the north demolished in 1976. An unusual feature is the former Imperial stairway, which would look more at home in a palace. An observer once noted that the Berliner Dom clarified the fact that there was no genuine piety in the city. Repair of the heavy damage of the Second World War was completed on the exterior in 1981. This involved a simplification of the central cupola on the cordon, which was rebuilt lower than the original. The four flanking cupolas are also plainer. The recreation of the interior was largely completed in 1993. Since 1999, the restored Hohenzollern vault with 90 sarcophaguses of members of the House of Hohenzollern has been open to the public once more.

Kaufhaus Wertheim (137)
Wertheim Department Store
1906
Leipziger Straße/Leipziger Platz
Alfred Messel

DEMOLITION The main structure on Leipziger Platz formed the crowning element of the 500-feet long front of Kaufhaus Wertheim in Leipziger Straße. Messel retained the already developed system of end-to-end pillars, leading up to the roof from a minimal plinth and with the intermediate space fully glazed. The ground floor area consisted of a four-trestled hall with arcades and solid vaulting. A bonnet-like mansard roof completed the building. The structural decoration played second fiddle to the monumental effect of the soaring columned facade. Despite a degree of contemporary criticism with regard to the stark contrast between stone and glass, this "department store gothic" style of Messel remained a dominant feature of Berlin department store architecture until the First World War. The enormous department store complex was gutted by fire in the Second World War, although the facades in Leipziger Straße and on Leipziger Platz remained. They were demolished to provide a clean line for the division between East and West Berlin. After the fall of the Wall, the Italian architect Aldo Rossi designed a new structure for the plot, with references to Messel's Wertheim department store. The building was planned to house a permanent home for the Canadian Cirque de Soleil theatre group. The project failed to be implemented following difficulties with the investor.

this complex was retained in its historic substance. Following a heritage conservation analysis, the complex was comprehensively restored and reconstructed to its original state in 1995.

Pensionat Steinplatz (138)
Steinplatz Boarding House
1906
Uhlandstraße 197
August Endell

This building, originally erected as a residential house, is one of the few Art Nouveau structures in Berlin. Once used as the Hotel am Steinplatz; today it is a home for the elderly. It was restored in the 1980s, according to the plans of the architect. Endell also designed a festival room in the Hackeschen Höfen (no. 144).

Helenenhof (139)
Helena's Courtyard
1906
Holteistraße 28–33, Simplonstraße 41–51,
Sonntagstraße 17–22, Gryphiusstraße 1–8
Erich Köhn

This group of five-storey rendered buildings on a limestone plinth aimed to fracture the standard monotony of the tenements, with various render forms, window types, loggias and bay windows. Art Nouveau elements can be noted. In addition to the green space of the courtyard, the project was also the first occa-

Geschäftshaus (140)
Commercial Building
1906
Klosterstraße 64
Georg Lewy

This four-storey, sandstone-clad building covers an area of two courtyards. It contains distinctive Art Nouveau elements. The facade is accentuated by a central projection with a large arched window on the top floor and sweeping eaves. The parapet of the projection is decorated with ornamentation depicting mask and dragon motifs. The left portal includes an intricately decorated, original iron door leaf.

Ludwig Hoffmann
* 1852 in Darmstadt, † 1932 in Berlin (141)

"All those of us who have dedicated our lives to building are unified by the same goal: we wish to give form to the yearning for beauty."

Ludwig Hoffmann

Ludwig Hoffmann built more structures in Berlin than Schlüter (no. 18), Knobelsdorff and Schinkel (no. 44) put together. He was the great organiser of the Wilhelminian construction projects and the most significant architect of municipal Berlin.

In the era of great economic expansion in the city, schools, hospitals, bath houses, fire stations and administrative buildings were all erected under his leadership, as "Islands of taste in a sea of grey stone", as a contemporary critic put it. The majority of his buildings withstood the destruction of war and demolition almost untouched. They continue to exert their influence on the historic districts of Berlin to this day.

Hoffmann was born in Darmstadt on 30th June 1852, the son of a lawyer. He grew up in a middle class household. Af-

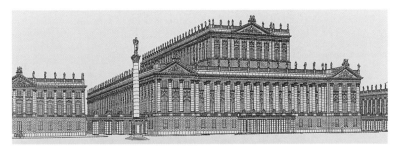

Hoffmann's proposal for a Royal Opera House at Königsplatz.

ter passing his Abitur school examination in his hometown, he left to study architecture in Berlin in 1874, together with his childhood friend Alfred Messel. He went on to become a favourite pupil of Johann Heinrich Strack, a former colleague of Schinkel.

Hoffmann's breakthrough came with his design for the Reichsgericht courthouse in Leipzig. His work was awarded first prize of 119 submitted works. The building of the 35-year-old also met with widespread acclaim on its completion, making him one of the most sought-after architects in the country. Despite this, he rejected the offer of the position of privy counsellor, the highest construction official in the land. Instead, he was elected construction counsellor of Berlin in 1896, attracted by the manifold construction projects of the capital.

Hoffmann soon detached himself from the convention that specific building types required a specific style: churches were Gothic, Museums Roman, courts of law in the style of the Renaissance. Hoffmann constructed his numerous schools in various styles; German Renaissance, Baroque style or the almost style-free brick structures of Schinkel.

Details that seem overloaded today were extremely modern for their time. The contemporary observer becomes aware of this at the latest on comparing Hoffmann's buildings with the more extreme creations of Historism. The architectural historian Julius Posener described Hoffmann's buildings as "likeable": "They were influenced by Wilhelminian optimism, and they wanted to generate confidence." This friendly impression was achieved through two rou-

tes. One of these was surprising, picturesque deviations from strict formality. Hoffmann was also more sparing in his use of historic style elements than his contemporaries, there is nothing petty about his buildings, contours and facades are clearly readable: large roof surfaces with gently sculpted gables are common, or walls with large surface areas. A clear reference to more simple country house architecture is often noticeable. Perhaps the most typical example of Hoffmann's "likeability" is the Märchenbrunnen fountain in the Volkspark Friedrichshain (no. 91).

Hoffmann's most significant buildings include the Stadthaus (no. 159), incorporating motifs from the Gontard towers on Gendarmenmarkt (see no. 13), the Märkisches Museum (no. 146) with its collage of Brandenburg architectural references and the castle-like, neo-Baroque Rudolf-Virchow-Krankenhaus hospital. His œuvre is almost limitless, encompassing over 60 schools and sports halls, 13 hospitals, eight bridges and five bath houses.

Hoffmann was construction counsellor for almost three decades. When he left office in 1924, the revolutionary house of the printer Max Taut had just been completed. However, this breach, caused by the onset of the Modern and its social utopia failed to attract Hoffmann as a follower. His intention had not been to change the political situation, but to satisfy it. He died in Berlin on 11th November 1932.   rh

**Deutsches Theater und
Kammerspiele** (142)
*German Theatre and Kammerspiele
1906
Schumannstraße 12–13 A
William Müller*

Before the Second World War, both theatres were in the second row. The present-day forecourt was a rear courtyard for a long period; the road front in Schumannstraße was enclosed by a row of houses. It was only after these were destroyed that the complex was opened up to become an interesting forecourt. Of the original building of the Deutsches Theater dating from 1850 only the two-tiered auditorium by Eduard Titz remains. In 1883, the remainder of the building was redesigned in Renaissance style, including the facade. In 1906, Max Reinhardt, who led the theatre to worldwide acclaim, commissioned William Müller with the addition of a revolving stage and

the reworking of the fade in neo-Classical style. The same architect also converted the adjacent casino into a chamber music hall. The reserved Classical facades of the two theatres fit well into the adjoining mid 19th century residential buildings.

Kaufhaus des Westens (143)
*Department Store of the West
1907
Tauentzienstraße 21–24
Johann Emil Schaudt*

The KaDeWe was the only one of the large Berlin department stores to survive the Second World War – albeit in an altered form. The original building of 1907 was erected as a five-storey brickwork structure in the residential area of the Neuer Westen. Schaudt adapted his design to the area by rejecting a columned facade in favour of a closed facade with individual windows. A courtyard was not included in the design. Schaudt himself converted the building in 1930 for the first time, with, amongst other features, the addition of a further two storeys. Reconstruction in 1950 saw the hipped roof replaced by a flat roof. In the 1960s and 1970s, the building was subjected to further conversion work. The most recent alteration was in 1993, with a new, seventh floor added, with a glass dome and a return to the hipped roof.

Hackesche Höfe (144)
Courtyards Hackesche Höfe
1907
Rosenthaler Straße 40/41
Kurt Berndt, August Endell

The largest residential and commercial complex of its time in Europe reaches from Rosenthaler Straße, covering nine courtyards, to Sophienstraß at the rear. The Hackesche Höfe were constructed for mixed usage, with commercial space, amusement areas and festivity rooms, generously-appointed apartments in the front building, craft workshops, shops and workers' apartments in the courtyards to the rear. The architectural styles were also varied, ranging from rendering, white fascia stones and ornate, lazed tiling on the front of the courtyards, with styles varying between Art Nouveau and Art Deco. After reunification, the building, which had deteriorated during the GDR era, was initially rediscovered

by artists. Soon after, the entire complex was acquired by a private investor. It was comprehensively restored in a tenant-friendly manner, with new shops, restaurants, theatre and cinemas moving in. The Hackesche Höfe rapidly developed into a core feature of the pulsating life of the Spandau periphery. Nowhere else in Berlin boasts such a wide variety of shops, restaurants, clubs and cultural activities in such a limited area.

Wohnhäuser am
Kurfürstendamm (145)
Residential Buildings on Kurfürsten-damm
1908
Kurfürstendamm 56–60
Hans Toebelmann, Henry Groß

From 1880 onwards, the Imperial riding path to the Jagdschloss Grunewald between the villa district of the same name and Tiergarten-Straße was enlarged – on the initiative of Imperial Chancellor Bismarck, who dictated that the boulevard should have a width of 174 feet, with each street corner graced by the architectural highlight of a cupola. This prestigious street rapidly developed into the most expensive residential real estate in Berlin. The plots, the value of which increased three thousand-fold in the years up to the turn of the century, became the sites of a tight concentration of stately tenement houses in every conceivable style and mixture of styles. They often occupied 80 percent of the plots, reaching construction breadths of 66 feet. At that time, the buildings were also inhabited on the ground floor, which can still be seen today in the display windows at parapet height between Wielandstrasse and Leibnizstrasse. The apartments were enormous (in the building of Kurfürstendamm 60 for example, there were apartments with 4,40 and 6,200 square feet), with domestic staff entering via their own stairways, the narrow spirals of which appear to have been stuck to the courtyard facade as an afterthought. The layout of rooms was in accordance with the social mores of the age, with reception room, salons, closets and bedrooms, a layout that led to many of these apartments – often sub-divided – finding use as lawyer's offices or medical surgeries after the war.

Märkisches Museum (146)
Märkisches Museum
1908
Am Köllnischen Park 5
Ludwig Hoffmann

The new building of the Märkisches Museum, which was founded in 1874, is based upon an architectural concept that had previously been realised in the form of the Bayerisches Nationalmuseum in Munich: the works of art were to be presented in an ambience based upon the era in which they were created. The picturesque complex is grouped around two courtyards and displays references to various styles and structures. This also involved the integration of original historical components. The high, rectangular brick tower is similar to the keep of the Bischofsburg castle in Wittstock, the main section is a copy of a Gothic brick church. On the park side, a three-winged rendered building in late Renaissance style adjoins. In front of the building stands a copy of the Brandenburger Roland statue of 1474.

»Tacheles«-Ruine (147)
"Tacheles" Ruin
1908
Oranienburger Straße 54–56 A
Franz Ahrens

The present-day ruin was originally part of an enormous building complex built as an arcade department store in 1908. The high, round arched doorway on Oranienburger Straße marks the entrance to the covered arcade, which once stretched all the way to Friedrichstraße. The bold, reinforced steel construction of the building was unusual at the time, but never became economically successful. From 1928 onward, the building served the AEG company as a technology building. A cinema and artistes' school moved into the bomb-damaged building after 1945. In the early 1980s, approval was given for the ruins to be demolished. The occupation of the building by the Tacheles artists' association after reunification and the brightly painted walls raised awareness of the ruins beyond Berlin. Following the failure of numerous conversion schemes, the Fundus Group, which has already erected the Hotel Adlon (no. 401), plans to erect a mixed complex of offices, apartments, shops, restaurants and a hotel on the site.

Hebbel-Theater (148)
Hebbel Theatre
1908
Stresemannstraße 29 – 29 A
Oskar Kaufmann

The first of Kaufmann's theatres in Berlin is a peculiar mixture of intricate Baroque and a fortification style. Despite the narrow front, the facade succeeds in making

a monumental impression with a concise cubature and sturdy rusticated blocks, reaching up to the fifth floor. The most significant accent comes from the high wall alcove, from which a window area extends outwards in an arch. The ticket office area is equipped with mahogany panelling with boxwood inlay. The theatre area itself is furnished with dark woods and silk drapes; laid out on two levels, it has a very intimate character. After the war, the upper level was altered. Kaufmann went on to become one of the most important theatre architects in 1920s Berlin (see no. 172).

ehem. Gemeindeschule (149)
former Parish School
1908
Christburger Straße 7
Ludwig Hoffmann

A splendid example of one of Hoffmann's numerous pillar facades, incorporating ideas from Messel's Kaufhaus Wertheim in Voßstraße (no. 137). The elongated,

dark red brick building is set slightly back from the street line of the neighbouring buildings. The front is over 300 feet long, with 29 axes, from which five triple-axis projections emerge almost imperceptibly. These ledges and set-offs are continued in the steep mansard roof. The three-sectioned windows between the columns are connected using a bar construction. The parapets are ornamented with small, decorative reliefs. In contrast, the courtyard front is without decoration.

Wohnanlage (150)
Residential Complex
1909
Grabbeallee 14 / 26
Paul Mebes

This complex, erected for the civil servants' housing association, is an outstanding example of Reform architecture. The site is almost triangular in shape and is connected via a sweeping private road. Courtyards to the surrounding streets and the narrow width of the houses ensure adequate illumination for the apartments. The house entrances stand out with decorated, shaped block work and

95

reliefs. With this exception, there is an absence of structural decoration. With this complex, Mebes overcame the Historism of the Gründerzeit era, developing floor plans and facades based more upon function.

AEG-Turbinenhalle (151)
AEG Turbine hall
1909
Huttenstraße 12–16
Peter Behrens

Schule Görschstraße (152)
Görschstraße School
1910
Görschstraße 42–44
Carl Fenten, Rudolf Klante, Eilert Franzen

The largest school complex in Berlin from the turn of the century, it is grouped around a trapezoid courtyard in numerous wings. The curved front of the building forms a green area to the street side. The design, with stairway tower, corner bay windows and decorative gables in Renaissance style generates a picturesque overall image. The decorative figures appear somewhat opulent today.

The AEG turbine hall indicates the transition of industrial architecture from Art Nouveau to Modern. Peter Behrens, appointed AEG in-house architect shortly before, created a 394-feet long, unsupported hall and elevated the construction, visible in the side facade, to the dominant design element. The aesthetic presentation of the triple-jointed steel frame construction, emerging visibly from the facade at pedestrian height, underlines the dawning of a new era, in which industrial architecture was to witness a revaluation: from the design of simple workshops to the shop floors of the machine age. On the longitudinal side of the hall, the areas between the iron supports are completely glazed. The proportions of the building and its monumental appearance are analogous to those of ancient temples, with the consequence that this Behrens structure is also recorded in architectural history as "temple of labour".

Pergamonmuseum (153)
Pergamon Museum
1910
Am Kupfergraben
Alfred Messel

The Pergamonmuseum was the last museum to be built on the Museumsinsel (no. 50). It replaced a neo-Classical building for Pergamonian antiquities, erected by Fritz Wolff in 1897–99 on the same site as an interim solution. The new building was specifically designated for the artefacts from excavations in Pergamon and other locations in Asia Minor. It required extremely high halls with skylights. The monumental complex comprises three wings and is built in neo-Classical style, influenced by Greek designs. It opens toward the direction of the Kupfergraben. There, the side wings are concluded by two temple fronts, equipped with relatively steep triangular gables. The structure is faced with limestone and rendering. Following disruptions in its construction, the building was not opened until 1930, at which time the exterior was still incomplete. In the GDR era, a new entrance and a bridge to the forecourt were added. The Pergamonmuseum is to be reconstructed a further time, this time by Oswald Mathias Ungers.

ly impressive, rising from the pavement to the framework without a plinth, the spaces between the columns disfigured by the addition of small, glittery bric-a-brac in Istrian marble. Decades of exposure to the elements have the consequence that the surface now gives the impression of being coated with adhesive. The rear of the building, on Planckstraße, is also a joy to behold for lovers of exotic ornamental forms.

U-Bahnhof Rathaus Schöneberg   (155)
Underground Station at Rathaus
Schöneberg
1910
Innsbrucker Straße, between Freiherr-vom-Stein-Straße and Fritz-Elsas-Straße
Johann Emil Schaudt

When the up-and-coming district of Schöneberg (at that time still independent) built its U-Bahn station, it saw it as an instrument for attracting rich citizens, which is why the stations are more complex than those of Berlin. The most splendid of all was the station Stadtpark (today's U-Bahn station Rathaus Schöneberg) which was built in 1909. The U-Bahn, which ran underground to this point, came to the surface here in a design by the architect Johann Emil Schaudt, who also erected the KaDeWe (no. 143). He designed the station as a bridge between the two, higher-lying districts to either side, as well as between park and town. He connected Innsbrucker Straße to a play area using an open stairway, using the soil excavated in the tunnel building process to sculpt a valley landscape, filling the accumulating groundwater into a reservoir.

Metropoltheater
(»Admiralspalast«)   **(154)**
Metropole Theatre
("Admiral's Palace")
1910
Friedrichstraße 101/102
Heinrich Schweitzer

FLOP Although the original building with public baths and ice rink was not converted into the Metropoltheater until 1922, the unchanged facade of 1910 was pure operetta from the very beginning. The Doric, granite columns are essential-

97

**Seniorenwohnsitz
(ehem. Hotel Baltic)** (156)
*Home for the Elderly
(former Hotel Baltic)*
1910
Invalidenstraße 120/121
Hans Bernoulli

The site of the Hotel Baltic was in the vicinity of Stettiner Bahnhof. Destroyed in the war, it was later pulled down. The present-day S-Bahn station Nordbahnhof is the sole reminder of this once vibrant lodging. The facade is faced with Silesian sandstone with fine profiling and is unusual for Berlin. Windows are almost at room height, with small French window-style decorative step-out areas with finely woven balcony mesh. Medallions between the windows of the first floor symbolise different towns and cities of the Baltic coast. The interior and the ground floor, which formerly housed shops, were altered in the GDR era. In the course of the conversion into a home for the elderly, the building was reconstructed after reunification, with the facade renovated.

Wettbewerb Groß-Berlin (157)
Greater-Berlin Competition
1910

In 1909, two Berlin architectural associations launched a competition to compile ideas for a "basic plan for the development of Greater Berlin". The aim of this was to control the development of the rapidly expanding city, upgrade problem districts, create more green spaces and improve transport connections. The prestige of the metropolis was also to be reflected in its urban planning. The number of inhabitants was estimated at five million. The 27 drafts submitted were directed predominantly towards the redesign of Potsdamer Platz and Leipziger Platz. Martin Mächler's design for a north-south axis was blown up into gigantic proportions by Albert Speer in the 1930s (see no. 225). One of the proposals of that time (an underground connection of the Lehrter, Potsdamer and Anhalter railway stations (no. 95)) was actually implemented following the fall of the wall (no. 301).

**ehem. Geschäftshaus
Tischbein & Mendel** (158)
*former Commercial Building of
Tischbein & Mendel*
1911
Lindenstraße 44–47
Hans Bernoulli

The facade, with its ten axes, is dominated by columns beginning just above the ground and rising up to the eaves in an almost uninterrupted line. Where the ground floor contains one display window each, the upper floors are fitted with three narrow windows. The layout of the interior dictates that the two round arched windows do not lie at the very centre of the building, which bears no references to historic construction forms. The copper windows form a striking contrast to the limestone facade.

Altes Stadthaus (159)
Old City Mansion
1911
Klosterstraße 47
Ludwig Hoffmann

With construction beginning in 1902, the Stadthaus was not only planned to accommodate 1,500 municipal servants unable to find room in the Rotes Rathaus (no. 83), a further purpose was to reinforce the community spirit of citizens. With this in mind, construction counsellor Ludwig Hoffmann (no. 141) erected this administrative structure, spread over four courtyards, with a "hall for large public festivals, which the city had previously lacked" (Fritz Stahl, 1914). The characteristic symbol of the building was a 260-feet tower with a cupola that at the time was the highest in the city, based upon the cathedral on Gendarmenmarkt

(no. 13). The barrel-vaulted crypt was decorated with aphorisms and a bronze bear by Georg Wryba. The decoration was in Roman style, in order to underscore the claim to permanence of the young metropolis. After the war, the GDR government used the Stadthaus for the Council of Ministers, turning the building into a fortress. Starting in 1996, the building was restored under Gerhard Spangenberg. The restoration work has now been completed.

Haus de Burlet (160)
House de Burlet
1911
Schlickweg 12
Hermann Muthesius

This small, single-storey brick building is the most consistent and, in the opinion of

many, best executed country house to be built by Muthesius, who studied the English role models of this construction type intensively. In contrast to the then-dominant, prestigious villa style, characterised by strictly regimented floor plans, Muthesius arranged his rooms on an L-shaped plan, with each room an individual space of its own. The ground level position of the rooms, the integration of a loggia and a large terrace leads to the garden being incorporated into the living area. The bedrooms are located in the converted attic space.

Zollernhof (161)
Zollern Courtyard Building
1911
Unter den Linden 36–38
Bruno Paul

With its profiled, limestone column facade, the Zollernhof is an outstanding example of elegant, pre-First World War commercial architecture. The original building was only half as wide as the present structure and marked the corner of Unter den Linden to Kleine Kirchgasse. Following the First World War, the building was acquired by the Hugenberg-Ver-

lag publishers, the Jewish shop owners had their property expropriated. In 1938, the company received permission to double the length of the Zollernhof by building over the Kleine Kirchgasse. Six additional window axes were added in the form of the original building. The seven large figures on the cornice were moved into the centre. Almost all the interior

was lost in the Second World War. Following reconstruction, the building housed the headquarters of the Freie Deutschen Jugend youth organisation – the central cornice figure was replaced by the FDJ emblem, with the consequence that this remains empty to this day. After reunification, the building was acquired jointly by ZDF and Veba, who planned to use the building as their Berlin headquarters.

Haus Wiegand (162)
Wiegand House
1912
Peter-Lenné-Straße 28–30
Peter Behrens
This residential house was erected for the director of the Prussian Archaeological

Collection. The neo-Classical style is oriented on the ancient world and buildings of the Schinkel era (see no. 44). The two-storey building is brick-built, faced with limestone. It stands on a sloping plinth. Visitors enter an open porch with Doric columns, with a vestibule and reception hall leading off. Symmetrical wings to both sides flank the central axis, which continues into the garden to the rear. The monumental building, almost without decoration, was an early portent of the neo-Classicism of the 1930s.

Weinhaus Huth (163)
Huth Wine Tavern
1912
Alte Potsdamer Straße 5
Heidenreich & Michel

Only two of the historic buildings on Potsdamer Platz (see no. 417) have survived war and demolition: a remnant of the old Hotel Esplanade (now in the Sony-Center/no. 472) and the comparatively intact Weinhaus Huth. The small plot between Alte Potdamer Straße and Linkstraße means that it has two street fronts. It is a typical example of Berlin commercial architecture at the beginning of the century. Two plinth-level floors are linked by round arches and followed by three vertically structured main storeys. The facade on Alte Potsdamer Straße juts out from the building and is highlighted by a small

tower. The construction work carried out on the new Potsdamer Platz required that Weinhaus Huth be propped up using complex technology. The architects of the adjoining new buildings consciously incorporated gaps to the old structure. The contrast between the elegant limestone facade of Weinhaus Huth and the industrial aestheticism of Richard Rogers' building could not be greater.

**Landesvertretung
des Freistaates Bayern** (164)
*State Representative of the Free State
of Bavaria*
1912
Behrenstraße 21/22
Richard Bielenberg, Josef Moser

This building was erected for the Schaffhausenschen Bankverein, a banking association. The three-storey natural stone takes a Classical form. On a rusticated plinth, broad Ionic colossal pilasters enclose two main storeys, crowned with an imposing cornice. Relief panels are mounted between the windows of the top floor. In the GDR years, the building was used to house the Deutsche Handels-

bank, before being converted for use as the Bayerische Landesvertretung after reunification. The covered atrium serves as an event hall.

Verwaltungsgebäude (165)
Administrative Building
1912
Wallstraße 76–79
Fritz Crzellitzer

Where the majority of commercial buildings prior to the First World War were built along neo-Classical lines, Crzellitzer designed this facade, decorated with majolica panels. Resting upon a plinth, later altered, the windows of the three main storeys are aligned above one another and encompassed by a frame. The parapet area is clad with copper. Above this are lunette reliefs with nudes.

Cathedrals of Work (166)

The first industrial companies in Berlin emerged at the beginning of the 19th century to the north of the Oranienburger Tor, along Chausseestraße. The district was known as "Fireland", due to the furnaces and smoking chimneys. One of the first large factories to be established here was the Maschinenbauanstalt August Borsig, an engineering company, founded in 1837.

The development of the electrical industry in Berlin was even more dynamic. In 1847 the company Siemens & Halske began production in Kreuzberg. The M. Weber plant in Chausseestraße was also to later play a significant role in the development of electrical engineering: in 1867 it was purchased by Emil Rathenau and later renamed "Allgemeine Elektricitäts-Gesellschaft" (AEG).

By the 1860s, the new residential districts were already clustering tightly around the production workshops. There were few possibilities to expand the sites in their original locations. Consequently, with the growth of the industry the companies often moved to the peripheral areas of the city. A cluster of industry grew up in Wedding, to the north, with the AEG plant, and later on the upper Spree in Schöneweide. The Borsig plants moved to Tegel, Siemens & Halske, with Loewe, moved to Spandau, later also expanding down the Spree in Oberschöneweide.

A key figure in the development of industrial architecture as an independent form was the entrepreneur Emil Rathenau. The design of the new factory in Ackerstraße (see no. 110) was not entrusted to the company's own architects, but handed to Franz Schwechten, one of the best-known architects of the time. In 1907, he not only entrusted the less well-known architect Peter Behrens with the AEG structure, but also with the design of important product lines and even the company writing paper – an unparalleled position, and the harbinger of what was later to become known as Corporate De-

sign. Two years later, Behrens erected his first factory building, the groundbreaking AEG turbine hall in Moabit (no. 151).

In his industrial buildings, Behrens sought to combine "serial opportunities of Classicistic form with the industrial requirements of standardisation". The principle of arrangement in colossal order is seen most clearly in the front of the small-power motor factory in Voltastraße, where a column front was repeated over four sections between 1910–13, taking its form from Schinkel's Altes Museum (no. 62). The tectonic assembly of the facade was accentuated by Behrens by cladding the steel joists with clinker stone. Large window surfaces enabled copious amounts of light to enter the shop floors. This procedure was adopted by Alfred Grenander in his industrial administration buildings, such as the Loewe armaments factory in Moabit or the Knorr brakes plant in Friedrichshain. The melting together of Classical forms with new steel and glass construction techniques led to the creation of the new "cathedrals of work".

The industrial complexes of the Gründerzeit era and early Modern age continue to characterise many districts of Berlin to this day. After reunification, their powerful architecture and the open, flexible floor plans made them particular attractive real estate for companies in the fields of the New Economy, design and modern services.

At the birthplace of Berlin industry, north of the Oranienburger Tor, stands a unique administrative building of the Borsig company, erected in 1899: Chausseestraße 13. In a partially preserved former locomotive factory between Chausseestraße and Novalisstraße, many young companies from the media and advertising sectors have made their home.   rh

103

Hochbahnanlage (167)
Elevated Railway
1913
Schönhauser Allee
Alfred Grenander

The U-Bahn line that once ran from Potsdamer Platz (no. 417) to Pankow continued overground from Senefelderplatz onwards. However, the continuation of the line as an elevated railway was hindered by influential Pankow inhabitants, which is why it disappears back below the surface shortly afterwards. The elevated railway viaduct that was required was designed by Grenander, with the structure incorporating two stations. It remains unchanged to this day. Grenander managed to lend the bare, riveted arches a form of high aesthetic quality. The station halls have an equally functional design.

U-Bahnhof Wittenbergplatz (168)
Underground Station at Wittenbergplatz
1913
Wittenbergplatz
Alfred Grenander

In 1902, the first electric municipal railway was opened in the Neuer Westen. The town of Charlottenburg, at that time still autonomous, pressed for the lines to be placed underground, with the first underground station, Wittenbergplatz, built as a consequence. As it soon became a junction point for two lines, the station building was to be a prestigious structure. With his concise, neo-Classical design on a cross-shaped floor plan, Grenander incorporated forms from the era around 1800. The facades are clad with limestone slabs. Following the purification of the railway station in the 1950s, the station hall was largely reconstructed in 1983, decorated with advertisements from the turn of the century.

Bundesministerium der Verteidigung (ehem. Reichsmarineamt) (169)
Federal Ministry of Defence (former Imperial Navy Office)
1914
Reichpietschufer 74–76
Heinrich Reinhardt und Georg Süßenguth

The Bundesverteidigungsministerium occupies a building in Berlin that was twice used by the German military staff to plan offensive wars in the 20th century, but that was conversely also the centre of German resistance. The architecture of the building is therefore all the more a warning from the past. In the direction of Reichpietschufer, the building is laid out symmetrically, with a prestigious limestone front. The core of the building in the southern Tiergarten district was used as the Reichsmarineamt in the time of the Kaiser. Beginning in 1938, Krupp and Druckenmüller extended the then Reichsmarineamt with the addition of an administrative section on what is now Stauffenbergstraße. The name of this street is a reminder that this was the headquarters for the resistance movement of 20th July 1944 (today Gedenkstätte Deutscher Widerstand, a memorial to the German resistance). The two components of the building have long since grown together, and are known today as the "Bendlerblock". Following the destruction of the Second World War, the expansive building on the Landwehrkanal stood in complete isolation. The reconstruction for use as a ministerial building trod a fine line between the often almost irreconcilable positions of heritage conservation and security requirements.

Stadtbad Neukölln (170)
Neukölln Municipal Baths
1914
Ganghoferstraße 5
Reinhold Kiehl

Around 1900, the construction counsellors in and around Berlin regarded themselves as having a social calling. With these public baths, Kiehl, from Rixdorf, put Hoffmann (no. 141), his colleague from the capital, in the shade. Behind the Biedermeier facade are two swimming pools (the smaller of which was once reserved for women), with mosaic-covered apses, Ionic travertine columns and marble floors reminiscent of an ancient

basilisk. With its vaulted chambers, surrounding a circular pool room with skylight cupola, the Greco-Roman sauna beneath the roof recalls images of the Imperial baths. The educational programme also included a municipal library. The 10,000 visitors that used the Apollinic temple on a daily basis almost broke the record for Germany at that time. Following a long period of renovation, the baths have been reopened to the public since 1984.

Staatsbibliothek (171)
State Library
1914
Unter den Linden 8
Ernst von Ihne

Following several 19th century attempts to initiate the construction of the new li-

brary, pressure from Wilhelm II resulted in the construction of the new Staatsbibliothek, in a severe Baroque style. The enormous, rectangular building encloses numerous courtyards, the first of which has a particularly pleasant ambience, characterised by fountains and ivy. Almost at the centre of the complex was a splendid octagonal reading room, with a cupola that stretched up above the building. After its collapse in the Second World War, the entire reading room was demolished. A new reading room was built to plans by the architect HG Merz, who subjected the building to a comprehensive restoration.

Volksbühne (172)
Theatre Volksbühne
1914
Rosa-Luxemburg-Platz 1
Oskar Kaufmann

The initiative for the construction of this building came from the social democratic organisation "Neue Freie Volksbühne", founded in 1892, which pursued the concept of a theatre of the people, with equal admittance prices for all. The building was erected to plans by Oskar Kaufmann, and was fitted with stage technology that was the most modern to be found in Berlin at that time. With its lightly curving, monumental entrance front of six colossal columns, the building follows the axis of Rosa-Luxemburg-Straße. The high stage area is flanked by functional areas. The theatre was completely de-

stroyed by fire in the Second World War. It was rebuilt in 1954 in simplified form, without the original ornamental figures and historic roof form. The auditorium was reduced in size.

Nordstern-Haus (173)
Nordstern House
1914
Badensche Straße 2
Mebes & Emmerich

With its vibrantly rounded corner, the former administrative building of the Nordstern-Versicherung insurance company makes effective use of the pointed

floor plan. The reinforced steel skeleton was clad in travertine slabs. The horizontally accentuated facade is finely profiled and decorated with discreet ornamentation. The recumbent, prestigious, character of the building moves up a scale on the interior. An oval vestibule leads to the main stairway, with the secondary staircases also elaborately designed.

Mitropa-Haus (174)
Mitropa House
1914
Universitätsstraße 2/3a
Johann Emil Schaudt

This unusually long commercial building was constructed by the architect of the Kaufhaus des Westens (no. 143) as the Handelshaus Hermes, on a relatively narrow plot. The five-storey, light, natural stone facade boasts twelve axes in a form strongly derived from neo-Classicism.

The central projection is accentuated by a triangular gable and sparse ornamentation. The institute building of the Humboldt University opposite is also worth looking at. It was built in 1904 by Otto Richter, and incorporates elements of Art Nouveau.

Wohnanlage (175)
Residential Complex
1914
Rüdesheimer Platz 1
Paul Jatzow

The district around Rüdesheimer Platz was the site of one of the most significant contributions to residential housing in Berlin prior to the First World War. The blocks of residential houses are fronted by slightly upwardly sloping lawn areas. The buildings were constructed by Terraingesellschaft Südwest, which had also erected the Bayerische Viertel district. The centre point of the district is formed by the artistically designed Rüdesheimer Platz, with its fountain complex. According to the plans of the architect, Jatzow, the buildings were largely intended to house middle-class apartments in the English style. As a consequence, despite the variety of the facades, the overall image was a uniform one.

107

Knorr-Bremse   (176)
Knorr-Bremse Building
1916
Neue Bahnhofstraße 9–17
Alfred Grenander

This five-storey complex with numerous courtyards was built as the principal plant of Knorr-Bremse-AG, a manufacturer of brakes. The clinker front on the street side is divided into two sections. To the south is the administration building with sandstone facade, the ground floor is particularly accentuated through sturdy column arcades. The factory building that adjoins to the north assumes the round arched motif but is on the whole plainer, with the facade reliefs shallower. Between 1922 and 1927 an additional complex was erected on the other side of the rail tracks, which was reached via a tunnel. The design for this building also came from Grenander.
A further addition came in 1995, with the Ostkreuz service centre of JSK Perkins & Will followed in 1995.

Bosch-Haus   (177)
Bosch House
1917
Bismarckstraße 71
Richard Bielenberg, Josef Moser

This commercial building of the Bosch company was one of the few privately financed buildings to be completed in spite of the limitations imposed by the First World War. The most characteristic feature is a semi-circular porch, effectively highlighting the street corner. The prestigious limestone facade was not fitted with any of the decoration prevalent at that time. The transition from vertical axes and horizontal elements led to an unusual layout. The building is enclosed

by a high-hipped roof. The ground floor has been simplified over the course of the years.

Charité (178)
Charité Hospital
1917
Schumannstraße 20/21
Kurt Diestel, Georg Thür

Berlin's oldest hospital and most renowned medical training facility was founded in 1710 by King Friedrich I as a building for plague sufferers, in 1727 it received the melodious name "Charité". The oldest remaining building of the original structure is the Pockenkrankenhaus, the pox hospital, of 1837, which lies to the south of Invalidenstraße. The most significant buildings on the hospital site, three to five-storey brick buildings with sandstone formwork and rendered facing, were built between 1897 and 1916. In most cases, the floor plan is Baroque, whereas the facades, broken up by large windows and loggia-style open halls, show the first indications of the encroaching Reform architecture. The interior of the buildings also incorporated new technical solutions for lighting, ventilation and heating. The range of vistas and the ivy growth creates a picturesque overall image. A hospital community grew up here, turned into a Mecca of science and research by doctors performing groundbreaking operations, fighting bacteria, tuberculosis and germs: Rudolf Virchow, Ferdinand Sauerbruch, Robert Koch, Christoph Wilhelm Hufeland and Karl Bonhoeffer all worked on this site. Numerous memorials in the grounds pay tribute to these personalities. A number of the buildings damaged in the war were reconstructed in the late 1970s, a period that also saw the erection, on the other side of Luisenstraße, of a 21-storey tower block with a surgical centre and 26 operating theatres. On its inauguration in 1982, it was the most modern clinic of the former Eastern Bloc.

Weimar Republic, the Metropolis of Berlin: The 1920s (179)

The 1920s were characterised by democratic emancipation, unparalleled levels of inflation, technical progress and an upheaval in the fields of art and architecture. However, these were anything but secure times. Until 1923, Germany experienced a level of inflation that had never been witnessed before. The situation only calmed down following the currency reform in 1924. However, the Weimar Republic was once again plunged into crisis towards the end of the 1920s due to the world economic depression.

The economic and political instability had an almost inspirational effect upon the fields of art and architecture. Berlin is the central point between Paris and Moscow. While impulses from the fields of fashion and theatre come from France, the focal point in the young Soviet Union was focused on the fields of painting and architecture. The constructivists joined forces in Moscow. Their utopian designs, in which buildings seem to lose their earthly connection, had their counterpart in Germany. Between 1919 and 1921, the architect Bruno Taut published the Frühlicht magazine, in which he propagated

the new form of architecture. He drew up designs for buildings under the title of "Alpine Architektur", which were copies of crystals as it were. The Bauhaus style of architecture was founded in Weimar, which would develop a new type of architecture for a new society from there. However, hardly any building work was carried out due to the economic situation. Only the young architect Erich Mendelsohn managed to build the so-called Einsteinturm, an architectural envelopment of a solar telescope, in Potsdam.

It was only from the middle of the 1920s that the long yearned for construction boom in the Weimar Republic began. The new commissions included the following: residential estates (see no. 194), high-rise buildings, sports complexes, film palaces, filling stations, airports – technical progress demands new types of buildings. The 1920s began in a very utopian manner, yet the first buildings were very conventional. Only ideology remained. "Our age is not full of pathos; we do not value the great leap forward but rather reason and functionalism" is how the architect Mies van der Rohe expres-

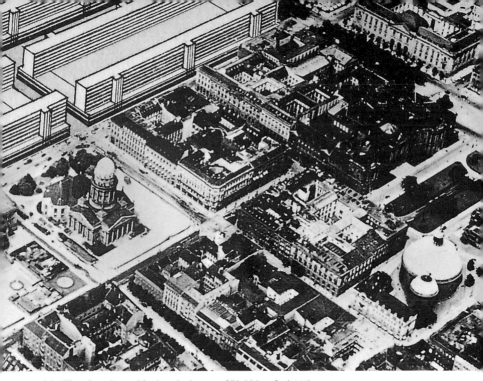

Ludwig Hilberseimer: Proposal for the redevelopment of Friedrichstraße (1929).

sed this idea. The greatest challenge constituted the construction of housing for the completely overpopulated cities. Berlin became a centre of council housing buildings.

In architectural terms, Berlin experienced a boom in architecture, which would only be repeated again 70 years later. The engine behind the urban development is the state, which created the basis for the expansion of the city through large infrastructure projects (the extension of the U and S-Bahn railways, the Tempelhof airport (no. 249), power and water supply buildings. Berlin is on the brink of being promoted into the Premier League of world architecture. A competition is announced for a high-rise office building at the Bahnhof Friedrichstraße, at the same time as a competition for the new construction of a high-rise building of the "Chicago Tribune" in which 263 architects throughout the world take part. While a Gothicised draft, typical of the time was selected and realised in Chicago, the realisation of the project in Berlin became of victim of inflation. The most significant projects of

this age are realised by architects in the form of detached houses and mansions for major industrialists. They did not embark on the social task of building economical housing for the masses until the second half of the 1920s.

The 1920s also revealed themselves to be extremely heterogeneous in terms of historical architectural styles. While the early projects are still characterised by expressionist styles, the "new objectivity" is beginning to assert itself, which for its part was replaced by a certain degree of recourse to more traditional construction forms towards the end of the 1920s. Within a period of ten years, the architecture in Berlin had developed a degree of diversity, from which it still thrives today.   meu

Large infrastructure projects: Tempelhof Airport.

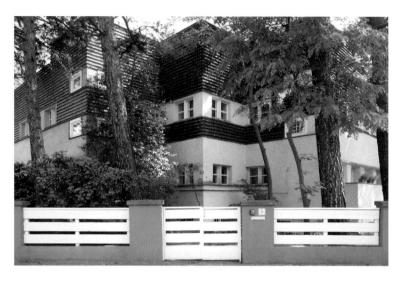

Doppelvilla (180)
Double Mansion
1922
Karolingerplatz 5/5a
Erich Mendelsohn

The city oasis is located between the heavily trafficked island of Theodor-Heuss-Platz and the trade fair site. The double mansion is located at the tip of the Westend mansion estate. The complex is comprised of two houses, arranged as mirror images of each other, which rank amongst the first flat-roofed buildings in Berlin. Each half of the house has four storeys; the exterior of which is decorated with plaster, hard fired bricks and ribbon windows. The clear line of the facade design is continued on the interior. The economic areas are located in the basement; the ground floor is inhabited, the bedrooms and the roof chambers ensue. A generous sun terrace forms the crowing conclusion.

Gebäude des ADGB (181)
Buildings of the General German Confederation of Trade Unions
1923
Wallstraße 61–65/Inselstraße 6–6 A
Max Taut/Franz Hoffmann

Max Taut and Franz Hoffmann built the first house with a facade made of a rein-

forced concrete frames within the giant complex, which the General German Confederation of Trade Unions had had built on Wallstraße. The exterior is accordingly characterised by a strictly rectangular grid. The fields between this space lattice with double windows were lined with bricks, plastered and ultimately painted in different colours. This makes the supporting and non-supporting structural components effectively stand out from one another. While the construction did not leave any more doubt that the rationalism of industrial

standardisation would determine how buildings were constructed in the future, a great love of expressionistic artistic work emerged in the interior architecture. The impressive meeting room has been preserved on the side of the building facing Inselstraße to this day.

Mosse-Haus (182)
Mosse House
1923
Jerusalemer Straße 46–47/
Schützenstraße 18–25
Erich Mendelsohn

This building is a manifest of the optimism of the early Weimar Republic. An explosion during the November revolution in 1919 blew out a corner of the building from the early modernist monumental building by Cremer & Wolffenstein (1901-1913). Mendelsohn transferred the tempo of the road traffic into the architecture with a lively new transverse module, emphasised effectively by the ribbon windows, which are covered with black ceramics and that fan out like

wings. This makes the building take on a completely new external appearance. The cambered facia construction intensified this dynamic impression and may also be understood as the articulation of the citizen's self-consciousness at the dawn of Germany's first democracy.

Borsigturm (183)
Borsig Tower
1924
Berliner Straße 35
Eugen Schmohl

The nervous desire to move of the twenties usually found expression in horizontal structures in architectural terms. This was not the case with Borsig. The largest German locomotive manufacturer underlined his economic power with a symbolic gesture. The Borsigturm, measuring 213 feet, was the first high-rise building in Berlin. The clinkered steel skeleton construction made it possible to partition each storey into six equal-sized offices or one open-place office. The expressionist, zigzagged structure with neo-Gothic ribbon windows stands in stark contract to this rationalism. The construction, which was renovated between 1977-79, is now a landmark of a new city quarter (see Hallen at the Borsigturm, no. 440).

ehem. Reichsschuldenverwaltung (184)
former German Debt Administration
1924
Oranienstraße 106–109
German Bestelmeyer

The fact that one of the monumental structures of the young Weimar Republic was the Reichsschuldenverwaltung is one of the ironies of history. The building characterises the street scene through its facade with expressionist decoration. The radiance of the house can be compared to the Chile-Haus in Hamburg. Despite all the modern allusions to the "nautical architecture" of those years (see no. 281) the house continued to follow the classical citizen's city tradition, primarily due to its inner courtyards.

115

Martin Wagner
* 1885 in Königsberg, † 1957 in Cambridge/Mass. (185)

"The playgrounds must not be more than 10 minutes away from the living quarters, the parks notmore than 20 minutes away, the sports grounds must not be more than 30 minutes away."

Martin Wagner, 1915

The name of Martin Wagner is generally associated with two things. On the one hand, he is associated with the dissertation "The sanitary green of the cities. A contribution to the open spaces theory", which he submitted in 1915. On the other hand, he is known for the residential es-

tates that were constructed in Berlin in the second half of the 1920s. The theoretical work, which had already made him famous and caused much sensation by the age of just 30, can nevertheless be taken as the basis of his practical work at the Zweckverband Groß-Berlin, the council of Berlin and its surrounding communities, and then as Stadtbaurat, which is the head of the office for municipal planning and building control, first in Schöneberg, then in Greater-Berlin. In this function, Wagner, in contrast to all his predecessors, attempted to view urban development as an integrated discipline and to incorporate green spaces and parks as obvious elements. This may be viewed as a reaction to Berlin's urban structures, which were solely oriented towards exploiting plots of lands and frequently led to catastrophically unhygienic living conditions. Wagner's bold initiative consequently met with a more positive response from the politicians than from the private property developers. He did, after all, state in his academic work that the neighbouring proprietors – both private and state – would have to bear the costs of the green spaces.

His five guiding principles became a kind of manifesto for planners of green spaces. The demands expressed within it have characterised the design of open spaces to this day. Above all, Wagner's reflections that there should be an "average of 260 square feet of children's playground, 17 square feet of sports fields, 5 square feet of promenades, 22 square feet of parkland and 140 square feet of city forest" for each inhabitant, were deemed as being the dictum for urban green space planning offices in the form of so-called reference values until just a few years ago.

However, Martin Wagner has predominantly left behind visible traces of his work as an architect in the city. In his just seven years as the head of the municipal planning and building control office (his predecessor had actually managed to serve 4 times as long), he was responsible for significant building projects such as the Hufeisensiedlung housing estate

(no. 193) and the lido Strandbad Wannsee (no. 212.). In addition, Wagner designed the Kriegerheimstätten estate in Friedrichsfeld, which was the first attempt at large-panel building in Germany.

There is no doubt that Martin Wagner was one of the most significant construction politicians of the 20th century. The Berlin-based architecture historian Karl-Heinz Hüter wrote: "In Wagner, a personality committed to social issues assumed the office of the head of the municipal planning and building control office. It comes as no surprise that he was only able to assert himself in certain subareas but failed in many others when one considers the opposing political and economic interests and the organised opposition of reactionary circles. His greatest achievement was to have decisively applied metropolitan standards to all the construction projects in Berlin and to have brought the "pioneer of a form of German building" (Wagner) to the capital city. Without Wagner's leadership, Berlin would not have been able to become the most significant centre of the new form of building.

After leaving the German civil service in 1933, (he had previously resigned from the Academy of Arts where he had attempted to oppose their political Gleichschaltung, the method of eliminating all opposition) Wagner emigrated to the United States where he lectured at Harvard University as a professor from 1938 until 1950. Wagner died in Cambridge/Mass. at the age of 71.   meu

117

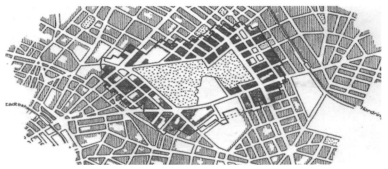

The sphere of influence of Volkspark Friedrichshain on its neighbourhood: according to Martin Wagner's analysis, this green area, which is a park, can provide for 81,500 people.

Haus »Dr. Sternefeld«   **(186)**
"Dr. Sternefeld" House
1924
Heerstraße 107
Erich Mendelsohn

Dynamism is the formal trademark for the optimism of the democratic avant-garde in the Weimar Republic. And it did not just find expression in the large representative buildings, but also in privately owned buildings. The residential building of the doctor Walter Sternefeld is an example of this. In the case of this building made of stacked cubes, the movement develops through forwards and backwards jumps, terraces that extend outwards and ribbon windows that are deeply indented and surround the building. While it is sealed in a fortified manner facing Heerstraße, the L-shaped construction on the side of the house facing towards the Grunewald city forest is all the more informal by way of a contrast. In terms of its facade structure, the residential house is reminiscent of the country houses of the influential American pioneer of the modern period, Frank Lloyd Wright. The mansion originally served the owner as his private house and doctor's surgery. The treatment rooms were separated from the living quarters by a supporting iron wall. They were located in the rear section of the house. The attic that was sealed outwardly was illuminated through a small inner courtyard and originally served as a storage and a drying room.

Wohnblock Thulestraße   **(187)**
Residential Block on Thulestraße
1925
Thulestraße 61/63, Eschengraben 54,
Hardangerstraße 1–5, Talstraße 1–2 A
Erwin Gutkind

A backdrop, which would have befitted Fritz Lang's metropolis: the three to four-storey block was the first modern housing estate in Berlin with iconographic qualities. It was also correspondingly controversial upon its completion, particular in view of the fact that Gutkind was a product of the contemporary style schools. The dark clinkered facades with white plaster bands and extremely small

windows anticipated the new objectivity. The cellar substitute rooms situated in the uppermost storey as well as the reinforced attics, were meant to accommodate a leisure time area (which was not realised) on the roof, assumed the aesthetics of industrial buildings. Set against this, the corner designs (in particular between Eschengraben und Talstraße, where the protruding concrete arch accommodates a filigree glass wall) correspond to the composition principles of expressionism. Such city-like aesthetics were never to form part of the estate construction again.

Versuchssiedlung Schorlemerallee (188)
Trial Estate on Schorlemerallee
1925
Schorlemerallee 7a–23a
Hans und Wassili Luckhardt mit
Alfons Anker

From a birds' eye view, the Berlin housing estate looks like a flock of migratory birds flying in formation. When viewed from the ground floor, the two rows of six houses structured symmetrically behind one another are an early example of residential construction in the period of new objectivity. While the houses were

constructed in a traditional manner in the first construction phase, the houses of the following two construction phases in 1927 and 1928 were already built adopting a steel skeleton design. At the same time, the complex is a chronicle of architecture at whose end are white cubes with glass brick porches. Even low earners were supposed to be able to fulfil the dream of a "mansion in the green areas" through this economical form of building.

Funkturm (189)
Broadcast Tower
1926
Messedamm 12–18
Heinrich Straumer

The city of Berlin in the 1920s could hold its own against Paris. A kind of Eiffel tower en miniature was created in the form of the Funkturm, which is 500 feet high and was built on the occasion of the 1st Great German Radio Exhibition in 1924. The Funkturm was opened in 1926 when Albert Einstein delivered the opening address on the occasion of the 3rd Radio Exhibition. The steel construction with a restaurant and a lookout platform served as the radio mast of the Deutscher Hörfunk, founded in Berlin in 1923, which broadcast its programmes from the Haus des Rundfunks (no. 209) opposite it from 1929 onwards. The Funkturm has been a listed building since 1966. The Deutsches Rundfunkmuseum, the German Radio Museum, has been located at its feet since 1967.

Heizkraftwerk »Klingenberg« (190)
"Klingenberg" Power Plant
1926
Köpenicker Chaussee 42–45
Walter Klingenberg, Werner Issel

The thermal power plants stand for the radical mechanisation of the municipal

Power demands a symbolic form of expression. And the architect who had already assisted the locomotive baron Borsig to achieve cathedral-like self-representation through a tower, now did the same for one of the largest publishing houses in Europe by building a printing house. The eight-storey Ullstein-Haus, the tower of which surpasses Borsig's tower by some 40 feet, was Berlin's first high-rise building to be made of concrete. However, this technical novelty was concealed by red brick facade with elaborate stone masonry work. The highpoint of the plastic decoration is the Ullstein owl.

organism in the 1920s. The large-scale Klingenberg power plant exceeded everything previous to it in order to meet the insatiable electricity demand of the metropolis. The core of the plant was formed by two boiler houses with eight metal smokestacks, a turbine room together with the eleven-storey high-rise building with administrative and social rooms. Apart from the boiler houses, the bare steel construction of the remaining buildings was clad in a cloak made of red clinkered bricks and vertically structured with pillars structured in close succession. The large-scale power plant is one of the outstanding performances in the field of industrial construction.

Ullstein-Haus (191)
Ullstein House
1926
Mariendorfer Damm 1–3
Eugen Schmohl

BVG-Betriebshof (192)
Berlin Public Transit Company
Operating Yards
1927
Müllerstraße 77–81
Jean Krämer

The operating yard was constructed from 1925 onwards for the tram. Its architect fulfilled the same role for this type of transport as Alfred Grenader (no. 213) had done for the underground. But while one architect created a purely functional design, the younger architect Krämer was much more fanciful: parallel arches, jagged oriels and triangular windows converted the tram depot into an example of expressionism, which only found its counterpart in Richard Ermisch's paral-

lel housing project in Spandau Zeppelin-straße. The work praises the general principle, which was only given up in the post-war period, of viewing transportation constructions as urban elements. Even the hall that is more than 12 hectares in size within the depths of the plot of land reveals gable and balcony facades. Garden terraces and block edges with 380 apartments make the tram town at Müllerstraße an almost normal address. It was converted for buses running in 1958/1960 in parallel with West Berlin's decision to dispense with the use of trams.

Hufeisen-Siedlung   (193)
Horseshoe Development
1927
Fritz-Reuter-Allee, Buschkrugallee,
Parchimer Allee
Bruno Taut, Martin Wagner

The joint project of Taut and Wagner is viewed as being the first major German housing estate with more than one thousand residences, of which no less than 480 were detached houses. The housing estate was intended for workers. It was therefore supposed to be an example of standardised construction and large-scale production techniques, with the objective of keeping the construction costs (and consequently the rent prices) low. For instance, the excavation of earth and transportation were mechanised. The workers were nevertheless still unable to afford the houses. Salaried employees

and civil servants moved into the houses instead. The core of the estate is formed by the white-plastered "Hufeisen", a horse-shoe which bends around a flat depression. This extensive "line" is formed from just one type of house, as the serial production required simple and cheap forms, that adapted as well as possible to the lie of the land and involved little earth excavation. The garden design is based on one of Leberecht Migge's drafts. The Britzer piece de resistance of the construction of workers' housing is delineated from a romantic, neighbouring housing estate of the Beamtenbauverein, the civil servants' construction association, through a "red front" comprising 32 identical residential buildings. Taut made intensive use of colour as a design element in addition to brick elements to structure the body shell. The formulation of road spaces and residential streets in the Hufeisen-Siedlung is deemed as being limited from a contemporary point of view due to rationalisation considerations, but was viewed as being a sign of progress at the time.

Housing Development: Hopes for a New Social Beginning (194)

Green space and parks included as a matter of course: the Hufeisen residential area (1927).

After the First World War, there was an enormous housing shortage in Berlin. Therefore, despite inflation and the economic crisis, the first Greater-Berlin council, which had been formed in 1920, declared the creation of affordable housing to be an important objective of their policy. Following the motto of "light, air and sun", new style housing estates developed not only in Berlin. In reaction to the construction in the Gründerzeit, which had been almost exclusively privately financed and had made as much as possible from the land plots, new residential estates emerged, in which colourful houses were scattered loosely in park-like complexes.

The housing development of the Modern age, to which representatives such as Bruno Taut and Martin Wagner (no. 185) belong, falls at the same time as the establishment of property developers, who were characterised by the trade unions, cooperatives or non-profit making organisations. As the owner and operator of the housing development, as well as the physical building of the buildings, they also took care of the collective approach in the operation of the predominantly worker-inhabited quarters. Large industrial operations, such as the AEG or Siemens, also built new residential areas in the immediate neighbourhood to the companies. Among the most well-known is Siemensstadt (no. 215) in today's district of Spandau. On the whole, all settlements were situated outside of the Berlin S-Bahn ring, as it was only here where large enough land plots were situated at reasonable prices.

Typologically, the architects broke with everything that had existed up until then. They said goodbye to the block-by-block development of the quarters and built their residential buildings in the form of ribbons or point blocks in the open landscape. With this anti-urban city model, they actually offered a counter concept to the traditional city of the 19th century. In the years between 1924 and 1930 alone, over 140,000 new apartments emerged in Berlin. This enormous building activity was accompanied by a debate on architecture, where the protagonists of a new Modern era fought with the traditionalists about steep and flat roofs. As National Socialism heralded the end of the Weimar Republic, even the modern housing developments were called into disrepute. From now on, new residential blocks lost their colour and were given steep roofs. However, ribbon development and open spaces with high proportions of green continued to be "en vogue".   meu

123

To each worker his own house: the development of housing estates also brought colour into the city.

**Schaltwerkhochhaus der
Siemens & Dunckert AG** (195)
*High-Rise Switching Device Building of
Siemens & Dunckert AG*
1927
Nonnendammallee 104–110
Hans Hertlein

In a number of respects, the 590 feet long "box" is a high point and turning point in the truest sense of the word in the field of

industrial construction. The ten-storey longitudinal structure was the first high-rise factory building in Europe. On both sides, the pane, which is a brick nogged, clinker brick-faced steel skeleton, is held in place by defiant stairway towers. These provide access to the continuous production storeys. The high-rise building is a rational construction that was specifically built with the goal of creating the "best and most expedient frame for working purposes" (Hertlein). To this end, the architect departed from perimeter block development and avoided the use of representative decoration.

Abspannwerk Wilhelmsruh (196)
Step-Down Station at Wilhelmsruh
1927
Kopenhagener Straße 83–89
Hans Heinrich Müller

Ordensburg castles built by the Teutonic Order to protect their territory or multi-bay basilica: depending on the location of

the observer, either one or the other of these associations will impress itself and prove that, based on the sum of the impressions, both will merge within one another. The step-down station is one of the numerous works, through which Bewag's in-house architect in the "Electropolis of Berlin" (Paul Kahlfeldt) created their sacred power generating buildings until 1930. Elements such as the stepped roofs from the side perspective or the powerful flank towers at the front of the central element of the building as well as the towers of the elevated distribution hall all have a sublime quality in terms of their expressionistic convergence with the brick Gothic style. It harboured the most sacred thing, technology, in its interior, which was necessary to convert heavy current into standard household electricity.

Wohnanlage Afrikanische Straße (197)
Housing Estate on Afrikanische Straße
1927
Afrikanische Straße 14–41
Ludwig Mies van der Rohe

This freestanding housing estate in the former worker's district of Wedding ranks amongst the smaller forms of housing estate construction, which was created in accordance with the programmatic guiding idea of modernism of light, air and sun. It belongs to the first generation of new building in the area of council housing. The 88 apartments, ranging from one to three rooms and 592 to 807 square feet in size, are located behind a facade, which apart from a row of clinkered brick and the panel windows with balconies and loggias, makes the functionality and the comfort of the apartments visible to passers-by. The fixtures and fittings of all the apartments with a bathroom and a kitchen-cum-living room represented a great leap forward for that time. The three-storey U-shaped complex was Mies van der Rohe's contribution to "accommodation for people on the bread-line".

Titania-Palast   (198)
Titania Palace
1928
Schloßstraße 4 – 5, Gutsmuthsstraße 28
Schöftler, Schlönbach & Jacobi

As different from distinct form the Universum cinema of the WOGA complex (no.217) the light of this Filmpalast does not just serve to make clear square hewn stones glow. Self-illuminating structures are also added to it: the high point is a light chamber, 100 feet in height. The narrow bronze-set strips of light made of opaque glass, which are set in a tight se-

quence, run horizontally like all corner elements, so that colossal pilaster vertically break down the fronts. While the exterior of the cinema has been preserved as a monument to this day, the interior was completely transformed in 1953 and also in 1969 and 1999. The Titania-Palast has only started serving as a cinema again in part since the last conversion. However, the interior aesthetics are still beneath the level of contemporary multiplexes.

Abspannwerk Buchhändlerhof   (199)
Step-Down Station at Buchhändlerhof
1928
Mauerstraße 78-80
Hans Heinrich Müller

This cathedral of "Electropolis Berlin" is very traditional and, for this very reason, spectacular. This is because the step-down station is located right in the middle of the perimeter block development of historical Friedrichstadt. The relations to the perimeter block development can barely be identified now due to the war. There are also only ruins remaining of the accumulator factory. Nevertheless, the entire complex is imposing. The smaller, northern section of the factory still reveals remains of the second block power station built in Berlin and has a similar significance in terms of the history of the city and technological history. In the southern section the positioning of the control room is particularly impressive. The steel construction stands in the corner like a wasp's nest, where its brick filling is reminiscent of classical half-timbering.

Gleichrichterwerk Zehlendorf   (200)
Rectifier Plant in Zehlendorf
1928
Machnower Straße 83
Hans Heinrich Müller

Rectifier plants served to convert the rotary current delivered from the step-down stations for the tramways into di-

rect current. These plants were standardised accordingly. However, the building supervision authorities demanded a functional building, which should blend in with the surroundings of the free-standing houses. Müller constructed a facade with triangular oriels. The transformer ventilation was installed in shafts in this construction. He succeeded in both reducing the cascading projection of the oriel consoles and the brick moulding formation in such a way that the two-storey building blends in with the environment. The construction is reminiscent of the relic of a medieval fortification system.

Villen am Rupenhorn (201)
Mansions on Rupenhorn
1928
Heerstraße 161, Am Rupenhorn 24
Hans & Wassili Luckhardt
with Alfons Anker

The detached houses rank amongst the most imposing examples of white architecture. At the same time, they set a new trend in the language of architecture. This is because the cubic steel skeleton

constructions no longer express a sense of dynamism due to their decorative facades. This is expressed instead from their body shells. In addition to the sliding strip windows, the stylish terraces also ensure that the mansions blend in with the gentle slope like two landscape sculptures. Even the interior is broken down in a functional manner and yet simultaneously in motion. The living room that consists of a large "flowing room" blends in so to speak with the garden. The two mansions have influenced the residential buildings on Schorlemerallee (no. 188) as their prototypes.

Musterpavillon »Dammwegschule« (202)
School Model Pavilion for
"Dammwegschule"
1928
Dammweg 216
Bruno Taut

FLOP The building is a relic of a design for a comprehensive school for 2,500 pupils in Neukölln in order to improve the educational opportunities for workers' children. The classrooms had a glass wall that could be folded away into the floor so that it was also possible to teach in external room that was roofed over. Surrounding upper lights and a broad strip of windows completely illuminate the room and, thus, permit the pupils a free seating order, making it possible for them to work in small groups. In addition, the steel concrete building is equipped with maps and projection surfaces that can be moved mechanically. The architecture was therefore designed to do away with the hierarchical teaching of children from the front. The school reform project failed due to the lack of support from politicians and the world economic crisis. It remained a trial construction, which has subsequently been renovated and has been used by an upper school, the Carl-Legien-Oberschule since April 2001.

Apartmenthaus am Kaiserdamm (203)
Apartment Building on Kaiserdamm
1929
Kaiserdamm 25/25a
Hans Scharoun and Georg Jacobowitz

The apartment block is an early response to the needs of an industrious singles' society. The single and double rooms are tailor-made to the needs of a clientele that has to spend a lot of time working in their individual professions. Even the very expensive fixtures and fittings were delivered at the same time. The fact that the apartments still offer an astonishing amount of space is due to the rationally considered room conception by Jacobowitz. Scharoun, who made his debut in the residential building with this house, was only allowed to design the backdrop. The facade has been broken down with exit windows and staggered stairway windows. Some of the studios on the attic floor in the new five-storey building are equipped with roof gardens. A sun terrace, accessible to everyone, is located above it.

Versuchssiedlung »Am Fischtal« (204)
"Am Fischtal" Trial Housing Estate
1929
Am Fischtal
Heinrich Tessenow

This reform housing estate with its conservative gable roofs is the counterpart of the neighbouring, new functionalist major housing estate Onkel-Toms-Hütte (no. 223) from the same period. And it is the result of the awful "pulling and tugging" of 1920s concerning which house roofing was appropriate for the German building culture, which peaked in the so-called "Zehlendorf roof war". The 120 mostly four to six room apartments of a maximum of 1890 square feet in size in the detached houses and apartment block buildings are located behind a facade made of panel windows with folding window shutters, wooden pergolas and wooden trellises. In 1928, the "ultimate form of housing for the middle class" was to be presented by this "Heimatstil", which was literally a domestic revival, at the "Bauen und Wohnen" exhibition . Schmitthenner and Poelzig were also involved in the project.

Volkspark Rehberge (205)
Rehberge Public Park
1929
between Schwarzer Graben, Windhukerstraße, Afrikanische Straße, Transvaalstraße and Dohnagestell
Rudolf Germer, Albert Brodersen,
Erwin Barth

GARDEN The sand, marsh and forest landscape of the Rehberge, 120 hectares in size, which was created from 1926 onward marks the climax in the development of public parks in Berlin – or to be more accurate the second generation of this type of gardens: seeing as the empire had still wanted to educate the workers about noble manners by "going for a stroll in the park" (Friedrichshain, see no. 191) the Weimar Republic attempted to strengthen their own momentum. In

this case, the 4-hectare, deep-laid high performance lawn formed the centre court. Playgrounds and tennis courts, a sports arena, a dance plaza, a horse-shoe shaped ridge with a toboggan run, lush meadows for relaxing and the first permanent colony in Germany were situated around this lawn. Set against these large scale uses, pure garden art can only seldom be found there. But still: An avenue of maple trees, a circle of poplars, a square of chestnut trees and the ponds are real gems.

Warenhaus Karstadt (206)
Karstadt Department Store
1929
Hermannplatz 5–10
Philipp Schaefer

Karstadt at Hermannplatz is an example of the architectural self representation of the department store giants from the 1920s. The seven-storey steel skeleton building formed a schematisation of the "department store Gothic" style, developed by Alfred Messel; a building which should do complete justice to the name of the square in a Teutonic monumentality. In this respect, the seven-storey building was a reaction to the typical functionalism of the age. The twin tower of this cathedral of consumption, set illuminated advertising columns has convenient devices to keep its customers mobile in

the form of fifty customer lifts and underground train connections in addition

to a roof garden with a restaurant. The reconstruction after 1945 has not given any of the building's former sublimity back.

ehem. Haus des Deutschen Metallarbeiterverbandes (207)
former building of the German Metalworkers' Union
1930
Alte Jacobstraße 148–155
Erich Mendelsohn, Rudolf W. Reichel

A clear aesthetic form was the character-istic style for this administration complex as well. Mendelson has planted this con-struction in the plot of land like a wedge and used its unbeneficial ground plan for a style-defining work of art in the visual language of the new objectivity period. A concave main building combines the five-storey side wings, which are linked with one another in the courtyard by a two-storey semicircular printing office build-ing. The building has the appearance of pliers, which hold a working part in place in the form of the main building. A masterpiece covered in travertine with bronze ribbon windows, a completely glazed double upper floor with a semicir-cular glass projection together with a flagpole emerged from the main build-ing. The writing of the trade union is very discreetly positioned above the entrance.

**Kathreiner-Hochhaus
am Kleistpark** (208)
*Kathreiner High-Rise Building at
Kleistpark*
1930
Potsdamer Straße 186
Bruno Paul

This twelve-storey building as a part of an H-shaped complex ranks amongst the avant-garde of the Berlin high-rise build-ing culture. The structuring elements of the administrative building of the Kath-reiner-Handelsgesellschaft für Malzkaf-fee, a malt coffee trading company, are cornering strips with panel windows. However, the aesthetic characteristic of the building is the optical interplay with Carl von Gontard's Königskolonnades that were set here from from Alexander-platz in 1910. They are not just a part of the main entrance. Reference is also made to the colonnade architecture through the columns and the ribbon win-dows. The Baroque building belongs to a collection of buildings, which documents the historic anchoring of the modern pe-riod.

Haus des Rundfunks (209)
House of Broadcast
1930
Masurenallee 10 – 14
Hans Poelzig

It was meant to symbolise the powerful influence of electronic mass media: the first German house of radio was built as a part of the complete restructuring of the trade fair site (no. 242). But it was not the imposing clinkered facade but rather the building concept which has set stan-dards. The three four-storey office wings form an inner courtyard in the form of a pointed arch, where the acoustically sen-sitive, sound-proofed studios are located. The three trapezium-shaped broadcast-ing halls are separated from one another and can be accessed through the large en-trance hall. The building has been used by the Freies Berlin broadcasting compa-ny since 1957.

Departure from Historical Continuity (210)

Hardly any other period in the history of architecture and art is more difficult to define than the "modern age". This begins with the very concept which suggests constant renewal but has now itself become historical. "Modernism" indicated much more of a distinct period which started around the year 1900. Charles Jencks, the British architecture historian and spiritual father of post modernism described the year 1972 as the end of modernism. At that time residential buildings were being demolished in the US city of St. Louis, which (although only 20 years old) had been constantly criticised by its inhabitants since the time they moved in. What had happened that an entire period could be declared over due to the demolition of one single building complex?

In architectural history terms modernism can initially be valued as the reaction towards the historicism that was and architectural point of view. Messel built the Wertheim department store on Leipziger Platz (no. 137) and attempted to provide a new type of building with a form through his monumental facade, which was based on an already existing formal canon. Behrens attempted the same thing with his turbine hall building in Moabit (see no. 151). Set against this, Gropius and his supporters tried their hands at constructions which radically rejected decoration and ornaments.Their projects were to go down in history as "white modernism". On the other hand, the expressionists applied more colourful and imaginative techniques. Their designs, which remained unrealised for a long time, now bear witness to the attempt to provide architecture with a new impulse through crystalline building forms and bright colours. The forerunners were primarily Bruno Taut and Hans Scharoun (no. 281).

A modern spirit which wanted to bring movement into architecture: Mendelsohn's sketches.

131

principally abounded at the end of the 19th century and its blunt copying of old building styles. The fathers of the movement, without being aware of the fact, were primarily Peter Behrens, Walter Gropius and Alfred Messel. While Behrens and Messel still attempted to develop new building types from old ones, Gropius shut his eyes to all forms of tradition and, as the founder of the Bauhaus style in Weimar, even had the library history books burned.The dispute was also carried out in Berlin from an ideological After 1945 the "Modernism" concept was resurrected following the period during the Third Reich when its trends had been predominantly surpassed. To this day, people are still considering which aspects of this movement can be salvaged for the future under the keyword of "second modernism". However, in many places, modernism has fallen victim to exactly the thing it had originally attempted to combat: historical continuity.   meu

Einsteinturm on Potsdam's Telegraph Hill, by Erich Mendelsohn.

Stadtbad Mitte (211)
Mitte District Baths
1930
Gartenstraße 5
Carlo Jelkmann, Heinrich Tessenow

By contrast with the older municipal swimming pools (see no. 170), the first example in the city centre reveals a transformed relationship with water. While it had once been used to celebrate hygiene, it now served as an exhibition of the body cult . The largest swimming pool of its time followed the bathing, massage and medical wings. The conservative modernist, Tessenow, surrounded the first competition-suitable 160-fet swimming pool with a glass case . Through the double walled beam to joint design as well as the facetted panes, swimmers have the feeling that they are still in the middle of the third element, even when they are above the water line. In this case, the elegantly cool interior does not pay homage to the fun factor of water in a way that the

baths of the 80s were to dominate (see no. 364). The director of the local structural engineering department provided the Stadtbad Mitte with a rigid sub-divided facade made of yellow brick with windows that sit flushly within the facade.

Strandbad Wannsee (212)
Wannsee Lido
1930
Wannseebadweg 25
Martin Wagner, Richard Ermisch

"Put your trunks in your bag ... and then hurry to Wannsee!": This evergreen about the way the whole city fled from its stone desert had its origins here. At the beginning, Martin Wagner wanted to create a cosmopolitan summer holiday resort where people could swim with an open-air theatre and a nursery school on a shoreline spanning approx. 2.5 miles. However, even the holiday resort that was created, which was just a third of the planned size, is still the continent's largest inland swimming area to this day. Richard Ermisch positioned a two-storey promenade, 1,750 in length and 20 feet wide with shops and restaurants between the Grunewald slopes and the shorelines which had been increased to a width of 262 feet. The steel skeleton construction that had been brick nogged with yellow clay bricks was expected to combine the "civilised and cultural needs of people from the city with their old-established perceptions of nature" (Martin Wagner). In actual fact, 1.3 million people visited the outdoor swimming area in the first season alone. 30,000 sun worshippers still flock here on hot summer days..

U-Bahn-Linie 8 (213)
Underground Line N° 8
1930
Gesundbrunnen to Hermannplatz
Alfred Grenander, Alfred Fehse

Grenander is the mastermind of Berlin's underground architecture. He designed

more than 70 stations, viaducts and service buildings between 1899 and 1931, which (like a constructed chronicle) tell the story of the change in history through to an abstract objectivity from the 1920s onwards. A few expedient elements have leant the stations of the U8 line a simple, but also deceptive calm. This is because the constant sequence of rows of columns, ceiling lights and station signs in all the stations, which differ in colour from one another, are set in motion when the train moves. Brakes and acceleration, i.e. speed, can be visually perceived as a technical journey through time.

Shell-Haus   **(214)**
Shell House
1931
Reichpietschufer 60
Emil Fahrenkamp

The building project almost collapsed due to the dispute between the proprietor and the authority responsible for the preservation of monuments. Now, at the end, a house which has been renovated in an exemplary manner fortunately stands. This is because the brick nogged steel skeleton construction is a jewel from the early modernism period. And this is for two reasons: the complex grows in a vertical cascading fashion from the fifth to the tenth storey from the neighbouring buildings, so that it can simultaneously

flow into the level ground in a wave-like form and seems to want to wash over the street to the Landwehrkanal. In visual language terms, the architecture makes an immediate allusion to the water. The building is one of the early and rare examples of organic architecture.

Siemensstadt Ringsiedlung   **(215)**
Sienmensstadt Ring Housing Estate
1931
Jungfernheideweg, Goebelstraße
Hans Scharoun, Otto Bartning, Walter
Gropius, Hugo Häring amongst others

The Ringsiedlung founded a new type of housing estate, which, in contrast to other major housing estates, consisted sole-

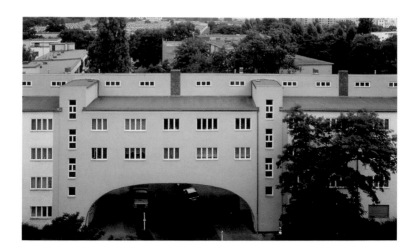

ly of high-rise apartments for the first time. The property developer was Siemens AG, who built this white housing estate for the rapidly growing red "Electropolis" for employees on low incomes. Scharoun provided the overall draft. The houses were designed by a team of progressive architects, who joined forces under the name of "Der Ring" in 1925. The four and five-storey buildings located in a line between the public parks, are arranged in a north-south direction or east-west direction, therefore ensuring that that all the apartments have as much light as possible. This meant they were to become the model design for the building of housing estates in the post-war period.

Weiße Stadt Reinickendorf (216)
White City Reinickendorf
1931
Aroser Allee, Emmentaler Straße,
Genfer Straße
Otto Rudolf Salvisberg, Wilhelm Büning,
Bruno Ahrends

This development ranks amongst the major housing estate projects, which were created under the supervision of the head of the municipal planning and building control office (no. 185) and carried out by architects from the new objectivity period. However, by contrast with the housing estates in Britz and Zehlendorf, the Weiße Stadt, literally the white city, only consists of apartment buildings. It was built on terrain, which already had a partially stipulated road routing due to an advance competition. Salvisberg, Büning and Ahrends were responsible for different parts of the housing estate. There were no uniform types of ground plans, but instead very different apartment designs and varied facades respectively have been integrated within an overall concept that is actually very homogeneous. The infrastructure provision of the housing estate consisted of 20 shops, nursery schools, a medical practice, chemists and a community laundry room. The description Weiße Stadt only applies in a limited extent as the buildings that are plastered in a bright white colour did indeed have fine colour differences on the windows, doors and the balcony railings. It is very true that colour was not such a dominant design element as it was with Bruno Taut, but modernism was not always as white as people liked to view it as.

Städtebauensemble »Woga« (217)
"Woga" Urban Development Ensemble
1931
Kurfürstendamm 153–156
Erich Mendelsohn

The ensemble right in the middle of the 'Gründerzeit', which was a period from 1871 of enormous industrial expansion in Germany, is the clearest example of the urbanistic visions of the avant-garde. An aesthetic unit for residential, business

and cultural purposes was built on the plot of land belonging to the Wohnhaus-grundstücksverwertungs A.G. (Woga) – with a cinema, theatre and cabaret. The complex integrated the perimeter block development of Jürgen Bachmann from 1927 on Albrecht-Achilles-Straße. The core of the miniature town is the Ufa cinema, that was converted into the "Schaubühne" theatre by Jürgen Sawade in 1981. A lively building, which slows down the speed of the road in a wedge and is reminiscent associatively of a sink – a comparison, which justifies the particular interior light architecture.

Berolina-Haus (218)
Berolina House
1932
Dircksenstraße/Alexanderplatz 1
Peter Behrens

Along with the adjacent Alexanderhaus, this building is the only remaining remnant of the ambitious new plans to convert Alexanderplatz (see no. 324) into a cosmopolitan traffic interchange. The twin buildings were planned to be gate houses, whose function is emphasised by glass light rows. The appearance of the houses is characterised by bay-like steel

windows and coquina stone panels. The completely glazed upper storey of the Berolina-Haus accommodated the legendary swing establishment "Café Braun" (later called Berolina), which, progressive as it was, could be accessed via escalators and paternosters. There was a garden with a lawn and a dance floor on the roof. Both gate buildings are an aesthetic example of the conversion of Alexanderplatz in accordance with the plans of the architect Hans Kollhoff.

Haus »Blumenthal« (219)
"Blumenthal" House
1932
Wilskistraße 66
Ludwig Hilberseimer

The property developer won the "Zehlendorf roof war" in favour of the new objectivity movement. A rectangular monopitch roof that slopes towards the road, practical and unsophisticated. The plaster-bordered door, visually linked with the small kitchen window through a cor-

nice of a door, and a ribbon window on the upper floor characterise the front side of the house. The other sides are characterised by a slightly advanced flue and panoramic windows. Hilberseimer's few buildings are a spartan variety of modernism, reduced down to the financially necessary features.

Columbus-Haus (220)
Columbus House
1932
Friedrich-Ebert-Straße 11–12,
Potsdamer Platz
Erich Mendelsohn

DEMOLITION The steel skeleton construction was conceived to be the "start of an equal-height ground wall, which was to be formed by the three corners – Siechen, Josty and Columbus-Haus. As the conclusion of Leipziger Strasse, as the gateway for the crossroads running across from the square" (Mendelsohn). But nothing came of the restructuring of Berlin's Piccadilly Circus. The ten-storey building with its curved facade and cantilever design continued to be the unique example. The Columbus-Haus housed offices, including the office of the architect himself, stores and restaurants until it was destroyed in the war. The house was a novelty with its new building technology, which included artificial ventilation. Makeshift renovations were carried out after the war, and on 17 June 1953, it was burned to the ground during the workers' revolt and torn down.

Haus Lemke (221)
Lemke House
1932
Oberseestraße 60
Ludwig Mies van der Rohe

Mies van der Rohe's last active year in Germany was in 1938, beofre which he had worked on several courtyard houses amongst other things. The country house for Karl Lemke is one of two house projects that were completed in this period. The country house sits flush on its terrace area as an L-shaped structure: all the openings are glazed at wall height. The individual well-proportioned rooms are linked to each another by room-height doors. The draft for the original garden design stems from Hermann Mattern. The small country house with an area of 1,722 square feet and a view of the Obersee lake was degraded to form a motor vehicle workshop after the war. It was later used by the state security service again and, following the reunification of Germany, it was turned into a municipal

gallery. Although the building has been greatly transformed over the years, it has been a listed building since 1977. The house is presently being renovated.

Kirche am Hohenzollerndamm (222)
Church at Hohenzollerndamm
1932
Hohenzollernplatz 202–203
Fritz Höger

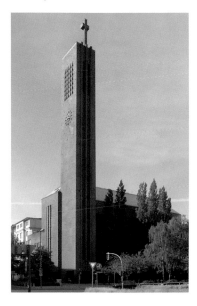

Fritz Höger's brick expressionism lived from pathetic elevations. Based on this basic conception, his Protestant church at Hohenzollerndamm certainly bears objective traits. It has a cubic appearance but its clinkered exterior has been partially decorated and covered with gold in the style of expressionist architects. In terms of urban development, the church building assumes an important function by closing the perimeter block. The inner space is entered through a flight of outdoor steps and a Gothicised portal, formed by thirteen pointed reinforced concrete arches. Reference should be made to the Kreuzkirche built some years earlier by Ernst and Günther Paulus at Hohenzollerndamm in conjunction with Höger's church and the expressionist works which are left in Berlin.

Onkel-Tom-Siedlung (223)
Uncle-Tom Housing Estate
1932
Argentinische Allee, Eisvogelweg, Riemeisterstraße, Am Fischtal, Reiherbeize, Waldhüterpfad, Im Gestell
Bruno Taut, Hugo Häring, Otto Rudolf Salvisberg

The "designer of solidarity", Bruno Taut, left one of his most significant urban extension works behind him in the form of the Onkel-Tom-Siedlung. The residential complex for low-income families, which was named after a tourist cafe in the vicinity, consisted of almost 2000 residential units extending across a total area of 3,7 million square feet and was built right in the middle of a middle class location on the initiative of Martin Wagner, who was the head of the municipal planning and building control office, and the landowner Adolf Sommerfeld. The development plan (by Bruno Taut) was developed while predominantly sparing the existing trees; the buildings were integrated between the pine trees and the birch trees of the Grunewald. Each of the three architects who carried out the work developed a certain type of house, which blended in with the overall appearance. The ground plan solutions follow the rules of the new objectivity period, are standardised and minimised in terms of their traffic areas. The use of colour is seen as the most conspicuous design element, which based on Taut's conception, should broaden or narrow the created exterior areas. This unique colour concept required special protection; however the story of its preservation was not always worthy of praise. However, today, sections of the original colours have now been restored.

137

Power over the Masses. Construction in the National Socialism Era 1933–1945 (224)

Does National Socialist architecture create a corresponding state of mind? Both German political systems in the post-war period were convinced of this, so all the architectural relics of National Socialism were removed. Even buildings with a politically neutral purpose fell victim to the wrecking ball, such as the Haus des Deutschen Fremdenverkehrs, the German tourism building, which once stood in the place of the Neue Nationalgalerie (no. 320). Where the post-war shortages compelled continued use, even pragmatism was faced with confrontation: for example, at the start of the 1960s, Klaus Tausendschön tried to retouch the effect of the Reichsluftfahrtministerium, the Reich Aviation Ministry (no. 229), which was used as the headquarters of the GDR planned economy, by putting a canteen as a glass box against the property in the yard. At the start of the 1990s, the prejudices were still maintained and the accusation of "fascist construction" in the Berlin architecture dispute (see no. 375) was used as a killer argument against tradition-oriented building. Of course, there were also counter arguments which put

National Socialist buildings in a global architectural history context. They set about revealing continuities or referring to the pluralism of forms of those years in which government buildings were constructed according to an antique archetype, with industrial buildings, for example, in the Bauhaus style and apartments and barracks in a conservative homeland security style. Were, then, the Nazi forms innocent in the final analysis?

Like many others, Adolf Hitler considered architecture as an "ideology set in stone". His regime saw itself, to all intents and purposes, as modern, which explains the so-called "white industrial boxes". But, the general opinion is that the modern age was hardly able to transport the ideological message of National Socialism. Like most rulers, Hitler therefore resorted to classicism for representational purposes. However, National Socialism was far removed from its humanistic impetus. Instead of the individual, it knew only the species "mankind", as presented in the films of Leni Riefenstahl. Unlike modern mass society, where it is the crowd which acts, the National Socialist

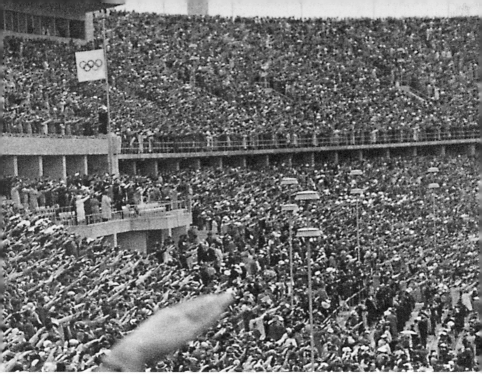

The masses as an ornament: homage to the "Führer" in Olympic Stadium (1936).

"national body" was subordinate to the "Führer". The mass was more solely an ornament and the architecture a means of gaining power over them. From classicism, they wanted to assume the "power of influencing people" (Albert Speer). The result was disparately oversimplified forms and dimensions increased to the gigantic. Hitler's Reichskanzlei, the Reich's Chancellery (no. 248) was the best example of this. The Long Hall, with its 480-feet length, had only one purpose: to keep the people small. Architecture was, most of all, a means of mass suggestion. Like the Lustgarten, many city areas were turned to stone to provide roll-call areas. The death of the young heroes was also effectively staged with the Langemarckhalle, which was the Hall of Remembrance (see no. 236). At the same time, almost as a sign of the preparations for war, barracks, comradeship, invalid residential areas and other paramilitary buildings were also built (see Nos. 251, 254, 255).

The National Socialist quest for a public demonstration of power and self-portrayal culminated in the "new design plans"

for the world capital "Germania" projected by Albert Speer "on the ideas of the Führer", which Speer was commissioned with in 1937. A gigantic, almost 1000-feet wide and 4.4-miles long Via Triumphalis flanked by monumental buildings was to be built as a north-south axis through Berlin. It was to have its exit in the south through a gigantic arch of triumph and lead to a huge 950-feet high dome hall with space for 180,000 people – the "biggest building in the world". The reconstruction was to be finished in 1950 and Berlin renamed "Germania": a gigantomaniacally oversimplified city which symbolised the "imperial perspective of the world domination being strived for" (Wolfgang Schäche). However, the outbreak of war ended the demolition work which had already begun.

Despite the total defeat of the National Socialist regime, the principle of city destruction continued in post-war Germany – even if it was under different signs.   hwh

Albert Speer
*1905 in Mannheim, †1981 in London (225)

"The apocalypse offered a grandiose spectacle."

Albert Speer, 1972

As the Reich Minister for Armaments and Munitions, who organised the "total war", and participated in the forced labourers programme here, he was sentenced to 20 years in prison at Nuremberg. Albert Speer became famous, however, as the "Adolf Hitler's architect" – and as one of the most dazzling personalities of the Third Reich. He actually built comparatively little in this time and even less of

this has been preserved. In Berlin itself, apart from his rather unspectacular residential house in Kronprinzessinnenstraße, there are only fragments such as the candelabra on Straße des 17. Juni and the redesigned Große Stern, the Great Star with the slightly higher Victory Column.

Albert Speer was born into an upper middle class family of architects in Mannheim. After his architectural studies in Karlsruhe, he became assistant to Heinrich Tessenow, a moderate representative of modernism whose architecture followed the criteria of simplicity, expedience and practicality, in 1928 in Berlin. In him, Speer found his "first catalyst".

He met his "second catalyst", Adolf Hitler, in December 1930 at his speech to students in Hasenheide in Berlin. One month later, Speer joined the Nazi party; the following year he took part in the election campaign. The party rewarded him for this with building commissions: before the assumption of power, he was allowed to rebuild two Berlin offices, later the bureaus of the Propaganda Minister and the Reich Chancellor. As "designer" of the May celebrations, the radio exhibition in Berlin and the Nuremberg Rally, he became known to Hitler again in 1933. A close relationship developed: for Hitler, Speer was the architect he had always wanted to be. It was only in discussions with him that the dictator, who was otherwise rather inhibited with his feelings, was relaxed, even laid back; he even tolerated being contradicted. Conversely, Speer endeavoured to accommodate the taste of the "Fuhrer". At the Nuremberg Rally site, he managed a synthesis between the classicism favoured by Hitler and the practicality of Tessenow: a facility of gigantic dimensions smothering the individual; the grand stand alone was to hold 60,000 people. Speer was clearly fashionable: at the Paris World Fair in 1937, he was awarded the Grand Prix.

To give his position as almighty "Führer" the appropriate backdrop, Hitler commissioned Speer with the construction of the Neue Reichskanzlei on Voßstraße (no. 248), which was deliberately conceived to intimidate foreign guests of state. The excessively long approach, which diplomats and guests of state had to make to the reception hall, did not fail in its effect. One of the first to realise this was the Czechoslovakian state president Emil Hacha, who, worn down by a nocturnal terror meeting and a heart attack, signed the consent for the occupation of his country by the Germans here in March 1939.

Speer's sphere of influence had expanded by 1937: Hitler appointed him "General Building Inspector for the Redesign of the Reich Capital". His responsibility was to rebuild Berlin into a 10 million metropolis "Germania" by 1950 (see no. 224).

In 1942, Speer was appointed Minister of Armaments. He energetically cranked up the war economy, which was essentially based on the employment of forced labourers and prisoners from concentration camps, and worked together with Heinrich Himmler and the SS to this end. Here, he clearly gave hardly any thought to the more far reaching consequences of his actions.

Unlike the other main players, Speer, at the Nuremberg trials, did not insist he was merely obeying orders. Instead, he assumed responsibility for the commands he had carried out. What he denied, even after his release in 1966 and until the end, was any knowledge of the mass shootings and extermination camps.   hwh

Worldwide effect carved in stone: model of "Germania" planning by Albert Speer.

141

Arnswalder Platz (Umgestaltung) (226)
Arnswalder Square (Redesign)
1934
Hans-Otto-, Pasteur-, Bötzow-,
Danziger Straße
Richard Ermisch

GARDEN To set an example in the fight against mass unemployment, from 1933, the National Socialists began to erect the huge "Stierbrunnen", a bull fountain with a diameter of 12 feet and a height of 15 feet, which the sculptor Hugo Lederer had created six years beforehand, at Arnswalder Platz. Richard Ermisch, who would later build the Berlin exhibition centre (no. 242), designed an arrangement around the fountain which used about 10,000 cubic feet red porphyries. With the strict axial nature and the frame-forming hedges and flowerbeds, the premises were absolutely monumental even though they had not yet been completely turned to stone as subsequent square arrangements of the Third Reich. Unlike the Lustgarten (no. 448) and the Gendarmenmarkt (no. 13), it has therefore remained almost unchanged to this day.

Haus Baensch (227)
Baensch House
1935
Höhenweg 9
Hans Scharoun

The Haus Baensch does not only represent the "different" style of architecture in the Third Reich. It also marks the beginning of a completely new form of architecture: Hans Scharoun (no. 281) realised the same anthropocentric design principle with which he became world fa-

mous with the construction of the Philharmonic Hall (no. 307). The one-family house only protrudes slightly on the roadside. Towards the garden, its characteristic ridged roof has little in common with the ground plan, which is fanned around a round-shaped dining area. The four segments stretch ever further out and follow the topography of the slope through a four-feet long projection. Almost in the middle of the space continuum is a concave sofa with an impressive view of the landscape.

Bahnhof Zoologischer Garten (228)
Train station at Zoologischer Garten
1936 (Suburban Station),
1940 (Intercity Station)
Hardenbergplatz
Fritz Hane

After the old stop from 1884 had long since reached the limits of its capacity, in 1934 the decision was made to replace this with a station in which city traffic and intercity traffic would be handled separately. The Reich railway's senior government building officer Fritz Hane designed two fully glazed city vitrines which were pushed against each other and made of almost right-angled box girders (max. span 115 feet). In contrast with the masonry of the old stop, they rest on a foundation which, like most of the buildings in the period, is clad in shell lime-

stone. The lively restaurant at Hardenbergplatz was built in 1957 in accordance with Horst Engel's plans. Subsequent reconstruction and expansion work always respected the quintessence of the design. The "traffic-attracting" effect of the station did not become the main motif of railway projects again until the 1990s.

Bundesministerium der Finanzen (ehem. Reichsluftfahrtministerium) (229)
Federal Ministry of Finance (former Reich Aviation Ministry)
1936
Wilhelmstraße 97, Leipziger Straße 5–6
Ernst Sagebiel

After a construction period of only two years, the Reichsluftfahrtministerium was completed as the first government building of the National Socialist administration. In the rigid shell limestone facade design which encased a steel construction, contemporaries saw a "signal of National Socialist desire". The eight-yard facility of Ernst Sagebiel was Berlin's biggest block of offices at the time with 2,000 rooms. In the neo-classicist Kleine Festsaal, the small festival room, Hermann Göring "conducted" the bombs against England. In 1949, in the radically reconstructed neo-classicist Grosse Festsaal, the large festival room, the GDR's constitution was adopted. As the headquarters of the Zentrale Planungskommission, which controlled the East German economy, the building eventually became the target of demonstrators on 17th June 1953. The incomparably cautious adaptation in 2000 to the Bundesministerium für Finanzen by the HPP office essentially made do with the restoration of the adopted facilities.

Deutsche Versuchsanstalt für Luftfahrt (230)
German Research Institute for Aviation
1936
Rudower Chaussee 4–6, Brook-Taylor-Straße
Hermann Brenner, Werner Deutschmann

If the conversion of Germany's first airfield for engine-powered vehicles in Jo-

hannistal was initially accelerated by the National Socialists, then the buildings on the aeronautical research field still fully followed the design principles of the Weimar period. Flat roof and white plaster facades of the research institute's administration wing demonstrate precisely the simple elegance which was characteristic of classical modernism. The experimental houses begun in 1932 on Brook-Taylor-Straße are manifestations of functionalism: the forms of the spin tower and engine test bench followed directly from the test arrangement. The large wind tunnel is a rolled-up tube of 26 to 47 feet in diameter and its reinforced concrete is a maximum of 3 inches thick. However, an inclination towards the mon-

143

umental can still be seen with symmetry. As part of the WISTA project (Nos. 432, 435), the facilities were restored appropriately for a monument in the mid-1990s.

Fehrbelliner Platz (231)
Fehrbelliner Square
1936
Otto Firle

The comparatively low land prices compared with the historic centre made Wilmersdorf, after its incorporation in 1920, the location for large-area administration facilities. In order to confine the uncontrolled growth between mansion suburb and the "Gründerzeit" residences, a competition was announced to "create one of the most attractive and, in its uniformity, perhaps greatest places in Germany" in 1934. All participants had to base their plans on the roll-call area with an SA monument which had already been created in 1933. In the end, the winner was Otto Firle, whose semi-circular scheme was largely realised, apart from the road superstructures (see Nos. 237 and 246, 262). Even if the connection between beauty and homogenous design may not have been really understandable, the Fehrbelliner Platz did at any rate continue to be the largest spatial municipal achievement of the National Socialists in Berlin.

Feuersozietät (232)
Fire Insurance Company
1936
Am Karlsbad 3–5
Paul Mebes und Paul Emmerich

The main insurance office of the fire insurance company in the province of Brandenburg was built around a curved courtyard in 1934. The building still shows the cautious modernity, which Paul Mebes and Paul Emmerich had already celebrated in many apartment facilities during the Weimar Republic, but which was

144

to be replaced by later representative buildings of the Third Reich favouring simplified neo-classicism. The characteristics of Mebes and Emmerich are visible in the horizontal window arrangement, the rows of stones that were set apart by means of their colours and the recessed balustrades on the ground floor. They also clarify that the shell limestone facade is actually held by a steel frame. The original condition and use have been largely preserved to date.

Haus des Sports (233)
House of Sports

1928 (Deutsches Sportforum – German Sports Forum),
1936 (Haus des Sports – House of Sport)
Friedrich-Friesen-Allee, Gutsmuthsweg,
Prinz-Friedrich-Karl-Weg, Jahnplatz
Werner March

The Deutsche Sportforum with offices, indoor swimming pool and gymnasium was designed by Werner March back in 1926. From 1934 he added the central "Haus des Sports". In the middle of the training camp, there is an auditorium for 1,200 listeners, which is crowned by a 56-feet high reinforced concrete dome and a hall of fame. Finally an open-air swimming pool connects the ends of the horseshoe complex which is bordered by arcades and colossal pilasters. In a further, very much simpler extension wing, the so-called "Friesenhaus", the recreation rooms of the athletes were located. In the post-war period, the easily shielded Deutsche Sportforum served as the headquarters of the British military administration. Since the end of the four powers status, it has been accessible to the Berlin sports clubs again.

Wettbewerb Umgestaltung
Kurfürstendamm (234)
Competition to Redesign
Kurfürstendamm

1936
between Breitscheidplatz and
Henriettenplatz
Arthur Peschel

Kurfürstendamm (no. 145), designed from the outset as a boulevard in 1886 and based on the Champs-Élysées, was initially a residential street which increasingly developed into an amusement mile after the turn of the century. Here the gardens were a disruption in front of the ground floor apartments, which were gradually replaced by shops. To give the boulevard a uniform appearance again up to the Olympic Games (see no. 235), a competition took place in 1935 among the great Berlin architects and garden designers, which was won by Arthur Peschel. According to his design, the pavements should be extended up to the houses and complemented by further display cases standing at crossways to the footpath, which are bordered by high walled beds. Although only the first stages of the plan were realised, the arrangement principle was still implemented after the war at least. It can still be seen today. In 1936, at the Kaiser Wilhelm Memorial Church, Paul Baumgarten constructed a remarkable Olympic Pavilion out of steel and glass, an unusual example of new construction in this period. The circular pavilion, which was to provide foreign visitors with information, was dismantled again two years later.

145

The Olympic Games in Berlin in 1936 (235)

The Olympic Games in 1936 were awarded to Berlin in the period of the Weimar Republic. The National Socialists made it into an event which will forever be associated with their rule. If with earlier games the event itself, the immediate sporting experience, was the main focus of attention, it was now used as a platform to put the NS state, which had been discredited internationally because of the boycotting of the Jews and race laws, in a good light, and to demonstrate cultural and economic strength and cosmopolitanism. This meant that for the first time in the history of the Olympic Games, all necessary financial and personnel resources for the its implementation were mobilised by the state. However, this expense was possibly not only for a one-off event: Hitler may have already thought at this point in time that, in line with his intention of creating a "Great German Empire", only one venue came into question for the games: Berlin.

With regard to the architecture, the aspect of value creation and therefore the associated question of continued use of the facilities also played a prominent role here. If temporary wooden houses were built to accommodate the athletes in 1932 in Los Angeles, then at the Olympic Village in Dallgow, stone buildings were built which could be reused as barracks.

The architect commissioned with the new buildings, Werner March, who had constructed the nearby Sportforum (see no. 233) in 1928, wanted to use reinforced concrete and glass to build the venues. But Albert Speer (no. 225) revised the plan and had ancient arenas and theatres in mind. The concrete construction was clad in natural stone and was given a strong finishing ledge. March was able to have his way in terms of functionality, though – and he did this so masterfully that the Berlin Olympic Stadium (no. 238) could still be converted today at much less expense than its counterparts in Wembley and Munich.

The Games and their design principle had an effect on the whole city. At a breathtaking pace, which was never to be reached again, the S-Bahn was supplied with electricity, the stations of Zoologischer Garten (no. 228), Schöneberg and Reichssportfeld were reconstructed, as was the tunnel facility of the north-south S-Bahn (no. 252). There were also large infrastructure projects such as the Tempelhof airport (no. 249). Finally, apart from the exhibition centre (no. 242), many squares and streets were also given a face-lift.

The Olympic Games of 1936 were a complete propaganda success for the NS state, which wanted to present to the world an illusion of normality which no longer existed. Their after-effect was ensured not least by the film director Leni Riefenstahl with her sensational documentary film Olympia in which she glamorised the athleticism in terms of the prevailing aesthetics of the time.

... *becomes a success for the Nazi state: sports and pomp in Olympic Stadium, 1936.*

147

Maifeld, Glockenturm (236)
Maifeld, Bell Tower
1936
Am Glockenturm
Werner March

The tower forms the western end of the Reichssportfeld, the Reich's sports field. At 250 feet, it is the highest of the pillars which mark the passages of the main axis from Coubertin Platz and Olympischer Platz, Olympic Stadium (no. 238) and Maifeld. The quarry stone foundation holds the so-called "Langemarck-Halle" where the fallen of World War One were once remembered. It passes over into a stepped wall containing the Maifeld that is designed for 250,000 people, which, in the accumulation of ancient building types, forms the "Forum" of the Reichssportfeld. Unlike the rally grounds in Nuremberg, the spectators' stand was not designed for a frontal theatre and instead surrounds the assembly area. In 1962, a public viewing platform was built at the pinnacle of the tower.

Senatsverwaltung für Inneres
(ehem. Nordstern-Versicherungsbank)
(237)
Senate Department of the Interior
(former Nordstern insurance bank)
1936
Fehrbelliner Platz 2
Otto Firle

As well as the state and party buildings of the National Socialist regime, which (if still in existence) are extremely formative of the townscape with their strict form vocabulary, corporate group buildings were also built in the same rigid characteristic style. The former headquarters of the Nordstern insurance bank forms the southeast segment in the U-shaped ribbon development, opening out towards the north at Fehrbelliner Platz. Otto Firle, who was also responsible for the overall concept (no. 231), began this project in 1934. In the middle of the T-shaped building is the main entrance, which is accentuated by a widely projecting canopy resting on two voluminous flagpoles. At the front ends of the building there are shaft-like arcades which

reach over the pavements. Typical for the period, the natural stone-clad facade of the steel frame construction is divided by overhanging window reveals. Their vertical and horizontal links are unusual, as are the countless allegoric reliefs which make the facade seem particularly martial. Today the building, which has hardly been changed is used by the senate department for interior management.

Olympiastadion (238)
Olympic Stadium
1936
Olympischer Platz
Werner March

Instead of the German Stadium and Grunewald Race Track, an elliptic arena was built for 100,000 people (today 75,000) for the Olympic Games of 1936 (no. 235). Its exemplary functionality goes back to Werner March. He lowered the field by 40 feet so that the spectators could enter the Olympic Stadium faster between the lower and upper ring and

could spread out more quickly. In the west, the stands are interrupted by the Marathon Gate which the athletes run through from the Maifeld (no. 236). The antiquating design, consisting of narrow colossal pillars with a wide cornice and the stone-pitched facing of the reinforced concrete construction, can be attributed to a revision by Albert Speer (no. 225). In 2004, the open oval was given a canopy in accordance with the design plans of von Gerkan, Marg & Partner.

Postamt N4 (239)
Post Office for the N4 District
1936
Am Nordbahnhof 3–5,
Invaliden-/Zinnowitzer Straße
Georg Werner

After the old building had to be knocked down as part of the work on the north-south tunnel (no. 252) for the benefit of the urban railway, the postal government building officer Georg Werner designed a building for an "independently-working large letter distribution facility" which had to serve the entire north of Berlin, in 1934. The fact that it took up almost the

entire second floor becomes clear with the anomalous facade pattern in this area. In contrast, the front, with its thoroughly simple form consisting of sanded travertine, recedes on Invalidenstraße as there were plans to broaden it at the time. When the Berlin Wall came down, the German post office built a series of new mail distribution centres in and around Berlin. Most offices were replaced by aesthetically inconsequential service stations so the building at Nordbahnhof is largely empty today. Externally, it has remained unchanged.

Waldbühne (240)
Open Air Stage
1936
Am Glockenturm
Werner March

On the premises of the Reich Sports Field is the Waldbühne at the Murellenschlucht exit whose slopes it uses. Four continuous flights of stairs each with 88 steps overcome a height difference of 100

feet. The arrangement of three circular stands made of limestone and tuff follows the example of ancient amphitheatres and provides space for 22,000 people. At the base of the middle ring, there is a VIP box with seven stone chairs. The fact that there were Germanic "thingsteads" as spin-off archetypes for the podium can hardly be seen since it was provided with a pavilion roof at the end of the 1970s. The Waldbühne is Berlin's favourite venue for open-air concerts and movie screenings.

Briefverteilamt SW 11 (241)
Letter Distribution Office
for the SW 11 District
1937
Möckernstraße 135–138
Kurt Kuhlow, Georg Werner

One could describe the building, in particular the interior, as a "forest of pillars". Along the frontage, there are four-storey high pilaster strips and pillars so close together that there is a "wall" of travertine and the windows look more like arrow slits. The two approximately 490 feet long rows are held together by a round corner facade in the same characteristic style, behind which is the oval stairway. The supporting structure is crowned by a fine cornice. On the top floor, whose facade is in the style of a perforated tape, there are official residences, while on the lower three floors a mail distributing machine works which can sort 2.9 million pieces of mail a day. The tunnel in the basement, which connected the post office with Bahnhof Anhalter (no. 95), is no longer in use.

Messegelände,
Palais am Funkturm (242)
Exhibition Centre,
Palace at the Broadcast Tower
1937
Hammarskjöldplatz
Richard Ermisch

The fact that a trade fair is a core function of the metropolis was depicted for the first time by municipal government building officers Martin Wagner (no. 185) and Hans Poelzig. However, from their overall plan from 1928, only the summer garden and a hall to the south of the radio tower (no. 189) were realised. Richard Ermisch included this in his new design in 1935, but he completely disassociated himself from Wagner's idea of an exhibition landscape. To give the exposition act an exalted character, Ermisch built, at the site which was reserved for a free-standing congress centre, a 155-feet high hall of honour with shell limestone cladding, coloured windows and colossal pilaster facades. At the palace at the radio tower, around 330-feet long halls and hinged buildings were connected alternately in the same characteristic style. Although the concept was only realised up to the radio tower and was foiled by the functional buildings of the post-war period, Berlin was given a new monumental trade fair which barely any city has managed since then.

ehem. Siemens Luftgerätewerk (243)
former Siemens Aeronautic Equipment
Factory
1937
Streitstraße 5–15
Hans Hertlein

About a mile of facade announce the energy with which Germany was armed in the middle of the 1930s. To be able to construct control-engineering equipment for military aircraft, the Siemens group, commissioned by Göring's Reichsluftfahrtministerium (no. 229), built a new factory in Hakenfelde from 1936. Architecturally the lack of innovation is striking: the aeronautic equipment factory demonstrates exactly the new objectivity, developing into the monumental, which had made up the state style of the Weimar Republic. The Third Reich adopted this,

even if they mainly used it for industrial buildings. Some of the building elements, such as the overflowing building cubature, the clock tower and the house-high pilaster strips, were used by the Siemens architect Hans Hertlein ten years before when he constructed the control unit tower block (no. 195).

Verlagshaus (ehem. Regionalverwaltung der NSDAP) (244)
Publishing house (former Regional Administration of the Nazi Party)
1938
Am Friedrichshain 22
Walther and Johannes Krüger

The building of the former "VII. Regional Administration of the Nazi Party in the Region of Berlin" illustrates the city hostility of the National Socialists: it does not really want to fit in properly with its po-

sition in a tenement quarter. Set back at an angle from the road, the two-winged plaster building, begun in 1937, with its stub flanks, dormer-occupied steep roof, solid basis, rustic stone decorations and Biedermeier portal, is reminiscent of the homesteads which Hermann Henselmann (no. 331) designed at the same time for the Warta region. The swastika eagle on the gable and the Aryan sculptures on both sides of the entrance archways were removed after the end of the war. Since then, the building has been the home of a publisher and was only recently renovated.

Großer Stern (245)
Great Star Square
1938
Straße des 17. Juni
Albert Speer

GARDEN As part of Albert Speer's plans for the "World Capital Germania" (see no. 225), the old west-east axis of Berlin was to be given a facelift as well as the north-south axis. The Grosser Stern was expanded from a diameter of 260 to 650 feet, the Victory Column (no. 86) was moved here from Königsplatz in front of

the Reichstag building and raised by one column segment. At the outer edge of the roundabout, the monuments of the military heroes of Prussia – Bismarck, Moltke and Roon – were set up. The temple-like tunnel entrances at the edge of the new facility and the drum lights, which were replaced by primitive whip lamps and candelabras in the direction of the west in the post-war period, are today the only works of Albert Speer (no. 225) which remain in Berlin. In its militaristic impetus, the Grosser Stern was typical of many designs for locations in the Third Reich. The Lustgarten, the Gendarmenmarkt and Wilhelmplatz were also redesigned at the time.

Bundesinstitut für Berufsbildung (ehem. Reichsgetreidekammer) (246)
Federal Institute for Vocational Training (former Reich Chamber of Cereals)
1938
Fehrbelliner Platz 3
Ludwig Moshamer

South of Fehrbelliner Platz, Ludwig Moshamer's Reichsgetreidekammer, the Reich's chamber of cereals, is connected to the Otto Firle building for Nordstern insurance (no. 237). With this building, the architect managed a somewhat more practical solution than four years later when he built the Japanese embassy (no. 259), which represents the spirit of the coarse dominant architecture of the National Socialists much more markedly. When developing Fehrbelliner Platz (no. 231), Moshamer based the construction on the ideas of Firle and structured his building equally axially, putting the main

entrance in the middle of the rounded square front. This show side was also more refined: it is clad in natural stone and window reveals and cornices are made out of shell limestone while the fronts turning away from the square were only plastered. The main building, similar to the former Nordstern building, was also provided with pedestrian arcades and, after the Second World War, a glass porch was added to accentuate the entrance. Today the five-storey building is the headquarters of the Bundesinstitut für Berufsbildung.

Umweltbundesamt (ehem. Zentrale des Reichsarbeitsdienstes) (247)
Federal Environmental Agency (former Headquarters of the Reich Labour Service)
1938
Bismarckplatz 1
Kurt Heinrich Tischer

The head office of the Reichsarbeitdienst, which was to be in a "relaxed environment", was realised as an office building with around 400 rooms. In order not to disturb the mansion colony of Grunewald, Kurt Heinrich Tischer designed a cautiously neo-baroque castle with the moderate height of three storeys as well as hipped and mansard roofs. The main portal of the plastered stonework building is in the inner courtyard which can be reached through a five-axis passage bordered by columns in the main building at Bismarckplatz. It is only here that there is a travertine facade. After the war, the idyllic complex was firstly occupied by the Allies. Today, it is the home of the Umweltbundesamt.

Neue Reichskanzlei (248)
New Reich Chancellery
1939
Voßstraße 4–6
Albert Speer

DEMOLITION From the outside the Neue Reichskanzlei looked rather respectable although its facade to Voßstraße, built in neo-classicist style, had the not inconsiderable length of 1,300 feet. The entrance, however, was on Wilhelmstraße. The room order behind this was designed so that the distance to the employers seemed even greater: following the forecourt and lobby there was the 52-feet high "Mosaiksaal" lit only by roof windows. Steps resounded here on the bare granite floor. Connecting with the "Runde Saal", the round hall, which counterbalanced the bend of the property, was the 480-feet long marble gallery which was inspired by the hall of mirrors at Versailles. Hitler's study was half way towards the garden. The Neue Reichskanzlei was knocked down immediately after the end of the war and its stones were reused in many different places (see Nos. 264 and 271). The State Representative buildings for the federal states are found here today (Nos. 468, 476).

Flughafen Tempelhof (249)
Tempelhof Airport
1939 (building shell),
1962 (civil initiation)
Platz der Luftbrücke 1–6
Ernst Sagebiel

Tempelhof airport was the biggest continuous building in the world. Built during the NS period as the eastern offshoot of the monumental north-south axis (see no. 225) as planned by Albert Speer, the airport was first used by the Allies on a provisional basis in 1945. On the city map, the ground plan has the shape of a huge coat hanger and still enables the exceptionally short access today as it did back then. One disadvantage of the shape is the limited number of aircraft spaces, which was particularly noticeable in the post-war period when air traffic increased immensely and the aeroplanes became bigger and bigger. However, in architectural terms, Tempelhof airport is one of the world's most significant transportation buildings.

Ernst-Reuter-Haus
Haus des Deutschen Gemeindetages
(250)
Ernst-Reuter House
House of the German Community Association
1939
Straße des 17. Juni 110–114
Karl Elkart

As part of Albert Speer's reconstruction plans for the Reich capital (see no. 225) there was not only going to be a new north-south axis; the existing east-west axis was also to be broadened. Some of the low cottages remaining here had to give way to new administrative buildings. Speer assigned the design and planning for the "Haus des Deutschen Gemeindetages ", which is the Ernst-Reuter-Haus

153

today – to the municipal government building officer of Hanover, Karl Elkart. Despite the integration in the plans for the future "World Capital Germania", the plan differed from the design principles of official National Socialist representative architecture. The building consists of three parts, with a court of honour formed by the recessed middle building. With the elaborate arrangement of the facade with rustic foundation, cornices and shoulder pieces, the house is closer to neo-baroque buildings than to modern mainstream constructions of its period. A third of it was destroyed in the Second World War, but it was rebuilt at the start of the 1950s.

Julius-Leber-Kaserne (ehem. Kaserne für das Luftwaffen-Infanterie-Regiment »General Göring«) (251)
*Julius-Leber Barracks
(former Barracks for the Air Force
Infantry Regiment of "General Göring")
1939*
Kurt-Schumacher-Damm 41–167
Senior government building officer Schneidt

With construction costs of 81 million Reichsmarks, this barracks, begun in 1936, was the largest of a total of ten armed forces projects in Berlin. At the heart of the facility consisting of a swimming pool, roll-call area and sports field, there is an approximately 1.600-feet long, continuously widening axis. Concentrically around this skeletal structure, there are sixty buildings which are a maximum of three storeys high. The uncomplicated design with steep roofs typical of colony complexes in this period, in this case made out of reinforced concrete but conventionally covered, was supposed to give the soldiers the feeling "that the nation wanted to provide them with a homestead during their period of service". In the post-war period, a base of French protecting powers, now the barracks are used by the air force of the German Bundeswehr, among others federal armed forces.

Nord-Süd-Tunnel der S-Bahn (252)
*North-South Tunnel of the S-Bahn
1939
between Nordbahnhof and
Bahnhof Anhalter
Richard Brademann (train stations)*

The city railway creator August Orth (see no. 98) had asked for this connection back in 1870. However, the narrow winding, 3.6 miles long tunnel route between Nordbahnhof and Anhalter Bahnhof (no. 95) was not realised until after the National Socialists came to power. During the Olympic Games (no. 235) though, 23 million passengers could be taken on the

northern section up to the stop Unter den Linden. Before this, the hellish construction tempo had taken its toll: on 20th August 1935 the construction on the west of the Brandenburg Gate (no. 40) collapsed and killed 19 workers. When the underground city line was completed in 1939, the Potsdamer Platz station (no. 253) marked a high point of Berlin urban railway architecture which is unparalleled to this day. To realise the long-distance traffic tunnel planned from the beginning, more than twice the construction time is needed today.

S-Bahnhof Potsdamer Platz   (253)
S-Bahn Station at Potsdamer Platz
1939
Richard Brademann

For the S-Bahn, Brademann was what Grenander (see no. 213) was for the underground. When he took over the office of head architect in 1924, the S-Bahn began to be supplied with electricity. To do this, Brademann built dozens of expressive brick transformer stations. Like his

colleague, Brademann proceeded noticeably more minimalistically, and Potsdamer Platz station was the highlight of his achievements. Although it is not designed as functionally as Grenander's later work, it puts it in the shade in terms of elegance: the walls were tiled with white opaque glass which glowed thanks to lights concealed in the orange and black coronas. After it was deformed by the war and no man's land passed over it during the Cold War, the underground stop has been developing in a more grandiose way than ever since 1991. Two new entrances by Oswald Mathias Ungers are planned in place of the old gate lodges of Schinkel (no. 44) at Leipziger Platz.

»Kameradschaftssiedlung der SS« (254)
"Comradeship Community of the SS"
1940
Selmaplatz
Hans Gerlach

A steep ridged roof, stub chimney, wooden pointed dormers, small square windows, folding shutters, plaster walls, a trellis and the entrance in the middle – the home of the German National Socialist "elite soldiers" was a simple idyll. Around 150 of these accommodation units were built by the in-house architect of Gemeinnützige Heimstätten AG from 1938 between Argentinische Allee and Quermatenweg. Detached, semi-detached or terraced houses were allocated according to rank. The planned community buildings, such as a casino, were not constructed. The "comradeship community of the SS" was therefore a typical project of the homeland security style. It was attractive on account of its position in the Grunewald and the generous distance to the neighbouring houses even in terms of this classy area. For this reason, the properties are still popular.

Polizei-Sportschule (255)
Police Sports School
1940
Hohenzollernring 124–125
Friedrich Schirmer and senior government building officer Götze

Simply plastered and with a high hipped roof, the Polizei-Sportschule is typical of the barracks buildings of this period. Particular emphasis was given to the portal with several frames over all three storeys

with the keystone in the form of a huge Reich eagle underlining the axiality of the complex. Despite the length of over 800 feet, the building complex only represents a small component of the project from 1938. According to the plan approved by Albert Speer (no. 225) there was to be, as well as the "National Political Reformatory" (Napola), both a sports school and also an officers' school, which would build completely on the 24 hectares between Hohenzollernring, Kisselnallee, Pionierstraße and Radelandstraße. The finished part was used as a military hospital during the war and since then has been used by the Berlin police.

Villa Schwatlo (Umbau) (256)
Schwatlo Mansion (conversion)
1879; 1940
Kurfürsten-/Derfflinger Straße
Carl Schwatlo (old building), Otto Sperber (conversion)

It looks like a miniature version of the Italian (no. 258) and Japanese (no. 259)

embassy buildings which were built in the 1930s in Berlin. But in fact it is roughly as old as its neighbours. While Café Einstein (constructed in 1878) and Haus Fromberg (from 1895) are the last remaining buildings which bear witness to the erstwhile Kielgan quarter, the Kindl brewery had the Villa Schwatlo on the corner of Derfflingerstraße rebuilt into its representative office in the capital in 1939. Limestone foundation and travertine facade indicate the style of the period just as much as the verticality of the windows emphasised by powerful reveals, the purely decorative exits on the second floor with, however, more solid smithery, the closed balustrade on the roof and the large absence of embellishments.

Wohnanlage am Grazer Damm (257)
Housing Estate on Grazer Damm
1940
Grazer Damm 127–167
Carl Cramer, Ernst Dannenberg, Richard Pardon, Hugo Virchow

The more than 2,000 apartments, with ground plans which were designed for families with a lot of children with simple furnishings (no central heating), corresponded to the target specifications compiled in 1935 for "people's apartments". The fact that they were part of the "Germania" redevelopment (see no. 225), where Grazer Damm was to represent one of the main arterial roads, is clarified by the archways on the front side of the residential estate heading out of the city, uniform facades with small windows and the "soldierly alignment" of the seven blocks on the building line which is emphasised by the setting back of its middle sections. Due to the fact that,

as part of Albert Speer's plans (no. 225), more apartments were to be knocked down than built, the biggest Berlin apartment building project of the National Socialists was just a drop in the ocean.

Italienische Botschaft (258)
Italian Embassy
1941
Tiergartenstraße 21a–23, Hiroshimastraße 1
Friedrich Hetzelt

The building was constructed (together with the nearby Japanese embassy (no. 259)) as part of the expansion of the Tiergarten quarter into the centre for diplomatic agencies. The size and also the furnishings of the embassy were to underline the significance of Fascist Italy for National Socialist Germany. The combination of representation rooms, resi-

dence and chancellery represented a new type of building at the time. The design of the monumental facades was based on palace buildings of the Italian High Renaissance. A fourth storey is concealed behind the principal cornice. The central projection jutting out on Tiergartenstraße with colossal pillars and a roofed driveway entrance marks the entrance for official receptions. Dark red plaster forms an attractive contrast to foundation and walls made of travertine. Shortly after its completion, the building was heavily destroyed and afterwards became one of the most picturesque ruins in West Berlin. After the Berlin Wall came down, Italy had the building restored as an embassy and residence.

Japanische Botschaft (259)
Japanese Embassy
1942
Tiergartenstraße 24–27, Hiroshimastraße 6
Ludwig Moshamer

The new building for the Japanese embassy was planned and built together with the Italian embassy (no. 258) and, as an agency of an ally of the "Third Reich", has a similar construction and status. Associations with Japanese art are brought to mind with vases and lion figures at the entrances, the channelled metal lattices and a golden chrysanthemum above the pillar portal. After suffering heavy damage during the war, the

building was left in ruins for many years before it was completely knocked down in the 1980s on account of the advanced status of disrepair. According to plans of the well-known Japanese architect Kisho Kurokawa, the building was rebuilt as a Japanese-German centre and the limestone facade and the vestibule behind it – once designed by Cäsar Pinnau – were reconstructed true to the original with the remaining parts of the building adapted stylistically and provided with discreetly classical interiors. To the rear, an attractive Japanese flower garden was created. With the latest expansion into an embassy with a consular department and residence section, a new side wing was added on Hiroshimastraße. The stylistic affinity with the neo-classicism of the main building is remarkable.

Großbelastungskörper (260)
Weight for Heavy Load Test
1942
General-Pape-Straße 2
Dyckerhoff & Widmann AG

FLOP To test the carrying capacity of the Berlin building ground which is not at its best in particular in the boggy Spreebogen area, where, as part of Albert Speer's "Germania" plans (see no. 225), the "Große Halle" was planned – the General Building Inspection had this solid reinforced concrete body constructed 33

feet in diameter and only a little less in height from 1941. Its weight of approximately 15 tonnes is channelled into the ground by only a quite small bearing. Although the gauge marks hardly showed sinking, the result could not to be stopped: of the buildings of the central axis (no. 225) only the Haus des Fremdenverkehrs, which, in 1962, had to make way for the Neue Nationalgalerie (no. 320), reached the building shell stage. As the only preserved testament of Speer's redevelopment plans, the weight for heavy load test is a listed building today.

Hochbunker (261)
Elevated Bunker
1943
Albrechtstraße 24/25

Since the late 1930s, many protective buildings were built in Berlin, offering

Rathaus Wilmersdorf
(ehem. Verwaltung der DAF)   (262)
Wilmersdorf Town Hall
*(former Administration Department of
the German Labour Front)*
1943
Fehrbelliner Platz 4
Entwurfbüro der DAF, Remmelmann

space for around seven percent of the
city's population at the end of the war.
After 1941, (the first bombs had already
fallen from planes) the work was intensified and it was mainly the less secure
high bunkers which were built. Among
these, this example stands out with its
particular design: the axial-symmetrical
construction is crowned by a powerful
console cornice. There are central projections on all sides. Towards both Reinhardtstraße and Albrechtstraße, there is
a round arch portico which is even
adorned with strips of imitation stone.
The concrete facades divide arrow slit-
style windows which are sometimes in
pairs. For cost reasons, demolition has
not been considered so far. In the mid-
1990s the bunker was the temporary
home of a club.

The German Labour Front (DAF) was one
of the main initiators of the competition
to redesign Fehrbelliner Platz (no. 231)
but was so dissatisfied with the result
that it postponed its construction plans
until 1941. However, at this point, the Second World War was already in full flow.
The fact that the building, which is now
used by the Charlottenburg-Wilmersdorf
district office, was constructed at a time
of material shortage can be clearly seen.
Unlike the older natural stone-clad reinforced concrete constructions in the
same place, it is conventionally walled
and plastered and is, in part, more finely
profiled. Quarry stone is used only on the
foundation, on the corner and side projections and on the window edges. However, the building seems generously proportioned in the interior: the round court
of honour lined with columns, which was
designed according to the example of the
Copenhagen police headquarters, and
the second square have gigantic dimensions.

159

Continuing Chaos – the Post-War Period 1945–1961 (263)

Today, there is still a conflicting relationship to the Berlin architecture in the post-war years. The so-called reconstruction has been rightly called a "second destruction" of the city. Yet a considerable number of these buildings have since been raised to the status of architectural monuments. From an architectural point of view, they often have little in common with each other as shown with the comparison of the "Hansa Quarter" (see no. 296) cityscape, kept in the modern style, with the monumental "Stalinallee" mainline (Nos. 274, 289, 297), which speaks a traditionalist language which National Socialism also used before. Its function also does not necessarily permit inference to the developers: the Hansa Quarter as a prestigious object of West Berlin is a social residential area, Stalinallee as the "first address" of the apparently "anti-imperialistic" "workers' and farmers' state" an imperial splendour mile.

In fact, the chaos that prevailed after 1945 is reflected in all these refractions. The former Reich capital was "the largest contiguous area of ruins in Europe". Around 40 percent of the living space was destroyed, two thirds of the city centre in ruins – in particular to the south of the Memorial Church (no. 302), between Potsdamer Platz and Ostbahnhof.

The first reconstruction plans were also subject to psychological paralysis. The consequence from the catastrophe of the Second World War, it was said, could only be dealt with by means of a radical break with the past. Large parts of the old city in which society's memory had become a fixed pillar were to fall victim to this thinking.

With regard to the formation of the future, there was a lack of conception, though, which is shown not least by the most radical design of these years: the collective plan, which Hans Scharoun (no. 281) introduced as the first Berlin senior government building officer after the war, did not succeed in creating a new aimed-for identity in terms of urban development. Air raids and disassembly had reduced the economic capacity of the once largest industrial metropolis of the continent by 85 percent. Of the 4.3 million Berliners (1939), hardly more than 2.3 million remained.

Tangibles in the west, ideology in the east: the Marshall Plan and "National Development Work".

Only the Marshall Plan introduced in 1947, the goal of which was an economic and subsequent political consolidation of Western Europe, brought about change. The American aid programme totalling billions did not just revitalise the economy: with material prosperity, it was possible to remove the NS ideology as well and, at the same time, it was to serve a policy of "containment" of communist influence. In the cultural sector, too, there were efforts to contain nationalism: the influence was again the modernism (see no. 210) of the Weimar Republic which now returned to Germany as an "international style" from America. The West's desire to be new again was typified in the virginal white of the residential communities.

For the Soviet occupying power, however, the communist society was the logical consequence of history. Since the sympathisers of this utopia had the power but no democratic or material basis, (the latter even being undermined by the USSR by its dismantling and clearing activities) they developed suggestive dialectics: "National in form, socialist in content" which should enable the revolution to succeed. This meant that as part of the "national construction work" (no. 296), workers' palaces, educational temples and countless monuments were built to promote the way of the East towards a different Germany.

At least, the competition between both systems had a positive effect for Berlin: building was done with twice the energy. But at the same time the conflict of interests of the superpowers prevented a mutual policy. And what is more: in 1948, as a consequence of the Berlin blockade, there was a division of the city government. Berlin developed into an international crisis hotspot. Finally, when the Berlin Wall was built in 1961, this indicated that it was not only in town planning that the ideological differences had become insurmountable.   hwh

Sowjetisches Ehrenmal   (264)
Soviet Cenotaph
1946
Straße des 17. Juni (at height of Simsonweg)
Lew E. Kerbel, Wladimir E. Zigal,
Nikolai W. Sergijewski

Overlooking the Reichstag (no. 106), where once the red flag had signalled the end of the Third Reich, and in the middle of the north-south axis (see no. 225) planned by the National Socialists, the Council of War of the Soviet armed forces erected a victory monument. In the centre of the 640,000 square feet construction is a six-axis, concave colonnade aisle made of granite squared stones which came from Hitler's destroyed Neue Reichskanzlei (no. 248). The production of the powerful central pylons is crowned by the bronze statue of a triumphant Red Army soldier. The pillars bear the names of dead soldiers. They are themes, recurring with many similar constructions. This also applies with the tanks on granite foundations which flank the entrance. On both sides of the main path, there are stone sarcophaguses with the names of the officers honoured as the "heroes of the Soviet Union". As the list was decided immediately after the surrender, the monument could be inaugurated on 11th November 1945.

Wettbewerb "Rund um den Zoo"   (265)
Competition "Around the Zoo"
1948
Between Breitscheidplatz, Fasanenstraße
and Augsburger Straße
Two first prizes: Paul Schwebes;
Ernst Müller-Rehm

In October 1947, the first post-war Berlin competition took place. What was required were mainly transport and town planning solutions for the area "rund um den Zoo". None of the more than 100 sub-

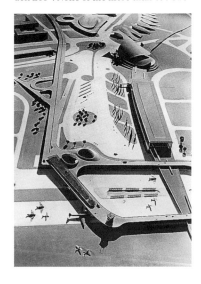

mitted designs tried to reconstruct the destroyed buildings. Suggestions were submitted which provided many more different building archetypes which were not even based on the existing roads. They also consistently pursued the ideal of a city suitable for cars with crossroads-free traffic junctions, pedestrian footbridges, etc. Sergius Ruegenberg even planned an airport instead of the Zoo. Although none of the proposals were implemented, the designs predetermined the complete reorganisation of the Imperial-Romanic forum into a modern city. In the broader sense the competition arranged the primacy of the "replacement new building".

Berlin (10 hectares in size) was created. Above stairs, wedge-shaped blocks made of red marble separate the rather horticultural half from the architectural. The highlight of the strictly axially symmetrical complex is the cylindrical mausoleum with the 45-feet high bronze sculpture of a Red Army soldier who is holding a sword and a child in his arms and is treading down a swastika, a much varied motif with similar constructions. 5,000 Soviet soldiers who died in battle have their final resting place under the five rectangular fields of grass lying in front of this. Thanks to a sturdy design, the cemetery of honour, despite being neglected, is still in good condition today.

Sowjetisches Ehrenmal
Treptower Park (266)
Pucliv Park Treptow – Soviet Cenotaph
1949
Between Puschkinallee and
Am Treptower Park
Jarkow S. Belopolski,
Jarkow W. Wutschetitsch,
Alexander A. Gorpenko, Sarra S. Walerius

Where in 1946 only a simple memorial stone had been set up, after a competition in the same year the biggest cenotaph in

Stadion der Weltjugend (267)
Stadium of the Youth of the World
1950
Chausseestraße, Höhe Schwartzkopffstraße
Selman Selmanagic, Reinhold Lingner

DEMOLITION On a parade ground from the 18th century a stadium for 20,000 athletes was built for the III. World Youth Games from 1949 with stands for 70,000 spectators, a sport house and an inn. The former Bauhaus student Selmanagic, who was to remain an outsider in the

GDR, and its soon leading garden designer Lingner, created a facility which is simple yet completely developed. Selmanagic's design plans went as far as loudspeakers, lamps and waste paper baskets. In one of the most embarrassing planning farces in Berlin following the reunification of the city, the complex was knocked down in 1992/93 as part of the efforts to attract the Olympics. When this failed, the plan for a new large sports hall proved just as unfeasible as the residential project of 1995. Today there is a golf course here making the most of the extremely central location.

Laubenganghäuser (268)
Access Balcony Houses
1950
Karl-Marx-Allee 102/104 and 126/128
Hans Scharoun, Herbert Klatt,
Ludmilla Herzenstein; Karl Brockschmidt

FLOP The modest residential area construction in immediate proximity to the Berlin centre may still be explained by post-war necessity. But the access balconies are the result of a planning process which was already in conflict with the development of the city in 1949. In this year Hans Scharoun (no. 281) drew the plan for the "Friedrichshain living cell" where he applied his idea of a new arrangement for the cityscape in the district, which was more than half destroyed. In only slightly modified form,

this concept was implemented by the house architects of the "Berlin Homestead" cooperative which wanted to provide its members with apartments as quickly as possible. When those responsible from the magistrate and construction ministry stopped the plans in the middle of 1950s, they already had five further modernistic lines realised in line with Helmut Riedel's plans behind them which would not fit in with the politically sponsored project "Stalinallee" (see no.

296) or with the "Friedrichshain residential community" designed by Hermann Henselmann (no. 331) next to the multi-storey building at Weberwiese (no. 274). The access balcony houses were later "concealed" behind a row of poplars. The situation has remained like this to this day. The development is provided with access balconies oriented towards the north. At the entrance, the kitchen and bathroom are located, and towards the south the living rooms are connected, sometimes provided with loggias.

Marshall-Haus, Erweiterung
Palais am Funkturm (269)
Marshall House, Expansion
Palace at the Broadcast Tower
1950
Summer garden, exhibition centre,
Hammarskjöldplatz
Bruno Grimmeck

The Marshall House was named after the initiator of the "European Recovery Programme" from 1947 which financed almost the entire post-war architecture of West Berlin. The show building site of the American activities was originally only meant to be as temporary as this itself. At the same time, the simple construction consisting of a brick-filled steel girder underlines the deprivation of these years.

While its eccentric position and spiral soaring entrance hardly face towards the oval of the summer garden, the extension of the palace at the Broadcast Tower, which is six years younger, is harmonised with the trade fair realisations of the Weimar Republic and the Third Reich (see no. 242). At the same time, the style of the Western 1950s culminated in its casual colourfulness and elegance as seen in large brass windows, dynamic stairs and the dance floor-like garden. The creator of both architectures commemorated the builder in 1957 with the America House in Hardenbergstraße.

Botschaft der Russischen Föderation
(270)
Embassy of the Russian Federation
1950
Unter den Linden 55–65
Anatoli Strichewski with Lebedinski and
Sichert, completed by Friedrich Skujin

With its Unter den Linden embassy, the former Soviet Union created stylistically a memorial similar to the USA at the exhibition centre (no. 269). The design of the architect of the Moscow foreign office was implemented in the place of the Russian embassy hotel destroyed in the war. The many-winged construction is

reached through a well-protected forecourt. A powerful projection emphasises the entrance hall whose cupola is crowned by a lantern reminiscent of the Lenin Mausoleum. After this, the no less embellished festival room is located. Overall, the stylistic roots are not clearly in Russian or in Berlin building history. The building therefore represents the international neo-traditionalism of the 1950s, which from now on was maintained only in Eastern Europe.

U-Bahnhof Mohrenstraße
(Umbau) (271)
Underground Station at Mohrenstraße
(reconstruction)
1950
Mohrenstraße, between Wilhelmstraße and
Mauerstraße
Alfred Grenander

The underground railway station was originally called "Kaiserhof" (after the hotel at Wilhelmplatz which Adolf Hitler later moved into as headquarters) and was constructed in 1908 by the young

Alfred Grenander (see no. 213) in the practical Art Nouveau style. Completely destroyed in the battles for Berlin in 1945, it was opened again five years later under the name "Thälmannplatz". With the new design of the floors, walls, pillars and foundations of the benches, marble from the former Reich Chancellery (no. 248) was used. Their impression of space can be perceived well in the dark coated shaft where steps resound. After the area was built on (no. 343) and a memorial park was created for Ernst Thälmann on Greifswalder Straße, the stop was given the name "Otto-Grotewohl-Straße" between 1986 and 1991.

Schiller-Theater (272)
Schiller Theatre
1951
Bismarckstraße 110
Jacob Heilmann, Max Littmann,
Rudolf Grosse, Heinz Völker

Only the technical foundations remained of the Schiller Theatre, built originally in the Art Nouveau style in 1906 as a people's theatre by Jacob Heilmann and Max Littmann, after the end of the war. On these in 1950–51, according to the plans of Rudolf Grosse and Heinz Völker, the "first cultural multi-storey building" in Berlin was built – named after the cubic stage block. Unlike the concert hall of the art college (Hardenbergstraße 33/34) planned in the same year by Paul Baumgarten, whose transparent facade was revolutionary, the foyer here looks more ordinary but also much more elegant: a double-shelled round of coloured glass which covers the main entrances swings from the otherwise closed travertine front. Behind this, there are divan-style seating locations made of red velvet. The theatre hall was redesigned in 1980.

Autohaus Winter (273)
former Winter Car Dealership
1951
Schloßstraße 38–40
Curt Hans Fritzsche

In the 1950s, the Volkswagen dealer Eduard Winter had several stores newly built or reconstructed, including two on Kurfürstendamm by Hans Simon. On Schlossstraße there is one of the first and, at the same time, one of the last still preserved originals. In terms of the corporate identity which has today become standard, its architecture is coordinated for the automobile brand: in the middle of the circular all-round glazed showrooms, there is a central cylinder towering up with a Volkswagen symbol which is also round. Slim columns carry a staggered flat concrete roof whose outer ring protrudes a long way. The cheerful appearance announces the great optimism of the 1950s.

An der Weberwiese (274)
At the Weberwiese
1952
Marchlewskistraße 25
Hermann Henselmann, Emil Leibold,
Rolf Göpfert (master workshop of the
German building academy)

The multi-storey building which Hermann Henselmann (no. 331) called a "lighthouse in ruins" dates back to Schinkel's (no. 44) structure for the Feilner House in southern Friedrichstadt which was not rebuilt until the 1980s. Plastered corner and recessed centre facades with ceramic cladding stand on a cross-symmetrical ground plan. The four apartments on each of the eight storeys each have four rooms which, at 215 square feet

each, are well proportioned. The generous development includes, as well as a lift and main staircase, two additional secondary stairways. If these top achievements could only be continued in Stalinallee, the adjacent "Friedrichshain residential community", which stretches up to Wedekindstraße, demonstrates luxury suitable for everyday use in entrance halls, reliefs, French windows and balconies. The same applies for the actual Weberwiese, whose design Helmut Kruse based on English landscape gardens. For the symbolic significance of the project, see Nos. 263 and 296.

Amerika-Gedenkbibliothek (275)
American Memorial Library
1954
Blücherplatz
Gerhard Jobst, Willy Kreuer,
Hartmut Wille, Fritz Bornemann

Knowledge is power, and the first German library in the post-war period clearly wanted to show what this means in democracy. With a donation of millions from the USA, the realised building is a point de vue at the end of Friedrichstraße. The plan which beat 194 proposals in the competition from 1951 can be seen by onlookers in the form of a six-storey, slightly curved repository section. It follows a pattern which is filled on the outside with a small stone mosaic. The entire ground floor is a reading room. Its fully glazed, trumpet-like barrel vaults formally carry the knowledge onto the street.

With 10,000 books lent each day, the library is the most-used in Germany today. A planned extension project by Steven Holl (1985) was dropped after the Berlin Wall came down.

Haus des Deutschen Handwerks (ehem. Zentrale der NDPD) (276)
House of German Craft (former headquarters of the NDPD)
1954
Mohrenstraße 20–21
Erich Kuhnert and Hans Gericke

The fact that the building policy of the GDR did not only follow Soviet examples is proved by the building of the former headquarters of the National Democratic Party of Germany, which saw itself at the time as representing the interests of craftsmen in the GDR. Its founding chairman thus campaigned for craftsmanship and national tradition. As the first construction minister, Lothar Bolz was also able to draw on plentiful resources for the party building which, according to the plans at the time, was built in a recessed location on Friedrichstraße. With plaster, indirect distribution of light, candelabras, ceramic cladding, exotic wood panels, natural stone floors and a shell limestone facade, his consultants, Hans Gericke and Erich Kuhnert, made it into an evidence room of building craft showpieces. Expanded in the yard in 1999 by a semicircular, glass conference bay window by Steinebach & Weber, the building today faces the central association of guilds in grandiose fashion. It is the only example in Berlin of continuity between the GDR and a unified Germany in terms of material and ideas.

Max-Kreuziger-Oberschule (277)
Max-Kreuziger Highschool
1954
Böcklinstraße 5
Hans Schmidt

Schools became key buildings of the recently established GDR because they were to serve the purpose of educating pupils to make them "new people". With several programmes, the East German state looked for the optimal type in the early 1950s. After countless unconvincing attempts, which can still be seen today in the districts of Mitte and Friedrichshain, the VEB building construction project II found the desired form: at

Wühlischplatz from 1953 there was a "clearly" aligned educational establishment which, at the time, meant that the entrance, assembly hall and gym followed a clear axial order: facades and common rooms have lots of pillars, ornamental strips and decorative reliefs in the style of the national tradition; some class rooms even have balustrades. The building ennobled into a "school palace" is still largely unchanged today.

Plattenexperimentalbauten (278)
Experimental Prefabricated Buildings
1954
Engelhardstraße 11/13
Richard Paulick, K. H. Schulz, Horst Bauer

Commissioned by the German Bauakademie, from 1953 the prototype for the prefabricated residential buildings of the GDR was built. In terms of construction, it corresponded somewhat with the first Berlin example of this building technique which had come about in 1926 on Ontarioseestraße: the roughly three-tonne concrete panels were cast onsite and assembled by means of a rotary crane. The construction both here and there was admittedly not used as a design element and instead disappears behind a layer of plaster. Relatively elaborate decorative elements are applied on this in the style of the national tradition, of which a relief, in turn, was to typify the prefabricated construction. In the year of completion, it was first in the Soviet Union and then in the GDR as well that the slogan "building better, cheaper and quicker" was announced. After this, the industrial prefabrication technique was to have priority everywhere.

RECOVERY

Ernst-Reuter-Platz (279)
Ernst-Reuter Square
1955 (competition)
Ernst Reuter Platz
Bernhard Hermkes (1st prize town planning), Werner Düttmann (open space)

GARDEN At 50 miles per hour around the square: the redevelopment of Ernst Reuter Platz set an example of how a city suitable for automobiles had to look. The junction, one day called "knie", literally "knee", gave way to a roundabout whose radius was designed for this speed. The earlier closed road development was removed in favour of solitary projects (Telefunken high-rise and architecture faculty see Nos. 299 and 319), which were positioned so that the rush of speed was accompanied practically by an "optical rhythm". The area reserved for pedestrians degenerated from 1960 into a decorated rest room: "pavements", flowerbeds and fountain follow a square pattern overall – but the traffic island can only be accessed through a tunnel.

Verwaltungsgebäude der Staatsoper (280)
Administrative Building of the State Opera House
1955
Hinter der Katholischen Kirche 1–2
Richard Paulick

The building behind the German State Opera House (no. 27) is one of the most interesting buildings of the early 1950s in the GDR. Among many reconstructions, the only new building fits perfectly in with the classic architectures of the Fridericianum Forum (no. 32), whose damage during the war the GDR tried to remove over three decades. Hardly anything is known about the history of origin of the administrative building. Before at the same place, there were several commercial buildings and residential houses from the 19th century which were destroyed in the Second World War. The architect Richard Paulick, who also headed the reconstruction of the Unter den Linden State Opera House, designed the administrative and rehearsal buildings of the theatre in a simple, classic formal vocabulary, and here he adopted architectural elements of the Knobelsdorff State Opera House. The original building is connected with the opera house through a passageway under the ground. The origin of the historic decorative parts has not been exactly clarified.

171

Hans Scharoun
* 1893 in Bremerhaven, † 1972 in Berlin (281)

"...make a world out of the smallest part."
Hans Scharoun 1954

In his outlook for the year 2008, the editor-in-chief of the architecture magazine, Baumeister, recently saw a few older people standing near the Philharmonic Hall. They are holding tattered slides up to the wind with the demand that the culture forum be completed in accordance to Hans Scharoun's plans! For this fiction it needed little fantasy: there really is a Scharoun society. That it also acts as a caller in the desert fits in with an ar-

chitect who created countless exceptional buildings – but no complete artwork which would have been continued. Hans Scharoun always stood as solid as a rock.

He was born in 1893 in Bremerhaven as the child of a trader who was always suspicious of the artistic tendencies of his son. He found the first encouragement of his talent from the neighbouring family of the architect Georg Hoffmeyer, whose daughter Scharoun would later marry. He completed his first plans at school: the seventeen year old boy gave the Bremen senior government building officer "fundamental considerations for the connection of land and sea".

He was not able to complete his architecture studies, which he started in 1912 at the Charlottenburg Technical College, because he was conscripted at the start of World War One. During the war, Scharoun was appointed assistant head of the building consultation office in Insterburg/East Prussia and dealt with the reconstruction of destroyed East Prussian towns. A member of the expressionistic "Gläserne Kette", a group of artists founded by Bruno Taut from the end of the war, from 1925–1932 he was a professor at the State Academy of Art and Applied Arts in Breslau but remained focussed on Berlin, where he opened his office in 1926 and joined the architects' association "Der Ring", which also included Walter Gropius and Hugo Häring. With the latter, the mentor of organic building, he remained associated all his life. For the German Werkbund he made several contributions, including in 1927 for the building exhibition at Stuttgart Weissenhof.

In Berlin, he designed part of the Siemensstadt large residential area: individual lines stretch into the sea of trees in Jungfernheide. A typical characteristic of Scharoun's architecture is the use of maritime motifs such as rails and portholes, like with the bachelors' house at Kaiserdamm (no. 203). Ship quotes and city hostility are completely typical of the period here. The unique thing is reflected in the varied ground plans. They are therefore more individual than the architecture of these years, which was primarily aligned towards collective needs. In this period Scharoun found his very own theme – understanding the individual as the centre of architecture: in 1932 fourteen villas were constructed full of refractions and material variations. Only the inhabitants function as a fixed point of the buildings (see Haus Baensch no. 227).

It is obvious that Scharoun's subject-centred architecture would have to come into conflict with the concept of art of the National Socialists. This is why he limited his activities to the construction of private detached houses during the Third Reich. The festival halls, railway stations and communal palaces which Scharoun designed for himself during the Second World War, however, make it evident that his architecture must also be seen as an attempt at a new social model. But above all, they radiate an optimism which is astonishing when we consider what was happening at the time.

So Scharoun became the man for Zero Hour. As the first post-war senior government building officer of Berlin, he presented in 1946 the (later mistakably titled) "Collective Plan". The plan he elaborated with a group of young architects provided for the creation of a new town structure coming from the position of Berlin in the glacial valley between Barnlm and Teltow. Only the historic Unter den Linden street of houses and individual historic buildings were to remain. The entire rest of the structural legacy was there to be used. The fundamental idea is the design of a "city band" which, running parallel to the Spree, would combine all political, economic and cultural functions. The motorways which were to pass through the cityscape were going to be created in terms of North American chess board road patterns. It was the most radical break with all town-planning tradition. Scharoun visualised individual freedom and a new beginning – and therefore fulfilled the wishes of many people, especially in the West. But ultimately his plan was so subversive that it could not be implemented.

Hans Scharoun is seen as an intellectual authority for this reason alone. Already in 1946, he was no more than the town planning professor at the Berlin Technical University. He remained President of the Academy of Arts until 1968. During this period, he built a great deal, but always in solitary projects. The highlight of his achievements is the Philharmonie Hall at the Kulturforum (no. 307). This provides the best evidence of the rich collective experiences which his anthropocentric architecture enabled.

hwh

Industrie- und Handelskammer (282)
Chamber of Industry and Commerce
1955
Hardenbergstraße 16–18
Franz Heinrich Sobotka, Gustav Müller

The Haus der Berliner Wirtschaft looks like a lot of administrative buildings of the 1950s. Built according to the plan of the architect duo Sobotka/Müller, there was, from 1954, a building whose facade of narrow, close standing columns made of expensive Italian travertine stands up high. The extremely thin, greatly overhanging concrete flying roof is held solely by the corner supports of varying solidity. The form of the Industrie- und Handelskammer building is therefore completely different to the adjacent new building from 1998 (no. 405), for which the six-cornered stock exchange pit in the court was knocked down, but it does have a similarly optimistic effect.

Stadtring (283)
City Highway Ring Road
1956
between AVUS north bend and Hohen-zollerndamm
Senate Office for Architecture & Housing, Underground Engineering Department

The fact that on 26th November 1956 the first two miles of city motorway in Europe were inaugurated in the tunnel under Rathenauplatz was not an accident. The associated circumvention of the western city centre according to an American example formed an important connection line for West Berlin, which was separated from the historic centre. Just one year previously, the Berlin senate had decided on the construction of a city motorway ring. For the fast ring road which, by 1960, had already reached Jakob-Kaiser-Platz and Detmolder Straße, entire city quarters were reinforced and bridges several hundred feet in length were built. Today the city ring road goes from Seestraße in Wedding up to Grenzallee in Neukölln. After the fall of the Berlin Wall, work started to extend it in the direction of Frankfurter Allee, even if there is no thought of closing the ring anymore.

Haus Hardenberg   **(284)**
Hardenberg House
1956
Hardenbergstraße 4–5
Paul Schwebes

On the basis of commercial building typologies which Erich Mendelsohn (see Nos. 179, 217) had developed in the 1920s for the Schocken department store chain, here one of the most successful Berlin builders of the 1950s (see no. 288) designed his liveliest building. The thin brass frames, the large windows and the balustrade sections made of black opaque glass are of exquisite elegance. The simple layering of the dark window bands and white intermediate floors underlines the curve of the facade on the ac-

tually trapezium-shaped plot of land. The momentum ultimately rises above the flat, thin, more-rounded cantilever roof. Reconstructed several times after 1974, the interior can no longer keep up with the external effect.

Haus der Kulturen der Welt
(ehem. Kongresshalle)   **(285)**
House of the Cultures of the World
(former Congress Hall)
1957
John-Foster-Dulles-Allee 10
Hugh Stubbins

It is not by accident that the boldest construction by far of the 1950s in Berlin comes from an American architect. The Congress Hall was built as a gift of the USA to the Interbau (see no. 296). It consists of a glazed foundation of 300 by 315 feet in which conference, exhibition and gastronomy areas are contained according to the open plan principle. The actual eye-catcher is reached through an outdoor staircase which rises above the functional main entrance: stretching out on the concrete platform is the auditorium for 1,250 people, which is drop-shaped in the ground plan but in section is wedge-shaped, meaning that there is space for the foyer underneath. The hall

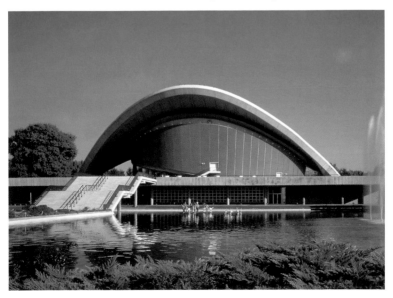

roof is in the form of a suspended shell. The effect of the building is underlined by its reflection in the water basin positioned in front of the entrance. One of the two eyelash-like supporting arches of the roof, which rest on only two supports, collapsed in 1980. During the reconstruction in 1987, slight changes were made to the roof form. In 1989 the Kongresshalle was renamed "Haus der Kulturen der Welt", the house of the cultures of the world. It is popularly called the "Schwangere Auster", literally the "pregnant oyster".

Schuhhaus Stiller (286)
Stiller Shoe Store
1957
Wilmersdorfer Straße 58
Hans Simon

The particularly unusual feature is the black facade of the office floors which is not only recessed but also runs concavely. In contrast with this is the convex concrete roof which protrudes more than six feet. The five circles which are cut out of this are repeated in the long, straight canopy of the shop on the ground floor. Although different reconstructions have weakened this appearance, the Stiller shoe store is still the purest preserved example in Berlin of the "Nierentisch architecture" of the 1950s. Together with the monumental rationalism (see Industrie-

und Handelskammer, no. 282), which was also widespread at the time, this typifies the attitude to life of the economic miracle that was gradually emerging.

Ignatius-Haus (287)
Ignatius House
1957
Suarezstr. 18, Neue Kantstr. 1
Johannes Jackel

The fact that the corner was only completed as one storey was not only typical of the period, it also accentuated the Chapel of the St. Canisius Parish (no. 506) which was planned at the same time but burnt down in 1995. There was a residential establishment for young Jesuits attached to the flat row of shops in Neue Kantstraße. Both here and there, the fronts were mainly tiled black and livened up with isolated pastel tones. Similarly decorative was the arrangement of the windows, doors and roof borders. Together with the Wilhelm-Weskamp-Haus in Suarezstraße 15–17, which was completed in 1960 by Völker & Grosse, the Catholic church is one of the most ambitious creative ensembles in Berlin in the 1950s.

Zentrum am Zoo (288)
Centre at the Zoo
1957
Budapester Straße 38–50
Paul Schwebes and Hans Schoszberger,
Gerhard Fritsche (cinema)

At the former location of the "Capitol" cinema, which Hans Poelzig had designed, and the "Haus Gourmenia" of Leo Nachtlicht, there was built, in 1955 with American funding, the first building of the new West Berlin centre. To strength-

en the relationship between the Zoologischer Garten and Breitscheidplatz, the 300,000 square feet office, exhibition, shop and parking area is divided into three tall segments. The long low connecting building was divided into a ground floor with shop arcade and three office floors lowered by a ventilation storey which has given the building the name "Bikini-Haus" in everyday speech. Different reconstructions have thoroughly dispossessed the curtain walls of their elegance. Since the "Zoo-Palast" cinema stopped being the main place of the International Berlin Film Festival in 2000, the West Berlin centre, which is facing the loss of the status of Berlin's city centre once again, has become increasingly neglected. A high-rise development plan for the west of the city centre, among other things, may counteract this.

Karl-Marx-Allee Block C   (289)
Karl-Marx Allee Block C
1958
Karl-Marx-Allee 71–91B, 72–90
Richard Paulick

After the young Egon Hartmann won the competition for Stalinallee (see no. 296) in 1951 and had elaborated on the final design together with the other prize-winners and Hermann Henselmann (no. 331), the individual areas of construction were allocated. Next to the Deutsche Sporthalle, Richard Paulick built the two adjacent, 850-feet long blocks and therefore the most ambitious boulevard section in architectural terms. Already raised to the status of a "Red Schlüter" by the reconstruction of the State Opera House (see Nos. 27, 280), he created historic pieces of scenery such as neo-gothic roof galleries or classicist portals in a superior way to his colleagues. After the sale of the entire former "Stalinallee" in 1993 for one symbolic Deutschmark to the Deutsche Pfandbriefbank, the German mortgage bond bank, the entire avenue was renovated in an exemplary fashion under the supervision of Olaf Gibbins. The bulk of the rooms in the Karl Marx bookshop on the south side of Block C are now taken up by the Berlin Architektenkammer.

Kranzler-Eck (290)
Kranzler Corner
1958
Joachimstaler Straße 5–9 and
Kurfürstendamm 18–21
Hanns Dustmann

From the "Victoria Area" competition in 1955, the most important West Berlin meeting point for strollers emerged. In the following year the former Bilka department store on Joachimstaler Straße and the corner of Kantstraße was completed: a cube crowned by a flat concrete cupola, without windows and clad in travertine slabs in a rhombic pattern which was quickly called "Groschenmoschee", literally "Penny Mosque" in everyday speech. Attached to the department store in Joachimstaler Straße 7–9 are two-storey shops whose widely protruding first floor is supported by a few brass-encased pylons. The fronts made of large-sized and elegantly profiled shop windows jut out like saw teeth on Kurfürstendamm. On the corner of Kurfürstendamm/Joachimstaler Straße, a round pavilion on the top marks the actual address: Café Kranzler, which had to close forever at the start of 2001, however. The high-rise building by Helmut Jahn (see no. 488), which was finished in the courtyard at the same time and was originally

planned in a different form, is generally considered as the biggest town planning transgression in reunified Berlin.

Unité d'Habitation »Typ Berlin« (291)
Unité d'Habitation "Berlin Type"
1958
Flatowallee 16
Le Corbusier

The urbane ideal of the modern – a vertical city as a large building in the middle of the landscape – became reality for Berlin as part of the Interbau (see no. 296) after Le Corbusier had already re-

alised similar residential house types ("Unités") in Marseille and Nantes. Without any relationship with the existing residential areas, a seventeen-storey building, whose east-west position is aligned solely with the sun, was built. Wedge-shaped supports lift more than 500 apartments above the Charlottenburg forest and villa region. Constructed mainly as maisonettes, they are positioned in an L-shape around nine internal roads 330 feet in length. The ground floor is left empty. The shops which are usually found there are accommodated at half the height. Other community facilities are located on the roof. Despite many changes to Le Corbusier's plan, the basic design has continued to prove problematic in business management terms today: in addition to frequently empty apartments, the shops are practically impossible to let.

Evangelische Kirche am Lietzensee (292)
Protestant Church at Lietzensee
1959
Herbartstraße 4–6
Paul Baumgarten

Towards Lietzensee, the five-cornered parish room with a wall of coloured but transparent glass opens up. It is crowned tent-like by a tetrahedrally folded concrete roof which touches the ground on both sides of the rear altar wall and is clad in long wooden planks. Similarly, the outsides are structured in a roughly linear way. The front consists of a wall which is closed off at the building height from the ground floor until below the belfry. The church at Lietzensee was only the prelude to a series of West Berlin chapels like the Memorial Church (no. 302),

Maria Regina Martyrium (Schädel, Ebert; Heckerdamm 230) or St. Agnes (Düttmann; Alexandrinenstraße 118) which are designed in terms of brutalism (see no. 295) and are an expression of an experimental approach to space.

Feierabendheim »Helmut Lehmann« (293)
"Helmut Lehmann" Leisure Time Home
1959
Andreasstraße 21
Heinz Bärhold

Old people's homes in the GDR operated under the euphemistic name "leisure time homes". They were essentially available for everyone who had finished working. In this leisure time home, which was, like so many similar institutions in the GDR, given with "Helmut Lehmann", a name from the midst of the population, around 205 residents could be housed, most of them in rooms with several beds. The four-storey building, which is in the middle of a park landscape, basically looks like a hotel with its continuous balconies and a dais. The entrance, which is in the middle of the slightly dented building segment, leads into a fully glazed hall with galleries and an outdoor staircase. However, the "Helmut Lehmann" leisure time home was the prototype for the "Berlin" series where the community facilities on the ground floor were bigger. The sculpture "Sitzender Vater mit Sohn", sitting father with son, by Wilhelm Haverkamp in front of the house at Andreasstraße 23 is the only evidence of Wilhelminian sculpture being used in the district of Friedrichshain.

179

Competing systems (296)

Intended to display one of socialism's most beautiful sides: the former Stalinallee.

The political division of Germany soon became a determining factor in Berlin architecture. In the western part of the city, they were forced at first to build those institutions which were traditionally located in the city centre and were now under Soviet control (university, people's theatre, business centre etc.). In East Berlin, the new social system also had to be given an architectural foundation.

In East Berlin, Stalinallee was meant to show socialism from its most attractive side (see no. 263). On the road, there were not only countless schools, sports locations and parks generously built, but its 5,000 apartments were also opulent in terms of size and furnishings and equipment (district heating, waste disposal unit). Stalinallee was created into a classic Via Triumphalis with grass verges and squares and a palace-like development. With a breakthrough at Alexanderplatz, not only the workers' district of Friedrichshain was linked directly to the centre, but there was also a representative connection going all the way between Unter den Linden and Stalinallee.

West Berlin reacted to the national construction work in the eastern part of the city with a competition (1953) to ele-

vate the resettlement of the Hansa Quarter, which had been destroyed in the war, to the core of an international building exhibition. Here it was discovered that the "international style" was harmonising best with the modern understanding of democracy. In fact, the ground plans for apartments were highly individual. The bungalow carpet, the rows of buildings and the high-rises which diverged radically from the old city formed a cityscape which created an all the more deep connection with the Tiergarten zoological garden area.

In 1957 the idea competition "Hauptstadt Berlin" was announced by the Federal government and the Berlin senate. Since the competition area also covered the eastern sector, East Berlin countered in the following year with the "idea competition for the socialistic redevelopment of the centre of the GDR's capital". While its intentions were implemented after the construction of the Berlin Wall, its western counterpart remained largely without consequence.

From now on the visions of the town planners in the east and west were restricted to their own part of the city.

hwh

In the Hansa quarter, a showpiece of the Interbau exhibition 1957.

Haus der Jüdischen Gemeinde (294)
House of the Jewish Community
1959
Fasanenstraße 79–80
Dieter Knoblauch, Heinz Heise

Today, this house still gives away the extent of the losses caused by National Socialism which decimated the Jewish community from 160,000 to hardly a thousand members by the end of the war. The community house was built in 1957 at the location of the synagogue from 1911, which was in the Romanesque-Byzantine style and was largely destroyed in the so-called "Night of Broken Glass". Part of its preserved portal is in

front of the main entrance of the new building which is a long way behind the building line on Fasanenstraße. The ground floor of the simple reinforced concrete framework construction contains school and administration rooms as well as a partly roofed memorial courtyard. Above this is the closed cube of the prayer room which is crowned by three modest domes made of glass bricks.

Akademie der Künste (295)
Academy of the Arts
1960
Hanseatenweg 10
Werner Düttmann

The project was begun in 1957 two years after the reestablishment of the Akademie der Künste in West Berlin. The three-part new building was constructed in the Hansa Quarter on a parcel of land left free by the Interbau (see no. 296). The blue plastered multi-storey building in the east contains studio and administration rooms. In front of this the washed-out

concrete square stone which protrudes over the ground floor holds the exhibition areas which are grouped together on the open ground plan around a garden court with a pond. Under the sharply curved folded copper roof reaching to the ground in the south, brick walls hold the auditorium with space for 600 people on both sides of the stage. The design principle follows the style of brutalism: the building is determined by the function of the structural elements where material and construction remain visible in their original composition. A new building is currently being constructed at the old location of Pariser Platz in line with plans by Günter Behnisch (no. 513).

Frankfurter Tor (297)
Frankfurt Gate
1960
Frankfurter Tor 1–9
Hermann Henselmann

After Hermann Henselmann (no. 331) had accomplished the prelude to the Friedrichshain major "Stalinallee" project with the high-rise building at Weberwiese (no. 274), he built the key buildings even though he was not officially taking part in the competition. While for the double high-rise at Strausberger Platz, he

again based his work on Schinkel (no. 44), at the Frankfurt Gate he proposed an approximately 130-feet high pair of towers in variants à la Schlüter (no. 18) or à la Gontard. Based on the examples of the domes of Gontard at the Gendarmenmarkt Market (no. 13), which Ludwig Hoffmann had already copied (see no. 141), building was finally carried out. The rotundas, in which Henselmann set up his studio in the meantime, are now the home of the Stiftung Denkmalschutz, the Berlin monument protection foundation.

Reihenhäuser (298)
Terraced Houses
1960
Radenzer Straße 3–61
Martin Wimmer, Wolfgang Kreischel

While with the house building of the Federal Republic the construction of detached houses was always the main focus, even in the immediate post-war period, the GDR produced around nine tenths of apartments in multi-storey constructions. The luxury of individual residences could, if ever, only arise if done on one's own account. The houses in Radenzstraße represent an absolute exception. This is because here the "collective" also planned the sought-after individual homes. The plan was tailored for a special target group: state secretaries were to move here. After a competition, individual and group interests joined forces in this project in which five apartments were connected in a row and had a shared garden. The small amount of privacy in front of the house was provided by low clinker walls carrying ample balconies. Apart from these outside seats everything else in the houses was highly conventional.

Telefunken Hochhaus (299)
Telefunken High-Rise
1960
Ernst-Reuter-Platz 7
Paul Schwebes, Hans Schoszberger

In accordance with the overall town planning from 1955 (see no. 279), according to which the square's walls were to be removed and in place of these individual high-rise buildings were to be built, an "eye-catcher" was planned at Ernst Reuter Platz between Bismarckstraße and Otto Suhr Allee. With the design for what at the time, with a height of 260 feet, was the highest office building in Berlin, the successful architect duo Schwebes/Schoszberger based their work on the PanAm building in New York and the Pirelli high-rise in Milan, which had been planned at the same time by Walter Gropius and by Giò Ponti and Pier Luigi Nervi respectively. The building was constructed on the ground plan of an elongated hexagon. The design of the high-rise, like with the Italian colleagues, is derived from its construction: the tips of the ground plan are accentuated by staircases on the outside. The four main supports show the variation of forces in the facade by tapering up to the 22nd floor. The contrast of the light-coloured supporting formwork with the dark secondary walls also gives an elegant effect. The balustrade sections were originally encased in green opaque glass. Today the house belongs to Berlin's Technical University.

183

Capital City and Waiting Status –
The Divided City 1961–1979 (300)

Hardly any Berlin constructions of the post-war period were as ugly and, at the same tlme, as famous as the Berlin Wall (no. 301), and none had such a drastic influence on the development of the city. Even today, long after it has disappeared, its repercussions can still be perceived: the Berlin Wall divided more than just a city; it also separated two different societies.

When it was built on 13th August 1961, the western part of Berlin, which had received around 200,000 citizens from East Berlin since the division of administrations, experienced a shock. Once the separation of the surrounding area became physically manifest, impulses from the outside were lacking. West Berlin lost almost a fifth of its inhabitants until the start of the 1980s. It was primarily the top performers who decided to flee. Industrial groups like AEG and Siemens relocated their head offices to the Federal Republic of Germany on the western side of the wall. The metropolis with the wall served more as an extended workbench. The property market collapsed. The elites said goodbye. "It is a not a culturally pes-

simistic exaggeration to describe the situation as apocalyptic," wrote the architecture historian Vittorio Magnago Lampugnani in 1980. What remained was the retreat into the private world: in the front line city an allotment holder mentality was established, and it is characteristic that the garden party of the building senator Harry Ristock from now on formed one of the main social events.

The view that was becoming increasingly widespread that the Iron Curtain was not just a temporary phenomenon was also fatal for the city's development. This did not only lead to the claim of the Federal Republic of Germany to Berlin as a "capital in waiting" being formulated more infrequently and half-heartedly. Even the inner city areas of West Berlin near the Berlin Wall were now treated as borderland in town planning terms, which actually amounted to recognition of the division. Politics were restricted mainly to sweetening the lives of the citizens in Berlin with perks: wage earners, for example, were given an eight percent Berlin bonus. Social housing was subsidised with billions. With a decreasing

It divided more than just a city: the Berlin Wall viewed from west and east.

FRISEUR

population, it produced around 20,000 new accommodation units each year. Trabant towns like the Märkisches quarter (see no. 330) and Gropiusstadt arose, each with 17,000 apartments. At the same time, the period of promoterism town so criticised by modernism was eliminated in great style by the clear-cut redevelopment in order to create further large residential areas. Innovative building types were required mainly for the ideal of equal opportunities announced as part of the educational reform of 1964. Thus the trendy high-level centre of Swinemünder Straße (see no. 342) became one of the few expressive addresses in West Berlin in the early years of the Berlin Wall.

It must be said that the egalitarian spirit celebrated its true triumphs where it had always been espoused: in the "capital of the GDR". If, since the foundation of the GDR, around one sixth of the citizens had turned their backs on it, it saw itself as consolidated by the construction of the Berlin Wall: the disruptive critics largely had migrated. At the same time, in one fell swoop, 80,000 workers who had previously been hired out in West Berlin were "brought home" to the "paradise" of the working people. The population losses before the Berlin Wall was built could be compensated for within the next two decades. Since the open competition of systems had ceased to exist, the collective could now develop in its pure form. As a key project the socialist city centre (see no. 309) was now realised. Since even the best comrade also sometimes needed a rest from the harmony of the collective, however, "dachas", the eastern variant of the allotment garden, soon began to proliferate into the city's surroundings.

So the division of Berlin basically had a levelling effect on both halves of the city. On both sides, a provision mentality also became established. When the Berlin Wall finally fell and normality arrived, there were therefore often hysterical reactions because of fear of a loss of traditional benefices.   hwh

Die Berliner Mauer (301)
The Berlin Wall
1961
originally 91 miles along the border
of the former western sectors

FLOP At 3 am on 13th August 1961 the GDR began to block the border to West Berlin with barbed wire, chevaux-de-frise and concrete barriers. Three hours later, the western sectors were sealed off, and at 3 pm the border was secured. It was going to be even more secure. The rolls of barbed wire were followed ten days later by improvisations from semi-finished parts from house building. In the following year the square concrete slabs with up to four layers of hollow square stone blocks on top were given a rear wall made of stacks of planks to the side held by concrete I-columns and crowned by a waste water pipe made of asbestos. From 1965, the front wall was also replaced by such a construction. These lines of defence – for propaganda reasons called an "anti-fascist protective wall" – were in no way for defending from attacks from the West, though, and instead (for example with effective vehicle blocks on one side) were solely against "attacks" from the East. The image of the Berlin Wall which people still remember

today, however, goes back to a special development of the 1970s: the white-painted, self-supporting prefabricated L-shaped concrete sections which, at 11,8 feet, were higher than ever, and were supposed to be not just "low maintenance" but "attractively shaped" as well in order to silence the verbal attacks from the West. The original "border wall 75" can still be seen at Bernauer Straße, where it was rearranged into a memorial in 1997 by Kohlhoff & Kohlhoff. Only markings in the road surface are there as reminders of the other miles of the Berlin Wall which disappeared after it came down. An impression of the mood of the "period of change" is given by the East-Side-Gallery in Mühlenstraße in Friedrichshain.

Kaiser-Wilhelm-Gedächtniskirche (302)
Emperor Wilhelm Memorial Church
1961
Breitscheidplatz
Egon Eiermann

The tower of the old building (see no. 107) has always been the symbol of West Berlin. Almost completely destroyed by bombs in the war, the "hollow tooth" remained preserved as a ruin after protests by civilians. The winning plan for the re-designing competition from 1956 initially proposed completely knocking it down. In the end, Eiermann replaced the neo-Romanesque church with a modern, liturgical composition consisting of five solitary sections connected only by a pedestal. To the east of the tower a square

stone chapel was built along with a hexagonal campanile which contained the bells, and to the west, an octagonal church room was constructed with a shoebox-like registry. The simple steel frame construction is mainly double-walled. The facade slabs made of blue glazed concrete honeycombs immerse the interior of the church room in a sacral light.

Müggelturm (303)
Müggel Tower
1961
Approach from Müggelheimer Damm,
Höhe Chausseehaus
Jörg Streitparth, Siegfried Wagner,
Klaus Weißhaupt

Unlike the "Grunewald Turm" which was built at its time as a memorial to Emperor Wilhelm I, the Müggelturm was always solely for distraction without any commemorative purpose. After the old wooden platform burned down in 1958, the look-out of the "Köpenick recreational landscape" (see no. 323) was built around 200 feet above the normal Berlin

level. Its northern horizon is marked by the Hellersdorf prefabricated buildings, and towards the south-east the view stretches to a forest landscape full of lakes. The concrete column with flying roof dates back to plans by architecture students of Selman Selmanagic who had been victorious in a competition. Glass surfaces stretching over the corner open the nine floors under the viewing level. The restaurants at the foot of the tower have space inside for a total of 240 people and outside for 500.

Deutsche Oper Berlin (304)
German Opera House Berlin
1961
Bismarckstraße 35
Fritz Bornemann

Only insiders know that there had already been a "municipal opera" at this location before the war. After the recon-

struction competition in 1955, only the stage area in the rear and the workshops of the building created in 1912 by Heinrich Seeling were maintained. The winner Fritz Bornemann built on the area with an elevated cube whose 320-feet front to Bismarckstraße is completely closed off with washed-out concrete slabs while the sides are fully glazed. In the corners of the foyer, which is as high as a house, there are powerful, self-supporting ascending roads. Staggered galleries enclose the auditorium clad in exotic wood. Its expanded sidewalls provide balconies on two levels. More than with its structural composition, the German Opera House soon impressed the Berlin public artistically with productions by Hans Neuenfels and Heribert Sasse.

ehem. Filmtheater Kosmos (305)
former Kosmos Film theatre
1962
Karl-Marx-Allee 131A
Josef Kaiser, Heinz Aust

The "Kosmos" cinema put the first emphasis of the international style on the former Stalinallee (see no. 296) where a world premiere cinema was planned from the start. The building forms a forecourt and underlines the functional classifications: a one-storey cube, whose main entrance forms a storey-high glass arcade, houses the foyer and adjoining rooms. In the middle here is the almost twice as high room which is egg-shaped in the ground plan with 1,001 (!) seats and is furnished in dark blue fabric and ebony. Like the adjacent buildings, the facade is ceramic but the quarter bricks are coloured. In 1997, the film theatre was expanded below ground by the architect firm rkw, making it a multiplex cinema. There are now nine further screens divided by the main room. Glass elements ensure a good connection everywhere with the historical building.

Gesellschaftliche Bauten (306)
Social Buildings
1962
Karl-Marx-Allee 32–36, 45/46
Josef Kaiser, Walter Franek (architecture),
Klaus Deutschmann (town planning)

The shops, which here come fully away from the main houses for the first time, became prototypes for all market halls and large inns of the former GDR. As social instead of commercial buildings, the two-storey pavilions are in the public space directly on the pavement. The windows were as big as could possibly be made at the time with glass. They were supposed to be showcases for what was created by the people, with an airy und visionary effect: now a place for strolling instead of the stone Stalinallee of the 1950s. The fact that it did not remain a matter of looking here is documented by the group "Team4" which landed a GDR cult hit with "It happened in the Mocca-Milk-Ice-Bar". That the range of goods on offer was usually small was compensated architecturally by the interior furnishings of the stores with luxury materials such as ash, maple or cebrano on the

organic architecture. In 1984, Scharoun's closest colleague, Edgar Wisniewski, completed the adjacent musical instrument museum, and in 1988 a chamber music hall half the size was then connected with the Philharmonic Hall, practically an offshoot of what was known in the vernacular as the "Karajani circus".

ehem. Staatsratsgebäude (308)
former State Council Building
1964
Schlossplatz 1
Roland Korn, Hans-Erich Bogatzky

walls and marble, silicate or lime freestone on the floor. Galleries and attached shelves are not in relation to the spacious rooms. Only the interior of Number 36 is close to being maintained today.

Philharmonie (307)
Philharmonic Hall
1963
Herbert-von-Karajan-Straße 1
Hans Scharoun

The Berlin Philharmonic Orchestra is still one of the leading orchestras in the world, but after the war it was without a home initially. The competition from 1956 arranged for a new building on Schaperstraße, where the Freie Volksbühne is - today. After a controversial debate, the winning design was finally realised in 1960 at the current location. Hans Scharoun (no. 281) put the music in the centre for the first time: enveloped in a tent-like roof, the 2,200 concertgoers gathered around the orchestra. On account of the geometry, which is based on three pentagons turned against each other at different levels, everyone sits practically in their own stand. This construction is considered a main work of

"1713/1963" – the gable cartouche suggests: this house is the "city palace" (no. 7). In fact, the original palace portal IV, from which Karl Liebknecht had proclaimed the socialist republic in 1918, became the central component of the front building at the former governance forum of the GDR on the Spree Island. The layering was also taken from the palace: at the bottom secondary rooms, in the middle studies and at the top festival rooms about 30 feet in height. Looking for international recognition, in 1962 the GDR built the headquarters of its main committee in the international style. With exclusive lights, richly structured wall and ceiling panels and a self-supporting "ascending road" over 50 feet, the stone-clad steel framework construction is East Berlin's best example of the architecture of the 1960s. Threatened with demolition by the Federal government in 1993 and then made accessible to the public for the first time until 1999, the "palace of everyone" is now the home of an international manager school after the chancellor left his interim headquarters in May 2001.

The Socialist City Centre (309)

No part of the city centre of Berlin has changed less since the Berlin Wall came down than the socialist city centre. Even the official planners who still spoke in the plans in 1997 only of one global location idea had difficulties. The reasons are commonly the lack of history and the immense scale. The image of the small, compact old town, which had stretched between the Spree Island and Alexanderplatz up to the Second World War, is used as an argument here.

After two thirds of Old Berlin was in ruins after the Second World War, there were, as a consequence, a lot of proposals to relinquish the centralistic city structure forever. The most radical came from Hans Scharoun (no. 281) whose "collective plan" aimed to align Berlin on the glacial valley. Against this, the GDR (in accordance with communist historical philosophy) saw itself as a constitutional product of historical development. In accordance with its principle of "socialistic centralism" it insisted on the primacy of the centre. In the year after its foundation, it passed a corresponding construction plan of Kurt Liebknecht and the reorganisation largely adhered to this over three decades.

He assigned the city centre its traditional function as a place of identification for the citizens, a term which was now confined to the working people, however. It was also new that the state instead of the city developed as a patron. This changed world view was to be manifested in a high-rise for party and government which was planned in front of the Red Town Hall in the early 1950s, not at the existent seat of the country's political leadership (the Spree Island).

The ideological demands shrank increasingly during the planning, however. After the East Berlin magistrate and the SED district management had prevented the high-rise, in the place of the castle destroyed in 1950 a house of the people was realised up to 1976 (Palast der Republik no. 337). An ideological message was therefore conveyed solely by the finally realised statues at the Marx-Engels-Forum (no. 357) which were hardly of superhuman proportions.

In contrast, the actual dominant building is as clearly urban as politically neutral: the Fernsehturm (no. 322) completed in 1969 centred the city similar to the church or town hall towers of the Middle Ages. The surrounding free space with its tightly formed square walls and purpose-free ground layout also refers to the form of the communal campus of the early modern times. The "heart of the capital" therefore represents a historical building achievement of the former GDR.

Even the leap in dimensions represented ultimately only a transformation of the oldest maintained testament from medieval Berlin at the scale of a modern metropolis: at 1,000 by 2,000 feet, the urban free space may be unmatched throughout Europe. But for the 3.5 million Berliners today, this is about as ample as the 140 by 210 feet of the old "Neue Markt" which was built at the same location in the early 13th century when the local population was only in the thousands. Only the consistently robust details proved to be system-specific, the apartments, above average in number and consistently designed for average households, and the generally accessible balustrades on department stores and residential houses. The GDR could afford this luxury solely thanks to the socialised land and the intended egalitarian society. In contrast, such a waste of space in pluralistic, market economy-based metropolises has no chance. So the challenge remains to enliven the incomparably large centre on a lasting basis.   hwh

In the heart of the East German capital: the Berlin Fernsehturm.

Restaurant Moskau (310)
Moscow Restaurant
1964
Karl-Marx-Allee 34
Josef Kaiser, Horst Bauer

Kulturforum (311)
Cultural Forum
1964 competition
1964 Wettbewerb
Matthäikirchplatz
Hans Scharoun

Once highlight among the many attractions throughout the GDR in Karl-Marx-Allee was the gastronomic embassy of the "big brother" Soviet Union. It was at the same time the only pavilion with an iconographic programme. However, the atrium-like cutout entrance corner with sputnik and wall-filling mosaic animated more passers-by to linger at the time than could be accommodated ultimately in the interior. The internal arrangement with inner courtyard and rose garden was originally planned as a "glass labyrinth". A "gastronomic reorientation" destroyed it in 1982 though: with three saloons, the hall bar and the dance café on the first floor as well as the Natascha bar and the Ukrainian and Russian restaurant on the ground floor, Gerd Pieper tried to come to intimate compartments from the "collective room". After the Berlin Wall fell, it was first used by different nightclub owners and now the complex, which has been empty since 1995, is falling increasingly into disrepair.

The return of the books which had been removed during the war required the construction of a state library in the western part of Berlin (no. 338). The building was also supposed to create a "Kulturforum" with the different architectures to the west of Potsdamer Straße in line with plans from the competition in 1964. Hans Scharoun (no. 281) came out triumphant against nine fellow competitors by extending his just completed Philharmonie (no. 307) into the city landscape. The second-placed Rolf Gutbrod was commissioned with the Muse temples to the northwest of the Neue Nationalgalerie and St. Matthew's Church (see Nos. 320 and 73) in 1967. After his car park-like applied arts museum had received heavy criticism, Hilmer & Sattler completed the Kulturforum (picture gallery, no. 408). Overall, the project developed into the most important municipal building site in West Berlin. The contrast with the socialist city centre (no. 309) is significant.

Haus des Lehrers und Kongresshalle (312)
House of the Teacher and Congress Hall
1964
Alexanderplatz 3–4
Hermann Henselmann, Bernhard Geyer, Jörg Streitparth

Until 1945, the Deutsche Lehrerverein, the German teachers' association, had resided at this location. In 1961, the twelve-storey high-rise was the first GDR project to be planned with a curtain wall. Up until 2005, the Congress Hall and the high-rise were reconstructed in exemplary fashion by Kerk-Oliver Dahm. Without the formulation of a roof, the symbol architecture typical of Henselmann (no. 331) concentrated more on Walter Womacka's mosaic of 410 by 23 feet which goes around the second floor of the library. The square, two-storey and fully glazed conference temple, with a round central hall with space for 2,000 people

under a flat cupola, became not only an icon of the international style but also a venue which Berliners from both parts of the city like to use.

Sportforum Berlin (313)
Berlin Sports Forum
1964
Weißenseer Weg 51–55
Walter Schmidt (town planning)

What, until the end, had been used as a metropolitan medal smith of the GDR, which was thoroughly successful in sports, today mainly documents the decline of its architecture. According to the winning design from the competition in 1954, the Sportforum is arranged around the central stadium. The boarding school, the Dynamo Arena, the gymnasiums and the indoor swimming pool (Horst Jekosch, Erwin Zitzke, Klaus Lindemann), which were built by 1964 in the west of the 44-hectare area, can still be considered as thoroughly reputably worked-on functional buildings. In contrast, the ice stadium on Konrad Wolf Straße, which was given a cantilever roof in 1986, looks like a banal tin can. It is no surprise that the Berlin ice hockey club "Eisbären", who plays here, urgently wants a new building. The throwing hall with sinusoidal wooden roof, complete by Jochen Jentsch in 1996, is an expression of an attempted revolution in this regard.

Europa-Center (314)
Europe Centre
1965
Tauentzienstraße 9
Hentrich, Petschnigg & Partners with Egon Eiermann and Werner Düttmann

In 1963, at the location of the Romanesque House of Franz Schwechten, which was destroyed in the war, the first multi-functional building complex in Berlin was built. On the foundation of three partly underground shop floors, four functional buildings emerge: a compact hotel, a rhombus-shaped, copper-pancled cinema and two office wings. The flat-front construction shows the typical Eiermann facade with suspended stainless steel support which, like the shopping mall concept, is also found with the Steglitz Forum. The recessed, 22-storey high-rise with dark steel facade based on the Seagram building (Mies, 1958) became a prototype for a series of equally inelaborate copies such as Kudamm-Karree, the postal cheque office and the Steglitzer Kreisel.

Karl-Marx-Allee,
II. Bauabschnitt (315)
Karl-Marx-Allee 2nd construction phase
1965
Karl-Marx-Allee 4–52
Edmund Collein, Werner Dutschke (town planning), Josef Kaiser (architecture)

In the extension of Stalinallee (see no. 296) the GDR found its ideal residential estate form from 1959. Here the placement of the 4,674 apartments may correspond with the international practice of the Athens Charter (positioning of the buildings according to most favourable exposure to sun), but specific social infrastructures such as summer baths or Kinderwochenheim, which were typical to East Germany and provided boarding care for children on a weekly basis, emphasise the collective idea. The "first socialist living complex" is characterised by the clear setting of the room which connects everything. A series of ten-storey, ceramic-clad house segments (Josef Kaiser with Klaus Deutschmann), whose slab construction had a structuring effect for the first time, characterises Alexanderstraße. The mainline, extended from 300 to 400 feet, becomes the

parade course for the 1st May with balconies pointed northwards. At the junction with the neighbourhood boulevard Schillingstraße, pavilion buildings, the international cinema, Café Moskau and the former Hotel Berolina (see Nos. 306, 316, 310) form one of the most exciting compositions of the modern urban development of the GDR.

Kino International (316)
Cinema International
1963
Karl-Marx-Allee 33
Josef Kaiser, Herbert Aust

Kaiser's second cinema on Karl Marx Allee (see no. 305) is probably one of the best in Berlin. The towering white concrete showcase, which is raised as a focal point slightly eccentrically above the Schillingstraße junction, makes the cineaste a stroller and vice versa. The ground floor opens up almost to the entire length through the glazed facade. The pavement slabs of the boulevard and the cleaving tile quarter bricks of the

foundation continue in the building. Countless lights in a gold anodised ceiling deny at the entrance that this is a hall at all. In the wide chairs in the high foyer, it is possible to sit practically on the street. Here, only one section of the front is not fully glazed: behind this, there is the bar and in front, the poster for the current film. In the hall, there is room for 600 visitors under a white wave band.

**Ministerium für
Auswärtige Angelegenheiten** (317)
Ministry of Foreign Affairs
1966
Schinkelplatz
Josef Kaiser, Heinz Aust, Gerhard Lehmann, Lothar Kwasnitza

DEMOLITION Monument curators began with the documentation only posthumously: when the building of the former foreign ministry of the GDR was knocked down in 1995, its interior was only known

to insiders. On the outside it formed not only the western border of the former GDR state forum on the Spree Island (see Nos. 337, 357) but also of the entire "so-cialist city centre" (no. 309). Like its counterpart, the former Haus der Elektroindustrie at Alexanderplatz, in which today the Bundesumweltminiterium, the Federal ministry of environment, among others, has its headquarters, it was a simple building: 476 feet long, 144 feet high. Only a conference hall protruded into the garden facing towards Friedrichstadt, only a powerful conical canopy above the way leading towards the Spree. The plastic facade made of blue plastic slabs and white, close-lying, folded pilaster strip sheets looked extremely clumsy. It was knocked down as a result of the desire to reconstruct the Schinkel Bauakademie (no. 65) and the Commander's House (see Nos. 87, 508), which had to give way to the foreign agency of East Germany in 1961.

Axel-Springer-Verlag (318)
Axel-Springer Publishing House
1966
Kochstraße 50
Franz Heinrich Sobotka, Gustav Müller, Melchiorre Bega, Gino Franzi

In the year the Berlin Wall was built, Axel Springer made a political statement with this building: for him the division of Germany was definitely not for good. He located his publishing house in the former Berlin press quarter which had completely lost this function since the end of the war. In the shadow of the "anti-fascist protective wall" a beacon of liberty therefore rose up: across from the Berlin Wall

(no. 301), 223 feet high and clad in golden bronze. His insights and perspectives were initially obstructed by four apartment blocks, which were even higher, on the East Berlin side from 1972. But the Berlin Wall finally fell and the publisher now moved many of its top people more quickly to Berlin than the federal government did. Lengthwise to the former border line, Gerhard Stössner and Thomas Fischer, in 1992, built a tower extension with a plate glass facade. By 2004, there was also a new city quarter in place of the demolished, once westerly situated print shop, and this stretched over the car park to the south of Kochstraße. This unambitious new building project is one of the biggest of its kind in the centre of Berlin. A public passage was built among other things.

Architekturfakultät der Technischen
Universität Berlin (319)
Architecture Faculty
of Berlin's Technical University
1968
Straße des 17. Juni 152
Bernhard Hermkes

With this ten-storey, three-section house, the master planner of Ernst-Reuter-Platz (no. 279) managed to create a fascinating inner life. The high art rooms which protrude dowel-like from the facade and the low office and seminar rooms are skilfully offset against each other. Three stacked atriums each on the face sides are connected to a continuous communication landscape with steps distributed in a Piranese manner. Through to details, the construction manifests, in textbook fashion, variation of forces and non-load bearing installations. Since the renovation in 1993, when the washed-out concrete slabs were replaced by granite slabs, the previously only functional facade has even shown a certain amount of elegance. The less inspired low building with auditoriums and a library was designed by Hans Scharoun (no. 281).

Neue Nationalgalerie (320)
New National Gallery
1968
Potsdamer Straße 50
Ludwig Mies van der Rohe

The building contract given to Mies van der Rohe was a gift from the Berlin Senate for his 75th birthday in 1961. With the Neue Nationalgalerie, the star architect, who had been active in Berlin until 1938, constructed his only building in post-war Germany – and also his only museum, although the design was based on a project for a company head office which had not been implemented in Cuba. Eight steel columns rise above the grey granite-clad foundation, which holds two thirds of the exhibition area. At the outer edge the crossed double T-girders touch the steel box roof which cantilevers more than 180 feet. Under this, there is an also square, almost fixed-point-free room delimited only by a glass curtain.

Walter-Gropius-Gesamtschule (321)
Walter-Gropius Comprehensive School
1968
Fritz-Erler-Allee 86
Walter Gropius
(The Architects Collaborative)

This building is the first comprehensive school built in Berlin after the educational reform of 1964 which wanted to give all

children equal opportunities for learning. Based on American and Scandinavian examples, it covers all levels of achievement from pre-school up to the school leaving examination. In exile in the USA, Gropius, to whom the original plan for the large, 50,000 people residential area of Britz-Buckow-Rudow also dates back, designed a main building for the classrooms and one to three-storey satellites connected by an arcade passage. The pavilions show the efforts for cohesion even in the ground plan: around an octagonal common area there are hexagonal classrooms, side rooms and staircases working in between as a buffer. In comparison with this formal

show of strength, subsequent comprehensive school types were degraded to pure "education factories".

Fernsehturm (322)
Television Tower
1969
Panoramastraße, Gontardstraße
Fritz Dieter, Günter Franke
(implementation planning),
Werner Arendt (construction)

Unlike its Paris counterpart, the Berlin "Eiffel Tower" was designed from the outset as a collective symbol. Parallel to Hermann Henselmann's form proposal from 1959 (see no. 331), a transmitter mast was first planned in Köpenick and then

in Friedrichshain. Both concepts were then brought together by the politburo member Gerhard Kosel. However, the later location of the Fernsehturm was then proposed by the president of the GDR Architektenbund, Hanns Hopp. Its completion was celebrated as a "work of the working people". Placed at the point of intersection of many radials, at 1,207 feet it is the second highest building in Europe and is clearly visible in the whole city. The universal effect is based on the "space design": the enthusiasm for space travel at the time gave rise to a hyperbolic concrete needle with a "skewered" steel facet ball with a diameter of 105 feet and a foyer in the tower shaft clad in vertical wooden slats and plaster chippings. The rotating telecafé 666 feet above the city is still the lookout point in Berlin, most frequently visited.

Freizeitlandschaft Köpenick (323)
Köpenick Recreational Landscape
1969
Between Elsenbrücke bridge and Erkner
Various collectives

`GARDEN` Long after the water and forest region in the south east of Berlin had been used for distraction and, in contrast to the "arcadias" between Charlottenburg and Potsdam, always by wide layers of the population, the GDR connected the isolated excursion destinations with each other. Even if there was neither an official term "Köpenick recreational landscape" nor a master plan, the roads were continuously converted into parkways here and even the waterside pathways

were created with several tracks. Entertainment was provided by the fun fairlike "Kulturpark Plänterwald" (1969). Walter Hinkefuss put all kinds of fairground rides next to the earlier people's park Treptower Park and the monumental Soviet cenotaph from 1949 (no. 266). The restaurants "Rübezahl" and "Müggelseeperle" were completed by Werner Hoffmann and Hubert Matthes (1977) and Achim Wolf and Margot Thomas (1981) with 500/1,500 and 684/1,400 inside and outside spaces respectively. For more see no. 303.

Alexanderplatz (324)
Alexander Square
1970
Joachim Näther, Peter Schweizer,
Dorothea Tscheschner, Dieter Schulze

In 1929, Alfred Döblin's novel Berlin Alexanderplatz created a literary monument for the traditional "gateway to the east". At the same time Martin Wagner (no. 185) tried to adapt the square for modern mobility requirements but this stopped at two new portal buildings from

Peter Behrens on the western side. The GDR then managed to achieve the smooth transition between central and eastern city. The pivot point was marked by the victorious design from the competition in 1964 with the 37-storey bed tower which is today's Park Inn Hotel (1970, Roland Korn, Heinz Scharlipp and Hans-Erich Bogatzky). The old roundabout has now been replaced by a tangent system, surrounding the square on three sides. The centre of the pedestrian zone is Walter Womacka's "Fountain of Friendship between Peoples" whose fountains continue in a spiral-shaped ground motif which points far away into the eastern city area. The 33-feet high "Urania World Clock" (also Womacka, 1969), a steel construction with etched aluminium panels and coloured enamel, has developed into a favourite meeting place at the square. According to Hans Kollhoff's plan from 1993, all post-war buildings should be replaced by a crown of nine skyscrapers with free space gaining in exclusivity here.

Warenhaus (325)
Department store
1970
Alexanderplatz 9
Josef Kaiser, Günter Kuhnert

Started in 1967, the former "Centrum-Warenhaus" is typical of the consumer temples of these years in East and also West Germany. White folded aluminium sheets, like the ones here which envelope the cube which is windowless from the second to the fifth floor, were also used by Egon Eiermann, among others, in a series of buildings in the West German Horten chain. Specific to socialism, however, are the balustrades which surround the fully glazed foundation on the first floor. With a single-storey canopy which forms a passage ("Alex Passage"), the department store is connected to the hotel. Today the location is still the most frequented in Berlin, even though after 1990 there were countless competitors all over the city. The Kaufhof group, which has run the building since the Berlin Wall came down, has carried out considerable modifications of the old department store, such as adding a completely new facade.

Fernsehturm-Umbauung (326)
Construction Surrounding the Television Tower Base
1972
Rathaus-, Gontard-, Karl-Liebknecht- and Spandauer Straße
Joachim Näther, Peter Schweizer (town planning), Walter Herzog, Heinz Aust (construction surrounding the television tower base), Hubert Matthes, Eberhard Horn, Rolf Rühle (open spaces)

The year of the completion of the Television Tower (no. 322) also saw the beginning of the construction of two-storey pavilions whose connecting bridges surround its shaft. From their roofs, pointed concrete folded plates (construction: Rolf Haider) reach up over 50 feet in height. In the pavilion buildings there are restaurants and exhibition rooms. The hexagonal pattern of the complex is continued in the free spaces. Its outside staircase pointing towards the west passes over into terraced fountains. In its axis at the height of the Red Town Hall (no. 83) is the Neptune Fountain which once stood at the palace square. Only the middle zone is therefore designed as would correspond with the significance of the biggest communal campus in Europe with an

area of 10,000 by 20,000 square feet, however. But attempts for formal revitalisation have so far been restricted solely to the pavilions.

U-Bahn-Eingang Fehrbelliner Platz (327)
Underground Station Entrance at Fehrbelliner Place
1972
Fehrbelliner Platz, south east side
Rainer G. Rümmler

Rainer G. Rümmler became head of the design department of the senate in 1964. He soon exerted his style with the western extension of the Subway line 7. He took back functionality and network continuity and took account of the spirit of the age. The reconstruction of this transfer station, which began in 1967, did not cater for either Fehrbelliner Platz (no. 231) or the main line from the time of the Emperor. On the surface, a ball of cylindrical cubes with glaring red small ceramic panelling sprouts out of the separate entrances. Underground, probably the most important pop art sculpture in Berlin has been largely destroyed by the "memorial-suitable" renovation since 1999.

Rathauspassagen (328)
Town Hall Passages
1973
Rathausstraße 7–12
Joachim Näther, Peter Schweizer (town planning); Heinz Graffunder with Lothar Köhler, Walter Wenzel, Dietmar Kuntzsch (building construction)

The complexes on both sides of the communal campus represent probably the

most urbane post-war buildings of East Berlin, with the south front begun in 1967 the more successful: at 551 by 223 by 138 feet the town hall passages take up the space like a mediaeval palace. The passages were designed as a counterpart to the development on Karl-Liebknecht-Straße and, together with the park-like free space, were supposed to spatially contain the Television Tower. The free-standing "market hall" building type was used here practically as a foundation whose roof continues the forecourt half-publicly and houses social infrastructure (balustrades, medical services and earlier also a day care facility for children). The nine apartment floors rising above this are developed collectively: unlike the access balconies or corridors usual in the West, here there are internal roads on every third floor, which, before the Berlin Wall came down, were practically furnished like living rooms with carpets. The plastic slab facades made of marble gravel are based on the adjacent Behrens buildings, the cleaving tile-clad front faces on the Red Town Hall (no. 83). The renovation by the architect firm rkw which converted the foundation into a shopping mall in 2004 proves that the continued construction of large buildings is often wrongly called into question.

Versuchsanstalt für Wasserbau und Schiffbau (329)
Research Institute for Hydraulic Engineering and Shipbuilding
1973
Müller-Breslau-Straße, Schleuseninsel
Ludwig Leo

Unlike with the Versuchsanstalt für Luftfahrt (no. 230), the machine which serves

as a structural model for architecture everywhere was drawn upon here for the first time intentionally as an aesthetic example. Contrary to the facilities usually arranged on one level, Ludwig Leo stacked the components of large-scale experimentation on top of each other. The inspection stands are accommodated in an elevated blue box which sits on the round surface of a pink tube around 25 feet in diameter. In the inside of the upper part, current experiments take place in a submarine-like ambience, and in the lower part there is the turbine which powers the water cycle. If the architectural design here is still in direct relation to the specific function, then it often becomes an end in itself with the later high-tech architecture.

Märkisches Viertel　　　　(330)
Märkisches Quarter
1974
both sides of Wilhelmsruher Damm
Werner Düttmann, Georg Heinrichs,
Hans Christian Müller (town planning)

From the "green slum" to the "long lament": with what, at the time, was the biggest new building project in Germany, the 1960s dictum "urbanity through density" was implemented literally. Unlike Gropiusstadt (see no. 300) which followed the same programme but was

much more sweeping, the Märkisches quarter was given the undivided attention of the German planners' guild. Involved in the implementation were the likes of Oswald Mathias Ungers, Ludwig Leo and several of Scharoun's pupils, but on the 370-hectare former gardenland, only largely replaceable tower block mountains were built which were heavily criticised at the time. According to the plan of 1962, there are 17,000 council apartments in four to 16-storey U-shapes in three arcs around Wilhelmsruher Damm, where the social centre and the longest metropolitan line of accommodation units in Berlin are found. In the 1980s extensive renovation work began which anticipated the programmes initiated after the Berlin Wall came down for the East Berlin prefabricated residential areas. The satisfaction of the residents has increased in the meantime mainly thanks to the increased consumer and leisure facilities.

Hermann Henselmann
*1905 in Roßla (Harz), †1995 in Berlin (331)

"People have nothing against being called typical citizens of a state but they have a lot against being called typified."
Hermann Henselmann, 1967

Whether retro style as with Stalinallee (see no. 296) or a futuristic form like with the Fernsehturm (no. 322): Hermann Henselmann predetermined what is today known as the best architecture of the GDR. Here he was rather unloved as a colleague, neither a perfect nor principled planner and (according to his own manifest) everything but a worker. Maybe his

success is explained by the fact that he represented the opposite of the type of person desired by socialism: the self-promoter.

Henselmann grew up in Bernburg (Saale) as the son of a cabinet maker. After an apprenticeship as a joiner he refused to take over his father's business, however, and went to Berlin to study interior design and architecture at the School of Craftsmen and Applied Arts. He led the life of a bohemian, reading the "Weltbühne", listening to lectures of the socialist art historian Max Deri and making his way as a draft illustrator. His main role model was Le Corbusier, whom he met in 1930. Near Geneva, Henselmann completed the Kenwin Villa, which could also have originated from his idol. It had, admittedly, been designed by the film architect Ferency who died during the construction work. However, Henselmann passed off the building solely as his own work.

However, Henselmann was unable to assert himself with his own powers. The four homes he realised by 1934 had to alienate planning craftsmen, civil builders and National Socialist "culture guardians": when the Kampfbund für deutsche Kultur, the battle league for German culture demanded the demolition of his work at Weinmeisterhöhe, which was disparaged as "bolshevist building", Henselmann knew that he had no chance in the Third Reich. In 1941 he was excluded from the Reichskammer der bildenden Künste, the Reich's chamber of fine arts, as a "half-Jew". Despite this, he still managed to manoeuvre by stealth and keep his head above water with civil contracts: with his talent for drawing he was soon decorating estates in the Warta region with blood and soil jewellery and therefore avoided army duty.

At the end of the war, Henselmann was forty. Now the communists were to enable him to pursue his longed-for career. In July 1945, the provisional supervision of the Weimar College of Architecture was transferred to him. When this was re-organised he tied in with the traditions of the Bauhaus style which had been founded in 1919 at the same location by Walter Gropius. Under Henselmann's supervision there were model plans for collective houses, and finally he was given a post in Berlin which had to be seen as strategic for the structural development of the GDR: at the newly founded German Bauakademie, he became director of the Institute for Theory and History of Architecture in 1951, which assessed German building traditions as commissioned by the state. So he was there when in the summer there was to be a signal for construction at the later Stalinallee: admittedly his visions for the high-rise at

Weberwiese (no. 274) were able to dissuade the SED leadership from embarking on its wedding cake style ideal just as little as those of his rivals. But just as vocal as Henselmann was in this discussion as a defender of modernism (so that only he was personally attacked in the SED-newspaper "Neues Deutschland"), he was equally quick to follow the party line afterwards. The alternative, already previously laid down by his colleagues, was awarded the contract and Hermann Henselmann was generally recognised as the main representative of GDR architecture.

He used his special position to exert influence. Soon nobody who was interested in East German architecture could get by Henselmann anymore. His residence in Pankow was one of the few open houses in the GDR. His attempts to keep the prefabricated residential areas away from the norm admittedly ended with the formal rounding off of Leninplatz. He was more successful in influencing the symbolism of the state: as an unofficial participant he designed, in the centre competition in 1958, the picture of a tower of signals in a place where a government high-rise was required. At first this move cost him his position as Berlin's chief architect which he had held since 1953. But finally it became apparent that only politically neutral city crowns could be implemented: so with the Television Tower (no. 322) a highly visible new statement was made which was never achieved in this form in the West. It is so universal that it is now appreciated by most people across all borders.   hwh

Universal instead of ideologic: Henselmann's vision of the socialist city centre (1959).

203

Flughafen Berlin-Tegel (332)
Berlin Tegel Airport
1975
Kurt-Schumacher-Damm,
AS Tegel airport
Meinhard von Gerkan, Volkwin Marg, Klaus Nickels

Not even 150 feet between the taxi seat and the aeroplane seat – that is a world record. With the decentralised check-in in the hexagonal ring full of automotive infrastructure, the rise of Gerkan, Marg and Partners (see Nos. 378, 426, 485), today the most successful architecture office in Germany, began. Back in 1965, when they were still students, they won the competition which was looking to solve the shortage of space in Tempelhof (no. 249) by expanding the former airfield of the French military administration from 1948. The prize-winning design provided for a hexagonal "drive-in airport" whose principle was to be exemplary for later airports all over the world. But while the facilities there were soon given further hexagons, the second building section planned in Tegel was not realised. After the Berlin transport agreement had shown alternatives to flying before the inauguration, the design which built continuously on a triangle pattern became more important at first. The brown clinker floor, the mustard yellow furniture and the red fittings fell victim to the expansion which reacted to the opening of the sky over Berlin. Today, the adjoining buildings show the serial slim-line design more in pure form. Since the start of the 1990s a new central airport in Schönefeld has been planned and gmp is also going to design this.

Mehringplatz (333)
Mehring Square
1975
between Franz-Kühs-Straße and Gitschiner Ufer
Werner Düttmann

The 171-year old Victoria from Christian Daniel Rauch looks from her peace column to a typical example of the town planning of the early Wall years in West Berlin. What was created in around 1730 as one of three geometric squares in the historic centre was to be rebuilt as an area of rest after the destruction of the war – this is how Hans Scharoun (no. 281), who was the only one who kept the round form in the competition from 1962, saw it, even if this was in smaller dimensions. The former flow of traffic over Stresemannstraße and Lindenstraße was directed past the roundabout, with

Friedrichstraße made into a pedestrian zone and covered the area up to the Landwehrkanal. From 1966, the senate building director Düttmann then implemented the programme which ran out in small apartments – supplemented by 16-storey blocks which were to protect the square in the north and east against motorways which were then, in fact, not built.

Stadterneuerung: Klausener Platz (334)
Urban Renewal: Klausener Square
1975
between Spandauer Damm, Schloss-, Knobelsdorff- and Sophie-Charlotte-Straße
Edvard Jahn, Wolfgang Pfeiler, Heinrich Suhr (working group for town planning)

The systematic urban regeneration in West Berlin began in 1963. The senate programme at the time aimed for 60,000 apartments of which ultimately 43,000 were knocked down, 24,000 were built as new and only 10,000 were refurbished. The first serious tenant protests ended this disastrous clear-cut policy: in 1973 at Klausener Platz, the oldest redevelopment area in Berlin, the block-by-block gutting of the back yards containing many buildings was also stopped. Between Schlossstraße, Seelingstraße, Nehringstraße and Neuer Christstraße, Hardt-Waltherr Hämer brought all existing houses for the first time up to standards tailored for the requirements of their inhabitants. The cautious urban regeneration was born and was also celebrated internationally. Its spiritual father Hämer later worked as Director of the International Building Exhibition (IBA Old, no. 355). More recent statistics show, however, that the social milieus which were actually planned to be preserved by the cautious modernisation were changed much more by this than by new buildings.

Bierpinsel und U-Bahnhof Schloßstraße (335)
"Beer Brush" Tower and Underground Station Schloßstraße
1976
Schloßstraße on the corner of Schildhornstraße
Ralf Schüler and Ursulina Schüler-Witte

Next to the Schlangenbader Straße motorway superstructure (Georg Heinrichs, 1981), which is on the extension of Schildhornstraße, the junction construction planned after 1964 has become the significant Berlin icon of the traffic-suitable city. It grows against the highway formally with the singularly original tower restaurant "Bierpinsel". The fact that the motorway runs crossways to the traditional Boulevard des Südwestens is reinforced by a glaring red, multiply constricted cone head. Technicistic forms can also be found under Schlossstraße. Blue and red plastic applications decorate West Berlin's only underground station designed by freelance architects, whose fair-faced concrete shaft continues the tunnel pipes. It is stacked two-high, additionally extending the paths for the passengers, for an underground line, which was never realised.

Komplexrekonstruktion Arkonaplatz (336)
Arkonaplatz Complex Reconstruction
1976
between Ruppiner Straße, Rheinsberger Straße and Schwedter Straße
Lothar Arzt (framework concept),
Klaus Pönschk (implementation planning)

Beyond the centres of the GDR, which were the scene of deeply symbolic projects of socialism, the reconstruction (inasmuch as there was one) was initially more cautious than in the West: whereas whole districts were rebuilt there, in the East they started with individual buildings. From 1970 the step into neighbourhood scale came at Arkonaplatz. With trade outsourcing, block demolition and resident involvement, which was permitted here for the first time, the strategies of both parts of the city came closer than at any other time (no. 334, Klausener Platz). The concept of the three blocks was transferred by Manfred Zache from 1973 to the ten times bigger area at Arnimplatz. That he proved the cost effectiveness of maintaining existing buildings compared with replacement for the first time here did not alter the fact that the GDR still built five times more new apartments than it modernised.

Palast der Republik (337)
Palace of the Republic
1976
Schlossplatz
Erhardt Gißke, (general supervision),
Heinz Graffunder, Karl-Ernst Swora (architecture)

DEMOLITION The Spree Island, which lost its government function during the Weimar Republic and also lost its stature with the destruction of the Palast in 1950 (see no. 7), became the centre of the country once again a quarter of a century later. Here, Erich Honecker, recently inaugurated, changed the plans of his predecessor in 1972 for setting up a socialist authority architecture in favour of a popular programme of grandiose mediocrity: a bronzed glass box was built with marble applications which went into the facades of the cathedral and stables (see Nos. 122, 136). The building opened onto the city forum, with terraces on the Spree side and to the former state forum, on the island side. The central component was the house-high loggia connecting everything. To the north, was the Kleine Saal, the small hall (Volkskammer, the people's chamber) and to the south the Große Kongreßsaal, the great congress hall, which could be adapted for everything

that a 5,000-capacity auditorium promised in terms of entertainment. The rest of the building was also devoted to entertainment, in particular the 13 theme catering sections for a total of 1,500 guests. After the Berlin Wall came down, there was an intense, emotional dispute on the further use of this "house of the people" after the government of the reunified Germany had become established in the Spreebogen area. Asbestos abatement left only a skeleton of the Palast remaining. The debate on the future of the Spree Island, which has now been running for ten years, is currently on an ethnological museum with a municipal library in the cubature of the palace and with post-modern architecture.

Staatsbibliothek (Haus 2) (338)
State Library (Building 2)
1976
Potsdamer Straße 33
Hans Scharoun, Edgar Wisniewski (interior)

The Staatsbibliothek, which was built from the Kulturforum competition in 1964 (no. 311), marks the turning away of the front city at the time from the Berlin unit. Turning towards the historic centre of an almost windowless back, it is set directly on the Alte Potsdamer Straße. Moreover, to the east of the cubic library, a motorway was planned which would run crossways to the traditional main route of the city centre. Even more remarkable are the user areas which fill the large anteroom facing in the direction of the West in broken geometries, folded levels and with various detailed designs. This "labyrinth of knowledge" is the only one of its kind in the world. The public passage going through the middle of the ground floor of the state library, which was planned as part of the Potsdamer Platz project (no. 417), failed in the meantime because of resistance from its users.

Versuchswohnhaus aus Stahl (339)
Experimental Residential Block
Made of Steel
1976
Schleswiger Ufer 6–8
Jochen Brandi & Partner

The dream of structuralist architecture to translate the faster and faster changing lifestyle alterations into flexible forms boomed in the 1960s. After such building block systems remained on paper for cities like Tokyo or were really quickly knocked down again in the West German area of Wulfen, the concept could be implemented here with lasting success. The 1965 competition of the European Coal and Steel Community resulted in a five-storey terrace building which was constructed as a steel structure with suspended composite slabs made of pre-fabricated parts. The ceilings accommodate

all installations and the walls are easily replaceable but this feature is hardly used. The residential house, which is still kept in good condition today, in turn became an example for new constructions in the 1980s such as the IBA "Wohnregal", the Dwelling Shelf (no. 359).

Block 270 (340)
Block 270
1977
Vinetaplatz 1–3, Wolliner Straße 43–46,
Bernauer Straße 67–68,
Swinemünder Straße 25–28
Josef Paul Kleihues

Enclosed on three sides of the former sovereign territory of the GDR, the quarter to

the east of Brunnenstraße in Wedding became the largest redevelopment area in West Berlin. After the competition for ideas from 1963 all housing estates were to be knocked down and many roads laid. Josef Paul Kleihues (Nos. 355, 356) won the competition for the southeast corner in 1971 by keeping to the traditional building line and leaving the courtyard completely free. The first block building in post-war Berlin shows adherence to the facade in the red clinker with white wooden window frames, loggias and angular cut corners, while apart from its 126 small council apartments it makes no contribution functionally to the urbanity. All things considered, the urban redevelopment concept of the critical reconstruction still valid today has therefore been formulated.

Sozialpalast (341)
Social Palace
1977
Pallasstraße 1-6, 28,
Potsdamer Straße 170–176
Jürgen Sawade, Dieter Frowein,
Dietmar Grötzebach, Günter Plessow

FLOP The 517 apartments of the building speculator Klingbeil, which were built as council apartments at the site of the legendary Sportpalast, which was knocked down in 1972, were a case for restoration right from the very start. The "accommodation at Kleistpark", as it was euphemistically called, never came into being: the necessary staircase on the south side of the main row, which is crossways to Pallasstraße and crosses high bunker ruins, was not given a building permit. Its wide passages waited for the once planned city motorway as much in vain as the play and sports areas on the roof waited for users. If they have left the daylight-free but more than 330-feet long development passages behind, then they can always still be pleased about French windows. But even this new feature is no replacement for the Sportpalast where, in its time, the six-day races were held and where Goebbels also made his infamous speech about "total war". Today, the complex can only be kept out of the headlines with all kinds of social management.

Oberstufenzentrum (342)
Comprehensive Highschool
1977
Putbusser Straße 12,
Swinemünder Straße 80
Pysall, Jensen, Stahrenberg & Partner

The intention of the educational reform from 1964 to ensure all citizens had equal opportunities for education is illustrated in exemplary fashion by this high-level centre which was begun ten years later and is located in the middle of the proletarian stronghold of the "Brunnenviertel" (no. 340). Along a public school path which connects Putbusser and Swinemünder Straße, there is a public library, assembly hall and lecture theatres. The development, which becomes increasingly mazy in the depths of the building, leads to a learning landscape in which, instead of the usual classrooms, there are departments with exercise rooms. The architectural exclamation marks of this new pedagogic concept are the colouring (bright orange and luscious green on the outside, dark brown on the inside) and the no less trendy slim-line design.

Botschaft der Tschechischen Republik in Berlin (343)
Embassy of the Czech Republic in Berlin
1978
Wilhelmstraße 44
Vera Machoninova and
Vladimir Machonin with Klaus Pätzmann

Originally located here was Wilhelmplatz with the Kaiserhof hotel, in front of which Hitler, who sometimes stayed here, let the masses pay homage to him. Ernst Thälmann, after whom the square was named in the post-war period, was commemorated in 1986 with a gigantic memorial park in Greifswalder Straße. At the same time in the northern half of the square, a part of the probably "most upper middle class" prefabricated residential area of the GDR was built. The first step on the contaminated terrain, however, was incumbent on the former ČSSR which built over the south side from 1975. How difficult it was, is proved by the almost complete elevation of its em-

bassy. The framework construction put on show, the cropped edges and the bronzed window bands show the technicistic brutalism which was spread throughout the world in the 1970s. The change of heart from spirit of the age to local patriotism did not come until the following decade.

Internationales Handelszentrum (344)
International Trade Centre
1978
Friedrichstraße 95
Ehrhardt Gißke (general supervision),
Kajima Corporation Tokyo Ltd. (realisation)

With this building began in 1976 the GDR congratulated itself on the international recognition from the UNO two years previously. To promote the settlement of foreign representatives, it commissioned the biggest Japanese building group with the implementation. The rough design goes back to the head of the main building office in Berlin. After competitions for the Friedrichstraße Bahnhof had vehemently demanded a high-rise building back in the 1920s, this shifted the project to the safer south side. The baroque Friedrichstadt (no. 32) was simply "tilted" towards the vertical: the white aluminium frame filled by a brown glass curtain is as thick as the eaves while its height of 307 feet corresponds with the depth of the property. The remaining forecourt of the high-rise has been occupied by conventional blocks since 2003.

Freizeit- und Erholungszentrum (ehem. Pionierpalast »Ernst Thälmann«) (345)
Leisure and Recreation Centre (former "Ernst Thälmann" Pionierpalast)
1979
An der Wuhlheide
Günter Stahn

Wuhlheide had already been rearranged into a "leisure landscape" (see no. 323) in 1950 by Reinhold Lingner with an open-air theatre, children's library, bathing lake and miniature railway. In the "Pioneer Park" Günter Stahn, who was also involved in the design for the Palace of the Republic (no. 337), began in 1976 to plan for the "GDR on a small scale" – with

this really big: at 390 by 700 feet and 140,000 square feet overall, the "Pionier-palast" exceeded all previous precedents. Chairs like in the big Palace or a spiral staircase to convey different step lengths were to aim at 'people who grow' while comparable projects in the West were re-alised in small proportions suitable for 'children'. Unlike the classicist culture houses of the young GDR, the building clad in larch wood celebrated less formal authority than it did "collective self-awareness": grouped around the foyer is a swimming arena, sports hall, theatre hall, puppet stage, space travel centre and a glass labyrinth of 60 specialist workshops. The self-discovery has con-tinued since the Berlin Wall came down with less but more multi-faceted direc-tion. Furthermore, almost 4,000 visitors a day make the leisure and recreation centre one of the few lasting cultural achievements of the GDR.

Internationales Congress Centrum (346)
International Congress Centre
1979
Messedamm 19
Ralf Schüler and Ursulina Schüler-Witte

In view of the global conflicts concen-trated in West Berlin and the correspond-ingly high expectations with regard to de-tente conferences, a multi-purpose hall which had played only a secondary role in the trade fair competition from 1965 developed into the biggest conference centre in Europe. In the end over 2,8 mil-lion cubic feet were enveloped and the city had its first billion mark building. The architects remained true to their machine aesthetics so that the cruise lin-er in the aluminium dress appeared "out of style" when it was completed. Domi-nating inside is a maze-like guidance sys-tem which contradicts all laws of intuitive user guidance: the largest of the nine halls (5,000 or 20,000 seats) is not reached using "staircase 1" but using number seven. The prominent communi-cation technology and the carpet lining ensured that the words spoken were "precious". In fact the annual running costs deficit totalled more than 15 million Euros, which led to discussions about knocking it down at the start of 2001, sim-ilar to with its counterpart in the eastern part of the city, the Palast der Republik. Changes are hardly possible in the house-in-house construction of the ICC in any case: this is because the shell is al-most free of fixed points so the internal tartan construction would fall like a house of cards. While, all things consid-ered, the ICC still works well today with large congresses or popular concerts, its technoid interiors are usually consid-ered extremely unsatisfactory during the many balls.

If the New Becomes Old,
then the Old is Renewed: 1979–1989 (347)

"Anyone who remembers the Eighties did not experience them", the Austrian pop star Falco summed up the widespread feeling that the penultimate decade of the 20th century ended like it was hit by lightning followed only by amazement as the changes in the reunified Germany took place.

In the 1970s, East Berlin experienced a huge improvement in its reputation thanks to the recognition of the GDR by Western states. The associated arrival of diplomats gave this part of the city a certain international flair. At the same time, however, the system comparison closed in again on the GDR increasingly: Western television did not stop at any wall. By arousing consumption desires in East German living rooms which could not be fulfilled, it put the standard of living in the East in a particularly unfavourable light. Since Erich Honecker had assumed office, the solution of the supply question therefore had the highest priority.

In the area of construction this led to the passing of the apartment building programme. In Marzahn (see no. 358) at the start of the 1980s the biggest resi-

dential area of the GDR was completed. The primacy of apartment building caused high deficits: thoroughly desired ideologically, the old building substance was systematically abandoned to decline so that in 1989 every fifteenth apartment was uninhabitable.

The immaterial damage was even higher though: the development of socialism had become a monotonous process which had to quench creativity. Normal citizens whom it helped get a new apartment did not see themselves as animated for involvement in collective ideals and instead were incited to withdraw into their private lives and consumption.

This is how the GDR increasingly lost support among the population. The SED heads became increasingly defensive and reacted with the expansion of the police informer system of state security. At the same time, they went without adhering too strictly to sublime ideological principles and thought increasingly of Prussian traditions. The symbolic act of the 1980s was therefore not the establishment of the Marx-Engels-Forum (no. 357) but the return of the monument of

Street fights for apartment buildings in the west, retreat into personal life in the east: Oranienstraße in Kreuzberg and Husemannstraße in Prenzlauer Berg, end of the 1980s.

the Prussian King Friedrich II, who was once vilified as reactionary, to its original home on Unter den Linden at around the same time. Generally the most remarkable efforts in the capital were geared towards the vedutes of the past. East Berlin was caught up by history.

West Berlin, however, had now recovered from the shock of the Berlin Wall being built. Life had largely returned to normal thanks to the ease of travelling through the GDR enabled by the Four Power Agreement. This development led not only to increased arrivals from the Federal Republic but also to the fact that West Berlin could now think of itself again. A real tourist boom also began now. And the visitors were also less interested in the newly built tower blocks than in the aura of Berlin – and this had its roots in history. So the determination of the past and no longer the swan song for the old soon dominated the discourse: "attempt at a balance" was the programmatic title of the large Prussia exhibition in 1981.

The young generation had also long since discovered the old, unrenovated parts of the city as free space. In Kreuzberg particularly, there developed an alternative culture whose spearhead was the Tageszeitung which had been published since 1979 – a new foundation in Berlin which there had not been for a long time! This scene was ready to start civil war to defend its way of life. But it did not come to this because the "Western system" – unlike the GDR – showed itself capable of reform. The clear-cut renovation was stopped. Mayor Richard von Weizsäcker pacified the city after 1981 by concluding contracts with the squatters and even making them owners.

A new, active cultural life developed. In 1984 the International Building Exhibition (see no. 355) was organised. The change became evident mainly in view of the fact that the once written-off outpost of the free world was named "European Capital of Culture" in 1988.   hwh

215

Wohn- und Geschäftshaus (348)
Residential and Commercial Building
1911 (old building), 1980 (reconstruction)
Kottbusser Damm 2/3
Bruno Taut and Arthur Vogdt (old building),
Hinrich and Inken Baller (reconstruction)

The ruins had been in decline since the war. According to the design from 1977 at least the front part of the six-storey house was re-converted in line with its listed designation. The building was complemented by a seven-storey half courtyard. The apartments in the entire complex are designed so that they include both the old and new wing and therefore convey the feeling of living in both epochs. New rear facade, balcony slabs, banisters, ground plans and spiral staircases show the typical Baller organic verve and can also be seen as an exaggeration of the arches and round bay windows with which the young Taut embellished the cautiously modern Art Nouveau facade. It was still seldom until this point that a built legacy was neither counteracted nor copied by contemporaries and instead was reinforced, but this became the rule in the 1980s.

Wohnbebauung Ritterstraße (349)
Ritterstraße Housing Construction
1981
Ritterstraße 55–60B, Lindenstraße 30–31,
36–37, Alte Jakobstraße 120A–121,
Feilnerstraße 1–4, 7–15,
Oranienstraße 99–105
Rob Krier (town planning)

On the strips of south Friedrichstadt, which had been deserted since the end of the war, one of the biggest projects of the IBA (no. 355) was realised since 1977. The concept of Rob Krier re-established the former building lines somewhat lower: around a (plastered) facade replica of the Schinkel Feilner house (see no. 44) was a structure with the form of a # symbol which divided the inner area of the 5-storey blocks into publicly accessible play streets and ornamental yards. The arched door constructions are reminiscent of the famous Vienna Karl-Marx yard dating from 1927. By 1988, eleven architect offices built a total of 46 postmodern multi-family residences with 400 council apartments. The opulently designed facades and the ample, spacious balconies and staircases are blatantly disproportionate to the rooms which are relatively small, however. A lot of form for little content, that should remain the predominant impression including with the following IBA projects.

into the wooden pole foundations so that the building had to be knocked down in 1985. As a replacement there was, from 1980 at the end of Reinhardtstraße, a boudoir-like "small revue" and a large hall for 1,900 spectators whose proscenium can be turned into a circus ring, water tank or frozen surface. The facade consisting of storey-high fair faced concrete elements with folkloristic reliefs and coloured glass prisms shows itself attached to the light muse and will characterise the further reconstruction of Friedrichstraße. The other "Kazakh main stations", as they are called in everyday speech, such as the Friedrichstadt passages, have since been knocked down (no. 372).

Friedrichstadtpalast (350)
Friedrichstadt Palace
1984
Friedrichstraße 107
Walter Schwarz, Manfred Prasser,
Dieter Bankert

"Friedrichstadtpalast" was once called the Great Theatre which Hans Poelzig had created out of the former market hall "Circus Barlay" next to the Berlin Ensemble in 1919 and whose stalactite cave hall represented an icon of expressionistic architecture. Lowering of the groundwater as part of the Charité project (see no. 178), however, led to the creeping

Wiederaufbau Schauspielhaus (351)
Reconstruction Schauspielhaus
1984
Gendarmenmarkt
Manfred Prasser, Peter Weiß

When, at the end of the 1970s, the GDR finally tackled the reconstruction of Friedrichstadt, which had been planned since 1950, the "civic" central buildings, such as at the Forum Fridericianum (no. 32) at that time, were to be re-established with no change to the exterior. This is how the facade of the theatre was replicated with detailed craftmanship in hardly six years, and its wall-free supporting

formwork with full glazing had been revolutionary in 1821. The interior of the romantic-classicist main work of Schinkel was already lost, however, before the Second World War destroyed the theatre temple altogether. In the central stage area there was, from now on, the concert hall with coffered ceiling which Schinkel had, at the time, accommodated in the side wing (see no. 54). The enlarged and closed-off square room emphasises the music less than the ceremonial act, however. Between two circulating galleries, a dozen crystal chandeliers and the hardly developed orchestra apparatus, the auditorium for 1,280 people experiences a kind of opera ball again and again. (For the other buildings at the Gendarmenmarkt see Nos. 370, 372.)

Stadtvillen Rauchstraße (352)
Rauchstraße City Mansions
1984
Rauchstraße 4–10
Rob Krier (town planning),
Valentiny/Hermann, Brenner/Tonon,
Nielebock & Partners, Aldo Rossi,
Giorgio Grassi, Hans Hollein

The first international competition of the IBA (no. 355) produced its most famous project after 1980. Behind a gate lodge

for which the Luxembourger Rob Krier quoted the Vienna Karl Marx yard much more grandiosely than on Ritterstraße (no. 349), city mansions were built in two rows of three, in the most cases by foreign architects in a post-modern style. At the eastern end Aldo Rossi, whose book *Architectura della Città* spread the idea of formal permanence throughout the world after 1966, constructed a clinker

fort as a counterpart to the former Norwegian embassy, the only old building on the premises. The cubature of this construction, which is oriented towards the upper middle class quarter from the 19th century that was destroyed in the war, contains 239 council apartments whose ground plans are varied and ample.

Wohnbebauung Fraenkelufer (353)
Fraenkelufer Housing
1984
Fraenkelufer 26, 38, 38a–c and 44
Hinrich and Inken Baller

Bücherspeicher der Staatsbibliothek
(354)
Book Storage of the State Library
1986
Unter den Linden 8

The block lost more than three quarters of its substance due to demolitions in the 1970s. However, by the end of the 1980s, there were even tourist buses in this area. To thank for this was the expressive, anthroposophically oriented architecture of the Ballers, who realised the most popular project of the IBA (see no. 355) on Fraenkelufer. They closed the gaps with a corner house and two door constructions which lead into an idyllic garden with pond, wild shrubs and meandering paths. Behind the heaped up hills the cars disappear in the rear part of the courtyard. Above the open parking spaces rises a 360-feet long fire wall construction on which three raised flat wings are installed. Like the front houses they display gothic dormers, balcony terraces curving pointedly upwards, curved walls and inclined concrete columns. With relatively inexpensive materials and elementation, the (at the time admittedly very ample) budget of the social housing scheme was adhered to. The 87 apartments with two to six rooms guarantee an optimal resident structure.

DEMOLITION 1986 showed how much the GDR, which saw itself as a "bastion of progress", ultimately put itself in the way of change. It denied the state library, which could have been a temple of the knowledge society, the constructive support it needed after the destruction of the war and let its cupola collapse in 1977. In the place of the large reading room a combine specialising in agricultural deposits built a repository from 1984 which actually resembled a silo. Here the four approximately 100-feet high towers were designed so carelessly that they – always damp – could not even function as a "refuge of knowledge for the sake of control". For this reason the state library, when reunified after the Berlin Wall came down, announced an architecture competition for a new reading room in 1999. Since then an angular variant of the old round hall is going to be built according to the design of the office HG Merz.

219

The International Building Exhibition 1984/87 (355)

As a result of the International Building Exhibition (IBA), approximately 4,000 publicly funded apartments and their infrastructure had been newly built. In the same way, many were repaired and a good dozen empty factories were reused as culture factories, in backyards greenery was planted and parks were created. Even if this only represented, at best, a fraction of that, which was built in the walled city of Berlin during this time, the IBA became the most important architecture project of the 1980s in the world.

Clear priority settings contributed to the success of the IBA: the Berlin Senate had sanctioned its programme as the "inner-city as residential estate". Subsequently, the IBA invested more than three billion Deutschmarks in the parts of the city, which the Berlin building policy had neglected in the post-war period. In over 160 individual projects, new city building concepts, which had only been realised as prototypes at best until then, were used for the first time on a broader front.

Hardt-Waltherr Hämer started a change of thought. As the director of the Altbau-IBA, which carried out the refurbishment of old buildings in Berlin, he faced up to the social present of the city in the east of Kreuzberg. He viewed the colourful mix of squatters, Turks and other fringe groups, who lived there and had been considered as part of the problem up to then, much more as part of the solution. He backed self-help, which made those concerned into property owners. In the course of the "Careful Urban Renewal", which he implemented instead of wholesale redevelopment, he succeeded in maintaining all the old buildings.

On the other hand, Josef Paul Kleihues (see no. 356), the director of the IBA-Neubau, the section of the IBA which carried out new development in Berlin, focused on western Kreuzberg, the Tiergarten district, Prager Platz and the Tegel Harbour, by rehabilitating the historical city structure, which had only been amputated over four decades, into the future model. In accordance with the method of "Critical Reconstruction", which offered compliance to the former plots, alignment and eaves heights, the city, craggy due to war and demolition, was expanded with (mostly post-modern) avant-garde architecture.

Through a multitude of publications as well as through numerous exhibitions and symposiums, which were organised in this context, it was guaranteed that the IBA and its methods were not only discussed by the trade public throughout the entire world, but also that it gained immense popularity with the public at large. He, who had never been past Kreuzberg before, could finally recognise the value of a Gründerzeit remise himself.

In fact, the multiplication effects were enormous, not just for Berlin. Not only that the written-off walled metropolis had caught up with the world level in the field of architecture. The city and its history were generally re-discovered. To develop it further instead of breaking with it has become a globally established strategy of urban planning since that time.

In the meantime, the star of the IBA shined so brightly that its failings were barely noticed. What urbanists are happy to label with the buzz word "sustainability" today, obtained at best at that time a formal corset: the IBA city continued to present itself without core functions. Industry, once an obvious part of urban multi-purpose use, continued to move into the industrial estates. This meant, in the end, the then so disapproved-of "sleeping sites of the modern age" were only prettied up into fixed locations which were just as unproductive. Because the IBA only built council apartments, which were then additionally subsidized, it even encouraged the illusion of a continuously progressing all-round welfare. hwh

IBA still life at Rauchstraße.

Josef Paul Kleihues
*1933 in Rheine (Westf.), † 2004 in Berlin (356)

*"The rediscovery of the laws of the historic
city was as obvious as it was essential."*
Josef Paul Kleihues, 1987

A discreet pair of glasses, a precise, but
by no means loud voice – the self-confidence of having written architectural history in this city was expressed in every
nuance. Josef Paul Kleihues was the
doyen of Berlin's architects. He had a decisive influence on what was built in this
city in the last two decades.

Kleihues came from the Westphalian
town of Rheine, a town whose Genius

Loci is determined by qualities such as
solidity, constancy and a certain down-to-
earth nature – qualities which had a considerable influence on the son of a building contractor.

The architecture studies in Berlin were
characterised by the late expressionist
anthropocentrics of Hans Scharoun (see
no. 281). After his degree, he went to the
Paris École des Beaux-Arts where, at the
time, the conflict was raging between the
defenders of the fine arts and the young
representatives of the enlightenment,
which, at the end of the sixties, would

encompass the whole of society. Kleihues dealt with all these trends intellectually – but never really warmed to them.

It was his own combination of savoir vivre and roots which helped Kleihues succeed in West Berlin, where he had opened his office in 1961. The experts were astonished when, in 1973 with the construction of the new Neukölln hospital, he preserved the substance of the old building and cautiously added to it – a real novelty at the time. Together with Wolf Jobst Siedler, he initiated a series of articles on town planning questions in the Berliner Morgenpost in 1977. This ultimately convinced the senate to implement the biggest support action conceivable for architects: the organisation of the International Building Exhibition (IBA) (see no. 355).

Kleihues became director of its new building section and here he was so undogmatic as to also invite architects whose aesthetic views he did not share – which helped make Berlin, with the IBA, one of the world's architecture capitals. The most promising heads of the world such as Daniel Libeskind and Zaha Hadid were thus given their first opportunity to build. Kleihues used the budget of 85 million made available to him here to a not inconsiderable extent in order to make the results of this workshop known worldwide. Soon even the US magazine Time was recognising "the organisation of the most ambitious display of this generation in world architectural standards".

Here, Kleihues gave the global spirit of the age only limited scope. The star architects were able to indulge in details – but he still largely provided the guidelines: the houses must be built on the basis of the traditional city, i.e. under consideration of the historic ground plan. The principle of "critical reconstruction" was actually revolutionary on the River Spree. This is because Berlin had, for at least a hundred years, been used to implementing every concoction without asking questions. But since 1968 the criticism of the modern had been articulated, and the resumption of historic continuity appeared as the only possible prospect for the future within the Wall.

When the "anti-fascist protective wall" then fell, the IBA director had already taken the critical reconstruction so far to success that there could be no alternatives to this. While senate building director Hans Stimmann (no. 400) accepted its implementation, Kleihues, as an "architect with an integrated building permit", was given dozens of opportunities to put his ideas into his own buildings. He was probably most successful in the balancing act between traditional and modern with the Kant Triangle whose weather vane roof has to be seen as homage to the dancer Josephine Baker, who celebrated her triumphs in the "Golden Twenties" in the Theater des Westens lying opposite. But usually he remained as strict as with his first building, Block 270 (no. 340).

Finally Josef Paul Kleihues also rendered outstanding services in another area: In 2000 with a much-visited exhibition, in which the Berlin architecture history of the 20th century was recapitulated, he prepared the foundation for a local architecture museum. The fact that he deserves an outstanding place in this is undisputable.   hwh

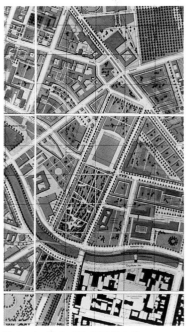

223

Master plan for the IBA, 1984 (detail).

Marx-Engels-Forum (357)
Marx-Engels Forum
1986
between Karl Liebknecht-, Spandauer,
Rathausstraße
Ludwig Engelhardt (general supervision),
Peter Flierl and Peter Kreuzberg (town
planning)

FLOP What had been planned as a "national monument" for the spiritual fathers of Marxism represented in the end "anything goes" more than pure doctrine. Already planned since 1951 for the Spree Island, it was to announce the power of socialism a long way away with its huge magnitude. Then, however, Erich Honecker rearranged the Palast der Republik (no. 337) and gave the memorial work to the Central Committee's secretary of cultural affairs Kurt Hager. Deprived of the basis and shrunk to hardly superhuman proportions, the planned Marx-Engels monument was also banished in 1982 from the square named after them on the Spree Island. On 4.4.1986, it finally came to the inauguration of a "real socialist double figure" which is bordered by stainless steel columns with incorporated photographs, neo-classicist marble relief blocks, French baroque waterside steps and English countryside.

Marzahn (358)
Marzahn District
1986
Märkische Allee, Blumberger Damm
Roland Korn and Peter Schweizer (town
planning), Heinz Graffunder (head
architect)

Marzahn was founded around 1300. In the late 19th century, James Hobrecht had sewage farms set up around the mediaeval village green (see no. 74). After 1975, as part of the GDR house building programme (see no. 347), the biggest new residential area in Germany was built on 600 hectares: a good 65,000 apartments for around 150,000 people. The town planning corresponded with the concept of the first "socialist residential complex" (KMA, see no. 296), but it was more associated with mass and less with expression (in particular in the quarter centres Marzahner Promenade and Springpfuhl by Wolf-Rüdiger Eisentraut and others). Marzahn differs from externally similar social residential areas in the West with production facilities constructed on a parallel basis and the "accommodation of all classes under one

roof". To maintain the social mix Berlin was the first federal state in 1993 to decide on an all-encompassing enhancement programme costing billions. This, however, could not prevent that – similar to in the Märkisches quarter (no. 330) – only more non-saturated groups and immigrants are looking for a home here, so Marzahn presents itself today as a "future Kreuzberg".

Wohnregal (359)
Dwelling Shelf
1986
Admiralstraße 16
Kjell Nylund, Christof Puttfarken,
Peter Stürzebecher

Admiralstraße was a stronghold of tenant self-help as propagated by the IBA (no. 355). But while the remaining projects (at least 20 of 330 feet) refurbished old buildings again, house number 16 was newly built in 1984. Similar to with Jochen Brandis' ten year older steel ter-

race prototype building at Schleswiger Ufer (no. 339), prefabricated parts (here made of reinforced concrete) form a rough structure which the 12 groups of residents then expanded with their own work and as they chose into maisonettes, snuggling mazes or large workshops. But while the forerunner building was a success both inside and outside, the trellis facade here, which leads over into a pitched roof with winter garden, represents an unreasonable demand aesthetically in the middle of the old buildings. It has still not been overgrown today.

Hofbegrünung Block 6 (360)
Planting Vegetation in the
Courtyard of Block 6
1987
Entrances: Bernburger Straße 22/23,
Dessauer Straße 14
Hans Loidl, Harald Kraft, Compactplan, AG
Ökologischer Stadtumbau

GARDEN "Green life" was the ideal according to which many sealed backyards were converted into living oases with ecological zeal in West Berlin in the 1980s. The special feature with Block 6: here there was extra arrangement for everything. While the block destroyed in the war, which was hardly occupied with residential buildings from the 1970s, was provided with ribbon development, in the newly-created open spaces tenants' gardens, hilly sunbathing areas and lus-

cious tree plantations were realised. Then there were also green roofs and a reed pool of 20,000 square feet which belong to a separate grey water cycle to save drinking water in Berlin for the first time "on a large scale". But neither the eco technology nor the living environment fulfil these expectations. And the demonstration project is absolutely representative in this.

The Westin Grand Berlin
(ehem. Grand Hotel) (361)
The Westin Grand Berlin Hotel
(former Grand Hotel)
1987
Friedrichstraße 158–164
Ehrhardt Gißke (general supervision),
Kajima-Corporation, Takeshi Inoue

The name of the hotel is deceptive, it was only given this by the American chain in 1997. Today the Westin Grand, formerly the Grand Hotel, is among the master achievements of the industrial (reconstruction) architecture in the GDR. It was built in a construction phase which must be called late socialistic and which is a contradiction to itself. On the one hand, trust was put in precisely detailed and expensive prefabrication and on the other hand, it used the neo-classicist form lan-

guage. Similar to the Nikolai quarter (no. 362), post-modern style quotes were used with the partial reconstruction of Friedrichstadt and with the Westin Grand. The structure is divided into foundation, main storeys and penthouse, and when viewed more precisely the pattern of joints which comes from the prefabricated construction really catches the eye. These "constructive necessities" were covered up with pilaster strips and cornices. The main entrance of the hotel, which is on the corner of Behrenstraße/Friedrichstraße, leads into an octagonal atrium which stretches out over all eight storeys and is concluded on the roof with a glass dome.

Nikolaiviertel (362)
Nikolai Quarter
1987
between Mühlendamm, Spreeufer,
Rathaus- und Spandauer Straße
Erhardt Gißke (general supervision),
Günter Stahn with Wolfgang Woigk and
Reinhard Reuer (architecture)

On the occasion of the 750-year celebration of Berlin, the competition from 1979 for the extension of the town hall passages (no. 328) led to the construction of a prototypical "history park" in the cen-

tre of East Berlin. After "Old Berlin" was affected in the 1930s and completely destroyed in the Second World War, a collage was now made of eight (in some cases in a new location) reconstructed testaments from history (Nikolai Church, Ephraimpalais, Knoblauchhaus see Nos. 2, 30, 31), as well as three- to seven-storey new buildings with a total of 780 apartments. The pre-casting plants produced a large number of special forms for the first time so that the channelled concrete facades show medium-sized town rows of balconies and arcades to the outside and neo-Gothic gables in the winding inner alleyways. Gerhard Thieme added relief allegories, which are supposed to represent the development of socialism and the "city of peace", seamlessly to museum-like interiors, guild signs and advertising pillars. The visitors to the 23-theme catering establishments with a total of 1,800 places still dominate the picture of the quarter today.

Spreeterrassen (363)
Spree Terraces
1987
Friedrichstraße 105
Karl-Ernst Swora, Gunter Derdau,
Dera Immaschmied

In the 1980s, twice as many apartments were built in the old centre of Berlin than after the Berlin Wall came down, with the council land making this unproductive use possible. Moreover, the slab production of the GDR was now well developed enough to come to terms with the grown city. So on Friedrichstraße on the corner towards the River Spree a complex of profoundly conventional urbanity was re-

alised from 1985. The two lower storeys were reserved for trade, and on the floors above there are 131 apartments attached almost "seamlessly". The restaurant in the basement stretches under the new waterside path up to the Spree. Unlike the countless iconographic attempts with other prefabricated buildings (see Nos. 350, 361), the new building parts look quite normally plastic here. Loggias on the top floor point to the inclined roof which is common in Berlin. Protruding artificial stone reveals let the pattern of joints on the prefabricated building retreat.

Spreewaldbad und Görlitzer Park (364)
Spreewald Bath and Gölitzer Park
1987
Christoph Langhof Architects (indoor swimming pool), Freie Planungsgruppe Berlin (parks)

Once the average green space of each inhabitant of the SO 36 area did not even suffice for the proverbial "bed in a cornfield", it was arranged to rearrange Görlitzer Bahnhof which, like all main Berlin stations since the Second World War, was waste land, in stages from 1984 into a collage of land art (sculptures), landscape garden (river courses) and a people's park (central green basin). Although the site was a sizeable 17 hectares, it was desirable to avoid any further sealing off of the area. So in the competition from 1979, a design won which lowered the swimming pool into the partially heaped-up ground. In the Spreewaldbad, there is now unexpected flirting between passers-by and bathers. Through the glazed side one can also see gold-coloured lattice girders – once an expression of a new "fun architecture" which has since then conquered not only Görlitzer Park (Pamukkale fountain).

Verlängerung der Linie 8 (365)
Extension of the Number 8 Line
1987
between Franz Neumann Platz and Paracelsusbad
Rainer G. Rümmler

In his thirty years of service as chief designer of the underground, Rainer G. Rümmler (no. 327) increasingly negated the network combination which had once been established by Alfred Grenander (no. 213) with the foundation of the Berlin transport services. In line with the spirit of the time he built increasingly in a postmodern style: with a simple association with the station name one can look at pictures with mediaeval washing scenes at Paracelsusbad, and the Bahnhof Residenzstraße in Reinickendorf shows views of old Berlin. With the total of around 40 stations which Rümmler designed the principle of distinctiveness had to lead into "over-furnishing". At the same time the tile sprees, gold-coloured wastepaper baskets and brawny installations of his later work underline that underground

station construction in West Berlin served less of a transport function than the provision of employment. The best proof is the project itself: the Number 8 line was taken further in the direction of Wittenau even after the parallel S-Bahn went in the care of the senate in the mid-1980s.

Wissenschaftszentrum Berlin (366)
Berlin Scientific Centre
1987
Reichpietschufer 48-58
James Stirling, Michael Wilford & Associates

After the competition victory of the British office whose Stuttgart Staatsgalerie made the post-modernist style presentable in Germany, a group of ground plan forms were created after 1980, for behind the former Reichsversicherungsamt: cruciform church, colonnade, cam-

panile and amphitheatre, like the palace-style old building from 1894 however, they house almost solely offices. The openings have bulky travertine frames which omit the windowsill of all things. A pineapple motif instead of the lost old building relief brings to the point the irony which Stirling had before his post-modern comrades-in-arms, which is shown by the cubic outline of the new parts as much as the pink and baby blue striped perforated facade. The fact that three academic institutes (ecology, economics and social sciences) are located here is known to only a few people.

Wohn- und Geschäftshaus (367)
Residential and Commercial building
1987
Friedrichstraße 56
Peter Meyer

East Berlin post-modern in somewhat different style. Unlike his neo-historically oriented colleagues, Peter Meyer adapted an icon of the modern at Friedrichstraße no. 56: above the two-storey foundation made of in-site concrete, a facade was built in 1985 analogous with Max Taut's "House of Typographers" (Dudenstraße 10, 1926) – but using the prefabricated slab method. However, the yellow small stone mosaic, in which the clinker used there was to be indicated, had to be re-

winter gardens, cites the Dessau Bauhaus style, its flying roof Le Corbusier. The new, barely vegetated neighbourhood area has, admittedly, remained fairly unenlivened.

placed by a coat of paint of the same colour because of sloppy production. Balconies, loggias and winter gardens stagger the apartments, which ably compensate for the lack of space with four apartments per floor. But the house, like its architect, has remained an outsider.

Wohnbebauung am Luisenplatz   (368)
Residential Development at Luisenplatz
1987
Luisenplatz, corner of Eosanderstraße
Brandt & Böttcher, Hans Kollhoff

The combination of two contrary competition concepts from 1982 vis-à-vis the Charlottenburg Palace (no. 21) resulted in a perfect example of the elaborate town planning in the 1980s. In the front section Brandt & Böttcher built a row whose hipped roof and three storeys correspond with the Knobelsdorff wing (no. 28), while with its colonnades it is displayed as a profane town house. The building contains the highly-trafficked Luisenplatz and duplicates it on the rear to form an agora for the residents, whose entrance is formed by an already existing mansion. The typological space innovation was given its backdrop by Hans Kollhoff: its six-storey fire wall construction – intersected by Eosanderstraße and an apartment house – swings from Otto Suhr Allee up to Schlossbrücke. It assumes the balcony band from the Schinkel pavilion (no. 28) here. Its gigantic window, which combines four storeys of

Block 103   **(369)**
Block 103
1987
Oranien-, Mariannen-, Naunyn-,
Manteuffelstraße
Winners: Stattbau, Luisenstadt e. G.,
Bauhof GmbH

Oranienstraße, since the plans from 1969 which wanted to replace it with a motorway, was plainly the stronghold of the house dispute. The following concept, which also intended to knock down the

majority of probably the most compact building blocks in Berlin, was toppled in 1980 by house occupations. After their legalisation, Block 103 developed into a model quarter for careful urban renewal: along with the resident-conducted repairs and planting of vegetation in yards came ecological installations with green roofs, composting, fire-wall wastewater treatments, solar cells and biogas plant. Unlike the rest of the IBA (no. 355) which continued to move trade out into new yards, measures in the portfolio doubled the number of businesses here. Since then the house dispute has been maintained "in folklore" every year on 1st May.

Randbebauung Gendarmenmarkt (370)
Gendarmenmarkt Perimeter Development
1988
Charlottenstraße 50–54, 55/56;
Markgrafen-, between Jäger- and
Französischer Straße
Manfred Prasser (complex architect)

When a 22-year-old concept from Günther Zimmermann was used for a ribbon development of the square in 1979 it was revolutionary in two points. First of all the small parcel structure remained and second the prefabricated slab design was changed so that there would be facades according to an historical example. On location, smaller concrete parts were cast which complement the old intendancy

building behind the theatre (no. 54), which was expanded with a passageway by Peter Kobe and Ernst Wallis. Further north in Charlottenstraße they decorate

two new steel framework constructions. The neo-baroque corner house on Französische Straße was built by 1983 according to designs by Prasser, Wallis, Wolfgang Sebastian and Dieter Bankert, the neo-classicist building at the Jägerstraße junction by 1985 by Günter Boy. Among the prefabricated buildings completed vis-à-vis in 1987 by Matthias Borner, Markgrafenstraße 39 shows an Art Nouveau small stone mosaic (see no. 374). The development at Gendarmenmarkt marks the highpoint of industrial construction in the former GDR.

Stresemann-Mews (371)
Stresemann Mews
1988
Wilhelmstraße 131–133,
Stresemannstraße 42–46
Klaus Zillich and Jasper Halfmann

The residential row emerging from an international competition in 1981 clarifies the small town dimensions in which West Berlin thought in the 1980s. A year before the opening of the Berlin Wall, terraced houses were completed within walking distance of Potsdamer Platz (no. 417), something one would normally expect on the periphery of a large city. At the time, it was a matter of reducing the size of the large block between two main roads from the war-damaged Friedrichstadt which had become cul-de-sacs. So to the north of a new green link a quite roughly detailed, four-storey plaster frame was built with sloping winter gardens protruding in front of the edge of the building. A counterpart originally planned in the south of the green space was not constructed in the end.

Friedrichstadt-Passagen (372)
Friedrichstadt Passages
1989
Friedrichstraße 66–78
Ehrhardt Gißke (general supervision),
Manfred Prasser

Tegeler Hafen (373)
Tegel Harbour
1989
Am Tegeler Hafen, Karolinenstraße
Charles Moore, John Ruble, Buzz Yudell
(town planning, library)

DEMOLITION The GDR tackled Friedrichstraße practically as the last component of the East Berlin city centre. The reconstruction of the shopping and amusement mile in historic cubature began in 1980 and initially brought about the block-style amalgamation of the small parcels of land. Between Mohrenstraße and Französischer Straße the head of the Berlin head building office, Ehrhardt Gißke, and the complex architect of the Friedrichstadt Palace, Manfred Prasser (no. 350), realised from 1984 three aesthetically similar reinforced concrete framework constructions with special slab cladding. The gastronomy and business blocks which were hardly staggered spatially were already completed on the outside when the construction work was stopped after the Berlin Wall came down in 1989. One year later the torso, which had been called "Tuntenbrosche" in the East Berlin slang, was knocked down. The irony of the story: the Friedrichstadt passages (Nos. 395, 396, 397) which were then built followed a very similar concept.

The most high-class new building quarter of the IBA (no. 355) was not realised in the city centre but on the eastern edge of Tegel. The victorious competition design, which eight mainly foreign architects implemented in a post-modern construction, provided for two rows building up serpent-like on the waterside. They open up a landscape of waterside promenade, green valley, residential yard, and water and fairground areas, which is connected to the old city centre by four city villas. The port basin extends the nave of the Humboldt library.

Praise for the Slab:
Industrial Building in East Berlin (374)

The industrial building goes back to research on the Bauhaus style in the 1920s. It is considered an attempt to connect social requirements in terms of mass residential construction with design elements. Through the rationalisation of the building process, the procedures in the construction of buildings were to be accelerated in order to provide as many people as possible in the shortest possible time with a newly built apartment – with the comfort of heating, running water and an inside toilet. On top of this was the aesthetic and ideological requirement to provide the simple workers and farmers with housing which would contribute to an area-wide visual improvement of the cities. The industrial prefabrication was pushed on so far that even special building parts were not produced on location at the construction site but instead already beforehand in the manufacturing facilities.

In the GDR it was Hans Schmidt who, in the mid-1950s as the main architect at the Institute for Standardisation, compiled theoretical principles which found recognition in the entire Eastern Block. Schmidt had already attracted attention back in 1924 as the publisher of the magazine ABC – Contributions to Building. He was convinced that the "new architecture could grow only on the technical basis of industrialisation and on the social basis of socialism" and propagated the design of buildings from industrially prefabricated components or even the assembly of repetitive facade elements as an architectural principle. Among his German colleagues, who still felt fully associated with neo-traditionalism at the time, the born Swiss was greeted with the head shaking and rejection at first. Nevertheless, with his theses, Hans Schmidt was able to initiate a development in the GDR which influenced the entire Eastern Block. The idea of saving time and, in particular, money from the rationalisation of the building process became the ideology of an entire generation of architects. According to Schmidt's ideas, the architects should learn in particular during their education to implement the "architecturally-conditional tectonics of industrial construction" in their designs. This is because the clear, simple and uniform correspond the best with the essence of socialistic society. But the repeatedly formulated demand to also help form an assumed new society with a new building process could be solved by the architects only with politically extremely high-ranking prototype residential areas. Material shortages and lack of workers, caused by erroneous calculations in the central plans of a rigid party and state apparatus, ultimately led to the fact that the idea of an area-wide architectural renewal of society ended in an economic and creative disaster. meu

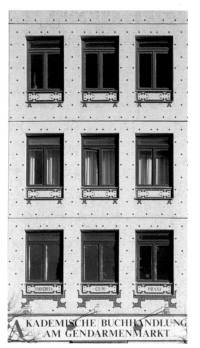

Panel style can be beautiful: facade detail on a residential building at Gendarmenmarkt.

An architecture with teeth: Canopy at the Haus des Reisens, Alexanderplatz.

Hildebrand Machleidt

Axel Schultes

Norman Foster

Daniel Libeskind

Joachim Näther

Roland Korn

Richard Rogers

Fritz Borneman

Rem Koolhaas

Hans Bogatzky

Zaha Hadid

Claude Vasconi

Hans Kollhoff

Dominique Perrault

Meinhard von Gerkan

Manfred Ortner

The New City of Berlin:
Construction Work in the 1990s (375)

The 1990s could hardly have had unified greater contrasts in terms of their urban development role models and economic expectations. While the city's population was expected to grow to reach a figure of five million citizens, the expectations that were excessive in some cases have markedly calmed down. No one wanted to speak of a booming city ten years after the fall of the Berlin wall. Berlin's population has decreased since 1996 and the population levels are presently equivalent to the levels at the time of Germany's reunification. The number of apartments that stand empty is well above 100,000; in the case of offices the figure is many times greater in square feet. The senate has incurred follow-up costs, which only future generations will be able to pay off, due to gigantic investments in infrastructure while the tax revenue was absent.

Despite this sobering end result Berlin has become a Mecca of modern architecture since Germany's reunification. You will hardly find any more markodly oon trasting philosophies of architecture anywhere else in the world – with the consequence Berlin is extremely polarised in terms of its planning and construction work. Passionate debates have been held about architecture and urban development especially since the reunification of Germany, which has provided Berlin with a surge in development activities that is unique in history. Upon the dismantling of the scaffolding a city has emerged following the boom of the 1990s, which is more modern than many others, which establishes links with long forgotten traditions and has revealed an astonishing level of diversity. In the past ten years numerous architects from all round the world have embarked on a search for a design for the city in competitions. Each of them has made a contribution ensuring that Berlin has found its own architectural style.

The Berlin architecture dispute, which reached its climax between 1993 and 1995 and at the same time also led to personal animosities arising between the architects, created a big stir throughout the world. This is due to the fact that Berlin has always been a trendsetter for contemporary architecture. This raised expectations in the modern architecture to

Building on the water: when the wall fell down, Berlin also received the opportunity to reconceive the Spree architecturally.

such an extent after 1990 that the response to the reconstruction of city that had been divided for decades had to be a sobering one. Rather than a city idea, which should have imitated the ideals of long since obsolete city utopias, the senate awarded a prize to designs, which had some elements that are typical Berlin, but which were nevertheless regarded as an absolute provocation by the international architecture sector, in numerous competitions and expert reports. Almost without exception the senate pursued a strategy of "critical reconstruction" during the reconstruction of Berlin in accordance with the role model of a traditional European city. In specific terms this means that the historic city ground plan has to be restored in those places, where it was meaningful from our current perspective. This applies for instance to the areas at the Leipziger Platz, Pariser Platz or in Friedrichstadt. A new city structure was developed where there were hardly any relics of the old city, whereby the houses are oriented towards the road, form a clear address and are based on the typology of Berlin's office blocks with

their characteristic cullis height of 72 feet. In addition there was the fact – and this really heated the debate up – a fundamental specification for the use of materials: The faces were to be designed in natural stone just like the historical models that they were based on. As a consequence this led to a situation whereby a lot of the new buildings were integrated quite naturally. Exceptions such as the Galeries Lafayette department (no. 397) are all the more conspicuous as a result. They form a kind of opposition in the "new centre of stone buildings".

In addition to the discussion about architectural details Berlin also initiated a series of major urban development policy decisions, which the urban planners had worked towards for almost 80 years as in the case of the Tiergarten tunnel. Berlin fulfilled the dream of a gigantic traffic hub right in the middle of the city centre through the decision to build the Berlin central station and the resulting necessity to create a north-south axis for transport.   meu

Haus am Checkpoint Charlie (376)
House at Checkpoint Charlie
1990
Friedrichstraße 207/208
Office for Metropolitan Architecture:
Elia Zenghelis, Matthias Sauerbruch,
Rem Koolhaas

Writing history with avant-garde means: The shed roof, which is precisely cut off in a north south direction and appears to be slanted from the grid of the baroque Friedrichstadt that is slightly offset against it. Within it, the residential form that were typical for the urbanisation process follow in accordance with their sequence in time: free penthouses, maisonettes that are more or less connected with a cradle walk and also apartments that are united by black strip ceramic tiles and windows. On the ground floor there were once parking lots, a bus turn-

around point, a control post that resembles a control tower and staff rooms for the Checkpoint Charlie. It was completed in the year the wall fell and the ground floor was converted for normal commercial traffic in the following years.

taz-Haus (377)
taz House
1990
Kochstraße 19
Gerhard Spangenberg

The Tageszeitung was the first newspaper to be newly founded in West Berlin since the 1950s. It initially regarded itself as the "Central organ" of the Kreuzberg squatters scene, which its location also still emphasises to this day. The editorial office resides in a trade building from 1909 that was formerly planned to be demolished, which was linked with an extension through development technology and basement heights. In aesthetic terms, the new architecture sought the type of contrast that was typical in the 1980s. The new building consists of composite beams, which are brick nogged with a few bricks and a lot of glass. Apart from the locally derived balcony arches, which are based on the recessed houses at the corner of the Charlottenstraße and can be interpreted as an ironic commentary of the once planned widening of the roads, the grid tower is reminiscent of the publishing house designs of the classic modernist period, such as the Chicago Tribune competition of 1922.

Salamander-Haus (378)
Salamander House
1992
Tauentzienstraße 15
Volkwin Marg (gmp)

In 1930 the Salamander company of Johann Emil Schaudt (architect of the KaDeWe) was already a futuristic store building at that time, which now, however, no longer exists. At the start of the 90s Volkwin Marg and gmp laid down an important foundation stone as part of the initiative to spruce up the department

store architecture only this shopping mile in the western part of the city through the construction of the Schuhhaus at am Tauentzien next to the Marburger Straße. In the immediate vicinity the Peek & Cloppenburg clothes shop (no. 389) that was designed the Architekturbüro Böhm was built just shortly afterwards. The Hamburg architects realised a concept in the form of the Salamander Haus which they also used for the Atrlum Friedrichstraße (quarter 203). The sevenstorey building forms a semi-public courtyard which can be entered from Tauentzien. The facade is strictly structured in a vertical manner, and opens up at the street levels to form arcades and is crowned by a corner tower at the edge of the down spout edge. A special novelty of the double facade of the building is its construction depth of seven feet, which is additionally illuminated in the company colours of white and green at night.

Focus Teleport (379)
Focus Teleport
1993
Stromstraße 1–7, Alt Moabit 91–96
Joachim Ganz and Walter Rolfes

The project marks the quintessence of Berlin industrial history to date. While the senate had already commissioned production plants for a new generation of IT founders since the early 1980s, this project marked the first time in a while that a private investor but built a new building. However, it was not until the fall of the wall that the project commenced in 1987 was able to occupy the entire Kampffmeyer-Mühlen area. Ganz & Rolfes organised the site community consisting of approx. 70 research institutions, established companies and startups in the form of the traditional Stockwerksfabrik. The twelve seven-storey complexes, which have a tower at the Lessing bridge as their hallmark, consist of a high tech prefabricate building made with concrete slabs. Exposed concrete blocks, terracotta ceramic tiles and dark blue metal frames add up to form a stylish aesthetic appearance, that the serial constructions have seldom been able to achieve.

Kant-Dreieck (Turmhaus) (380)
Kant-Triangle (Tower House)
1994
Kantstraße 155
Josef Paul Kleihues

The Kant-Dreick tower high-rise building was the only structural sign of the desire for high-rise buildings in west Berlin for a long a time following the fall of the wall. However, the design version of the tower was reduced in size by 120 feet following a controversial debate. The giant weathervane in the form of a shark's fin (a rotable aluminium sail) rises strikingly into the Charlottenburg skies. The allusion to the triangular plot of land is thus present in a number of ways. The combination of a tower and a flat roofed building in terms of its arrangement facing towards the Theater des Westens opposite (no. 111) and the Delphi-Filmtheater which disappears behind the row of streets. The modular design (59 by 59 feet) determines the gneiss basement as well as the metal tower with diagonal struts and flat roofed building that is extensively glazed in some areas. Kleihues had to define three free areas on the plot of land that had not been completely built on, in order to anchor the building within the area of the city. A square was built facing towards Kantstraße, framed by the edges of the building and a wall: a fountain was installed at the Fasanstraße; facing towards the railway line the free space and the Kant-Dreieck resonate along with the tram viaduct.

Geschäftshaus Kurfürstendamm (381)
Commercial Building on
Kurfürstendamm
1994
Kurfürstendamm 70
Helmut Jahn

The viewers must always ask themselves whether it is part of the facade or a proper house here. Stacked, banana shaped office floor space bulge to form a high-rise building over an area spanning three times 66 feet, in the direction of Adenauerplatz. Helmut Jahn built a functional building on the extremely narrow plot of land, which permits a lot of (quadratic) ornamentation for both the individual construction elements and also for its details. When set against Jahn's second coup at the Kufürstendamm some six years later, the Victoria-Areal (no. 490), the high-rise building on a corner seems to be more finely chased in overall terms and to be relatively more appropriate for the location. Despite the jump in scale compared to the heights of the existing buildings at the Kurfürstendam the buil-

ding represents a much less sensitive departure in terms of the style than the building around the Kranzler corner. At Adenauerplatz, Jahn let his building be concluded rib-like to the height of the fascia and stretched even higher to the sky with help from a filigree tower method. From Café Adlon which is situated opposite, the observer views an animated information reel, which should emphasis Jahn's interpretation of urban architecture with the night-time lighting concept.

Wohnanlage Seesener Straße (382)
Seesener Straße Housing Complex
1994
Seesener Straße 70 a–f
Hans Kollhoff, Helga Timmermann

The housing estate's plot of land is located next to the S-Bahn line and the city motorway and was thus deemed inappropriate for the construction of houses for a long time. The six-storey building closes the construction on the side facing the suburban railway by means of glazed winter gardens to keep the noise and exhaust pollution levels as low as possi-

ble for the sixty council apartments that have been financed in the second development scheme. The metal facade of the winter gardens has been folded slightly within itself. Connected apartments with interior kitchens and bathrooms face both the quiet inner courtyard and the width of the municipal traffic landscape. The entrance to the inner courtyard and the drive to the underground car park are restricted to access through the house with the number 79. The careful planning and design of the entire complex, typical of Kollhoff and Timmermann, is a remarkable feature. Although a simple, perforated facade that is slightly bent in reddish brown clinker faces towards the inner courtyard, wooden windows, dark square hewn stone in the stairways, oak wood doors and fittings made of brass and the green stone panelling of the house entrances do not speak the normal Spartan language of "minimal standards" in council housing.

Deutsches Architektur Zentrum (383)
German Centre for Architecture
1995
Köpenicker Straße 48
Claus Anderhalten, Assmann, Salomon & Scheidt

Upon the initiative of the Bund Deutscher Architekten (BDA), the association of German architects, this architecture pool was created in the construction phase of the "new Berlin", which was meant to stand as an institution representing the "capital city of construction in German". The BDA also set about transferring its Bonn headquarters to Berlin upon the opening of the Deutsches Architektur Zentrum (DAZ). Its construction and thus the refurbishment of an old textile factory in the middle of the former GDR border area, used for industrial purposes to an extent, threatened with decay, should become an additional motor for urban development in this part of the district. The concept grouped together professional representations with several event halls, rooms for permanent exhibitions, a coffee house and office spaces as well as studios for architects, designers and artists. Claus Anderhalten created a form of architecture for this mixture, which offers friendly and open room formations, and which modifies the industrial construction, while still restoring it in a manner befitting its status as a listed building. The white, clinkered facade that had been partially destroyed was renovated; the Assmann, Salomon & Scheidt's architects' office was responsible for the second construction stage. However the DAZ was unable to convert a hopeful starting position into a genuine success story after approximately five years. It thus announced that the exhibition area would be made smaller in 2000 as a strategic retreat in the form of a break to think things over.

Engelhardt-Hof (384)
Engelhardt Courtyard
1995
Danckelmannstraße 9
Kahlfeldt Architekten

The Engelhardt-Hof succeeds in re-establishing the old success model of inner city multi-use in the industrial yard in a contemporary form. The former brewery site in Charlottenburg only still existed in part with a brewery and an annexe from the 1960s. Essentially, three new building sections were added to the refurbished old buildings in the form of a U-shaped office building, a five-storey office tower and a residential building. The spatial configuration consisting of a double U-shape has been sealed by three-storey bridge constructions. These "glass boxes" made of steel trusses have been detailed in a masterful manner. Kahlfeldt Architekten have produced various facade concepts within the enclosed overall appearance of the building. The courtyard building characterises the ochre-coloured clinker wall that varies greatly in terms of its colouring. The office tower at the Danckelmannstraße sets itself apart by means of its glassy and steely appearance and the residential building was provided with a plastered perforated facade above the clinker basement. A solution that was very integrative in overall terms, and demanding in terms of its craftsmanship whilst discreet in terms of form was created here by way of a block reconstruction.

Haus Pietzsch (385)
Pietzsch House
1995
Unter den Linden 42
Jürgen Sawade

As one of the first buildings that were supposed to heal the wounds of Friedrichstadt after 1989 by means of a "critical reconstruction" (see IBA, no. 355) the Haus Pietzsch was built at Unter den Linden/Neustädtische Kirchstraße on a striking corner plot. Originally the road routing, at the point where the barely 50-feet wide building rises, was to be extended as the plot of land had not been developed after the war. Sawade showed consideration for the bordering neo-classicist neighbours and operated using the classical three fold division: basement, main storeys, roof junction. The perforated facade is lined with square hewn stone panels. However, the building clearly distances itself from the facade appearance of its neighbours due to the fact that a glass connecting member was inserted. This glass joint serves as an atrium and development area of the office block. The building differs from many subsequent buildings, which carried out reconstruction work by copying former constructions, by means of this delimitation. The narrow atrium is also used as a picture gallery. A branch of Café Einstein has been established on the building's ground floor, thus alluding to its use by a cafe and cake shop before the war.

Heinz-Galinski-Schule (386)
Heinz-Galinski School
1995
Waldschulallee 73-75
Zvi Hecker

A Jewish school building has been reconstructed in Berlin for the first time since the Second World War in the form of the Heinz-Galinski-Schule. The primary school has been in existence since 1986. When it needed reconstructing, the senate launched an architecture competition in 1990, which the Israeli architect Zvi Hecker managed to win. The school's concept in terms of its form was based on the abstract structure of a sunflower, whose draft had been revised several times. The individual structures are grouped around the dynamic centre point of the "flower". Hecker explained that the basic design had been selected because of a "longstanding interest in sunflowers: their everyday nature, usefulness, dynamism..." In structural terms, the concept is expressed by means of five wedge-shaped building sections, which, whilst pointing to the centre, form lanes and paths in the style of a small village. The building complex developed for up to 400 primary school pupils with 30 classrooms, sports and catering facilities as well as a multipurpose hall, which can also be used as a synagogue is also open to Christian pupils. In this sense, the building should serve to mediate between the cultures.

Info-Box (387)
Info Box
1995
Leipziger Platz
Till Schneider and Michael Schumacher

DEMOLITION The red Info-Box, which served as the information centre and a lookout platform for construction work at Potsdamer Platz (no. 417), should go down in history as the first building constructed in the 1990s to be demolished in the same decade. This box, which was built on stilts and resembled the constructions of Russian collectivism, was doomed to suffer this fate. Nevertheless, this provisional building, which nine million people visited, had managed to attract a number of guests, no PR strategist would ever have believed possible. Moreover this red box served as a model for similar huts, ranging from the "grüner Floh", the green flea directly opposite to the Info-Pavillon in Hellersdorf. Thus the initial building of the young Frankfurt architects could hardly have been a better form of advertising for the mother of all arts, architecture.

Wohnpark Malchower Weg (388)
Malchower Weg Residential Complex
1995
Malchower Weg 117–119,
Drossener Straße 1–4
Hans Kollhoff, Helga Timmermann

The residential complex consisting of 16 freestanding house cuboids was intended to integrate a clear constructional structure and statement within the disparate suburban area of Hohenschönhausen. This is because there is already enough structural uncertainty on the main transport axis of Hansastraße. Hans Kollhoff and Helga Timmermann have countered this by adopting the principle of "city villas": Cubic structures, which are 1.4 times longer than they are wide, four sto-

reys of two apartments each. This collection of villas simulates a block in a dense urban environment although it is set in more rural surroundings. The entire formation consists of the groups of houses that are arranged closely next to one another and which are made accessible by means of private roads. The houses even stand closer together at their narrow sides than is permitted in the building regulations, whilst the cantilevered roof overhangs emphasise the intention that the buildings should tilt towards one another. A brick skin with a lively appearance with dark grouting and prefabricated timber and concrete elements are the dominant materials. The living rooms were provided with room high glazing with French balconies and form winter gardens in the corners.

Kaufhaus Peek & Cloppenburg (389)
Peek & Cloppenburg Department Store
1995
Tauentzienstraße 19
Gottfried and Peter Böhm

The Peek & Cloppenburg department store has made an original gesture as one of the conversion and new building projects along the central shopping promenades in the western part of the city. In terms of the interior organisation, the master church builder Gottfried Böhm based his first department store on that typology, which was arranged around an atrium, from the imperial age. Grouped together the escalator access point leads upwards from here to then be coupled over at head height with a painting by Böhm's son. The structural resolution of the facade can be regarded as a very free interpretation of a curtain wall consisting of supporting and filling parts. Glass curtain parts, which behave like inflated

lengths of material swing between the slim concrete pillars that do indeed tower upwards. They form curved canopies, which firstly protect pedestrians and secondly represent a dual glass skin, which can be ventilated. At the eaves height, the concrete pillars link up to form a network of beams, which incline towards the roof junction like a hip roof. In overall terms, Böhm had adopted the type of monolithic department store in the form of the Peek & Cloppenburg building, which had already made the KaDeWe (no. 143) into a bastion of the retail trade a short distance from it.

Mauerpark (390)
Wall Park
1996
Schwedter Straße, between Ringbahn and Eberswalder Straße
Gustav Lange with Schweger & Partner (overall concept)

GARDEN People who now sit on the swings assembled on the slope can easily forget that the death zone once ran along here. In accordance with the senate's resolution of 1992, the site of division was to be made into a meeting place. In the competition that followed this, a minimalist concept won, which anticipated the garden design that would be typical in the era of unity: the victorious Hamburg architects have renamed the area between the apartment block districts of Wedding and Prenzlauer Berg into the "clearing in the city", the backbone of which would be formed by Schwedter Straße, along which the wall used to run. On the one hand, they positioned individual action islands in the back of the Jahn-Sportpark (for instance

an amphitheatre). On the other hand, a high quality lawn that was the size of five football pitches was created at the former Eberswald goods station. The northern annexe which was planned by Thomas Guba was completed in 2000. The western part is not any closer to being realised although the use of the wall park has now markedly increased.

Hamburger Bahnhof –
Museum für Gegenwart (391)
Hamburger Station –
Museum of Contemporary Art
1996
Invalidenstraße 50/51
Josef Paul Kleihues

In 1984 the Berlin senate obtained the right to have the "Verkehrs- und Baumuseum", the museum of transport and construction, at its disposal. Up until then, it had been administered by the GDR. Now the so-called Hamburger Bahnhof was expected to solve the confined situation of the Neue Nationalgalerie (no. 320) due to the fact that western Berlin had already been provided with a new transport museum. The late classical terminus construction (1846–47, no. 75) is the last remaining building of its type in Berlin. It actually only served as a train station for 40 years before it was turned into a museum after being supplemented by a glass hall. It was inaccessible after 1945 and exhibitions only took place in the house that had been partially refurbished from 1987 onwards. Kleihues addressed this situation by means of his actions (competition of 1989), left the three-aisle hall almost unchanged and, running in parallel with this, created a single aisle exhibition suite that is 260 feet in length with a light buoy. Art from the 2nd half of

the 20th century is on display in an exhibition area of approximately 107,000 square feet – exhibits from the state museums in Berlin and works of the Berlin Marx collection. The arguments that Kleinhues' work on the building was too "aesthetical" for a technology monument must be countered by stating that the station has also been used as a museum building in the past.

Hofgarten am Gendarmenmarkt (392)
Gardens at Gendarmenmarkt
1996
Between the Friedrichstraße,
Behrenstraße, Charlottenstraße und
Französische Straße
Josef P. Kleihues (urban development).

The fact that Friedrichstadt was planned en bloc between 1945 and 1991 violated the principles of critical reconstruction. The inventor of the urban development method, Josef Paul Kleihues (Nr. 356), therefore used the Hofgarten project, (the name refers to an underground car park covered in grass) for the revised parcelling of the land. The following constructions were built by autonomous architects whilst the investor did not comprehend the division in equal parts: Kleihues himself designed an aluminium house for the eastern side of the block as well as the shingle link travertine coating of the Four Season Hotel. On the southern side Jürgen Sawade created offices behind a delightful facade that is as smooth as glass made of black granite, whilst Müller/Reimann renovated the

Weinhaus Borchardt (Carl Gause, 1900). The baroque buildings in the west were rounded off by Hans Kollhoff by means of constructive acts of strength. In the north, the compulsory 20 percent quota of apartments in the capital city was fulfilled by the first veritable residential building of new Friedrichstadt: In this process, Max Dudler Le Corbusier's Unité concept (Nr. 291) imbued it with so much urbane grandeur, that it can hold its own with the ideal types of Kurfürstendamm (no. 145).

Königstadt-Terrassen (393)
Königstadt Terraces
1996
Schönhauser Allee 10–11,
Saarbrücker Str. 24
Thomas Müller, Ivan Reimann

The new building had to fit in with the existing old building from the turn of the 19th century that had been extensively restored on the grounds of the former Königstadt brewery. However, the two clearly outlined L-shaped building sections with their sober perforated facade do not attempt to embark on historical ingratiation, but are based on the strictness and objectivity of classical modernism. They form a two-winged complex, whereby its courtyard is concluded by a store facade set in front of it, above which a terrace covered with greenery is located. The collection uses the incline of the land and allows the users of the office and business floors a clear view of the beautiful surroundings.

Oberbaumbrücke   (394)
Oberbaum Bridge
1996
Am Oberbaum
Santiago Calatrava

The Oberbaumbrücke now no longer separates two extremely different city districts but is now instead the connecting element in the middle of the large district of Friedrichshain-Kreuzberg that has been merged together. Its name is derived from the word "Oberbaum", literally, the upper tree, which once cordoned off the river at the city boundaries here. The bridge based on the historicizing, Märkish brick Gothic style was built between 1894 to 1896 on the occasion of the Treptow industrial exhibition, based on the designs of the architect Otto Stahn (no. 108). The two towers were supposed to be reminiscent of a city gate, and the railway viaduct was supposed to resemble a cloister. As an important road link of the inner city the bridge was blown up in the Second World War and subsequently only provisionally repaired; only pedestrians were able to use the bridge from 1961 onwards. The towers were renewed and the railway viaduct section that had been destroyed was replaced by a steel construction based on the designs of Santiago Calatrava in the centre section (road bridge of König, Stief & Partner) as part of the reconstruction process. Calatrava had been commissioned with the task of producing an expert report on the entire bridge in 1991, but ultimately only the viaduct section was built based on his plans. This departs markedly from the old idea of the solid bridge by means of a new, elegant swaying element.

Quartier 205   (395)
City Block 205
1996
Friedrichstraße, Taubenstraße, Charlottenstraße, Mohrenstraße
Oswald Mathias Ungers

Quartier 2005 is the only building section of the Friedrichstadt-Passagen (see 396, 397) to fill out an entire block. In this process, Oswald Mathias Ungers covers the entire repertoire of urban elements by means of his quadratic module. The square is just as suitable for street facades, roof systems, courtyards and arcades as it is for apartments, offices and stores. The critics feel this large form consisting solely of individual squares is monotonous, whilst the fans of this style admire the potential variety of the combinations. The spatial structure under the facade cover is due to the core structure and the six individual buildings grouped around it. The projecting and recessed parts, which result for the development of the complex, simulate the former plot structure on Friedrichstraße. In functional terms the block does not offer anything other than the standard "Berlin

creamcake", which has stores on the lower floors, offices in the centre and apartments on the upper storeys. The ingredients of this cake do not really want to be mixed up in the Quartier 205. The living section of all places that is let for high prices with a view of the Gendarmenmarkt is rather more reminiscent of a fig leaf of the use mix. The Berlin building director Stimmann described Quartier 205 as the biggest planning error of the post-war period not least due to the huge effect of the building upon the Gendarmenmarkt (no. 13).

Quartier 206 (396)
City Block 206
1996
Friedrichstraße 71–74
Pei, Cobb, Freed & Partners

Quartier 206 is the most expressive and possibly also the most striking structure of the Friedrichstadt-Passagen (see no. 395, 397). The view of the building at night is particularly striking, the appearance of well-lit facade members is reminiscent of the electrical illumination of the city buildings of the 1920s and 30s. Pei, Cobb, Freed & Partners neither spared any costs in terms of the opulence and the keenness to base their design on former structures for the building design facing the road nor facing the courtyard. Light, material and the experimentation with shapes revealed a sense of drama, very untypical for Berlin. In the atrium, a curved stairway winds its way up to the first gallery on the luxuriously decorated stone floor. The underground design also differs markedly from the adjacent quartiers of 205 and 207; this is because the three blocks are linked to the Friedrichstadt-Passagen at this level. The roofing of the atrium assumes a folding structure, which has a rather complicated but inelegant appearance, which is made of glass and steel rounds. The street facades of the block fold, buckle, turn in-

side out and protrude, here and there they suggest a tectonic structure here and there and undermine it again at another point. The property developer built a luxurious form of architecture befitting a city of fun and excitement by means of this block.

Quartier 207 (397)
City Block 207
1996
Französische Straße 23
Jean Nouvel

The rounded corner of the Galeries Lafayette introduces a new element into the morphological vocabulary of Friedrichstraße. However, what is more noticeable to the eye is the entirely glass facade of the building which is apparently transparent but ultimately provides the impression of being grey or black in colour. It causes confusion with insights and reflections and also indicates the internal organisation of the block, which is fitted with a series of large and small lighting cones throughout, in the form of screen-print graphics. The office areas and the residual section that is laid down as a percentage are accessed away from the department store. You are plunged into the galleries upon entering the buildings and you are only confronted with two light cones of different sizes, spanning across all the storeys, when you are in the heart of the building. They hold the viewer in their spell, as a luxurious optical work of art, which is enhanced by the glass and mirror surfaces, is developed there. Therefore, the actual function of

the department store takes a step backwards; the sales floors appear to be low and seem to be ousted by the illusionist space conception. This block that is located furthest to the north is linked underground with two more of the so-called Friedrichstadt-Passagen (see 395, 396).

Willy-Brandt-Haus (398)
Willy-Brandt House
1996
Wilhelmstraße 141
Helge Bofinger

The Social Democrats were the first party to officially open new headquarters in the capital city of the reunified state of Germany. They actually celebrate their leaders as managers: After the Bonn "Baracke", a shack where the board meetings virtually took place on the streets, had made the SPD more democratic in 1970s converting it from a workers' party into a people's party, now a commercial representative structure in Berlin has superseded the Rhine's landscape of open policy. The chairman now sits powerfully, enthroned at the top of the compact office block, whilst the board hall located behind it presents itself in a more restrained light. The same-shaped atrium, in which exclusive events will take place, does not drive a wedge into the management floor. All the panes of glass are tinted blue and are not overly transparent. Helge Bofinger aesthetically imitated a trade union building of IG Metall that was constructed by Erich Mendelsohn in 1931 at a location that is a mirror image in terms of its city ground plan (no. 207).

Bürohaus Halensee (399)
Halensee Office Block
1996
Kronprinzendamm 15
Hilde Léon, Konrad Wohlhage

The inherited burden of the city motorways had dispelled any development notions up to this point in time. It became reality upon the construction of this new office building. The biconvex building was hoisted above the motorway where it now appears to float along the motorway above the rising stone basement in an elegantly curved form. Office floors with an abundance of natural light that are protected from emissions and noise are situated behind the double glazed windows. The bold charm that the building on the side of the motorway exudes is no longer just a characteristic of the entrance front at Kronprinzendamm. The special feature is solely the symbiosis of traffic and the curved glass facade.

Hans Stimmann
* 1941 in Lübeck (400)

"Berlin's key concern is sustained urban development, which relates history and the future to one another."

Hans Stimmann, 1999

The man with the snow-white hair has a fiery temperament! Berlin discovered this after Hans Stimmann had become the city's building director in 1991. A few weeks later, he dismissed proposals for the new development of Potsdamer Platz (no. 417), which renowned property developers had pressed ahead with, as "childish", "unrealistic" or "stupid". It may be the case that the state tasks are being privatised everywhere: Stimmann insisted upon public leadership. He wanted streets, square and blocks of houses that were based upon historical ground plans, lines of buildings and eaves heights.

The billionaire investor Eduard Reuter who had visions of an American city with high-rise buildings and shopping immediately felt as if he had been whisked away into a provincial "hamlet". In this process, the tradition of the European city was already successfully revived by

Josef Paul Kleihue (no. 356) during the International Building Exhibition at the start of the 1980s. Stimmann simply updated the strategy and implemented it in a more universal manner. He was able to do this because everyone wanted to invest in Berlin as quickly as possible at that time. And also because the city of Berlin had provided Stimmann with something that no Berlin building director had had before him – the rank of a state secretary.

However his biography ensures that this, by his own account, "powerful man" does not have his head in the clouds. The worth of the city was never called into question in his home city of Lübeck where he was the building inspector from 1986 until 1991. After his apprenticeship as a mason, he then went on to complete his training as a design engineer. The American office in Frankfurt/Main, in which he was only allowed to design refineries in the mid 1960s dismissed him as soon as orders became absent.

He moved to the turbulent city of Berlin in the politically heated 1970s, in which there were a lot of lively debates, in order to complete his doctorate in urban planning at the Technical University of Berlin.

He was called to Berlin in 1991 and governed in a decisive manner as the "aesthetic arm of the senator". He patronised purist Prussian master builders who had to rein in their imagination and work on the craftsmanship details as well as solid stone. Ultimately his diktat of taste made the term "New Berlin" into a trademark that could be recognised throughout the world, which is not anachronistic in the age of globalisation, but rather of essential importance for the city.

Stimmann made the most constructive contribution towards Berlin's inner city life after he was transferred to the urban development administration in 1996. He presented so-called "master plans" for the city as well as the outskirts of the city. They present the city in a form that could not be any livelier: as an organism with a heart and extremities, which both contribute towards its particular characteristics. This is revolutionary for Berlin,

which had lived in parallel universes at the time when the wall existed. The reactions have been correspondingly intense, not least due to the colonialist manner in which Stimmann dealt with the eastern Berlin milieu. Yet this time, he entered into dialogue with them because he did not have any power bar the power of his arguments. In an unparalleled process of co-determination, Stimmann's "master plan" became a generally accepted city agenda. The New Centre force had found itself in 1999 at least in the minds of those responsible.

Black plan (developed areas) of the historic centre, 2010.

Since then Stimmann devoted himself to the realisation of the "master plan" (no. 491). It was, of course, not the case that he was bound to be successful with this project, even though he had a stronger hold over the Berlin construction industry at the start of the year 2000 than ever before. This is because the city no longer built itself on its own. It was dying quicker than it was expanding ensuring that a governor was not required but rather a fisher of men – something that Stimmann has never been.

He has nevertheless transformed his government authority from being an implementation to a service tool and is now more moderate in his approach – particularly in terms of questions of style. It thus remains to be seen what Stimman will achieve in his third period of office. Irrespective of this, he has already achieved more for the city than any other building official of the current age. hwh

Hotel Adlon (401)
Adlon Hotel
1997
Unter den Linden 75–77
Patzschke, Klotz & Partner

The new Hotel Adlon has attempted to establish a link, by means of the old address, with the tradition of the grand hotel with the same name, which was one of the best establishments in the world in its heyday. The investor consciously decided in favour of a form of architecture, which was based on the historical hotel construction, but without copying it. The new Adlon is now double the length of its predecessor due to the purchase of the neighbouring plot of land on Unter den Linden boulevard. The new building wallows in retrospection but is not a match for its predecessor of 1907. The building with its facade made of light plaster and sandstone elements has a uniquely timeless air with its dormer windows, balustrades, and ledges next to the clear, modern new buildings in the neighbourhood. The intended grandeur of the interior suffers due to the fact the height of the storeys has been reduced as a result of an additional storey being added. Its traditionalistic architectural imagery has ensured that the hotel is one of the most hotly disputed new construction projects in Berlin.

Büro- und Wohnhaus
am Askanischer Platz (402)
Office and Residential Building
at Askanischer Platz
1997
Askanischer Platz 4/Schöneberger Straße
HPP Hentrich-Petschnigg & Partner KG
Berlin

On the former forecourt of the Anhalter Bahnhof (no.95), the former glory of which is now only indicated by the ruinous remains of the entrance portal, the new corner building unmistakeably proclaims the sobriety of the new age. The building with clear contours observes the stipulated eaves height in Berlin of 72 feet. Its two-faced facade structure provided high French windows on the facade facing the Schöneberger Straße, whilst there is a horizontal structure of office floors on top of one another on the side facing the square. The terraces that have been covered with greenery of the two-storey maisonette apartments are located between the outstanding stairway towers.

Debis-Haus am Potsdamer Platz (403)
Debis Building on Potsdamer Platz
1997
Eichhornstraße 3
Renzo Piano Building Workshop

Debis constructed its group headquarters on a plot of land on Potsdamer Platz (no. 417) spanning almost seven hectares. The elongated block, where the eaves is 90 feet high, has provided the city with a new landmark at its southern end in the form of the 280-feet high tower which can be seen from a distance. This does not remain a lone fighter, or at least not in the new city district. It marks out the territory of the global player along with the high-rise buildings of Kollhoff and Piano/Kohlbecker. The large group building itself does indeed exclusively accom-

A wide-ranging 13,000 square feet stretch glass roof, which is hardly perceptible from the outside, unfolds. The visitors view the hippopotamuses at a level beneath the water level, which allows them to view of the entire artificial living space of the animals. Even if the house does not compare with the magnificent tradition of the colonial zoo ar-

modate the standard office buildings, but its exterior does not really adequately reflect this functional monostructure. Its facade that is panelled with terracotta is given a rhythmic form by being subdivided into sections that are 150 feet wide respectively and becomes increasingly transparent due to the changing proportions of stone and glass as it rises upwards. The core of the building is the 260 feet long hall which 44 feet wide, which is rounded off with a glass roof at the height of the ninth storey. A range of reflectors provide light. The dimensions of this giant atrium correspond to the nave of Nôtre Dame in Paris. As a semi-public space, this cathedral of commercial success is accessible from the central square of the Debis grounds located to the north. The building will thus also be accessed from the northern side. Lifts lead up to the higher storeys whilst space has been reserved for the group's own promotion of art in the southern section. In addition, a cafe, canteen and auto salon can be accessed from the atrium. Orbiting arcades run along the length of the frontage to the north and the west of the building.

Flusspferdhaus   (404)
Hippopotamus House
1997
Hardenbergplatz 8
Jörg Gribl

The Flusspferdhaus is located right in the middle of the Zoologischer Garten (see no. 120) − slightly sunk into the ground.

chitecture, it is still an example of modern animal husbandry in which the hippopotamuses are no longer put on display on a stage but can instead look for areas where they can retreat in their enclosure. Solar collectors on the roof ensure that the water has a constant temperature of 18 degrees.

Ludwig-Erhard-Haus   (405)
Ludwig-Erhard House
1997
Fasanenstraße 83−84
Nicholas Grimshaw & Partners

Conceived in the form of a fish, described as an armadillo by the press and PR people, the Ludwig-Erhard-Haus turned out be a chameleon instead in the heterogeneous environment of the western part of the city. No matter how much people had wished for a building that had been in line with its zoomorphous structure between the Kantstraße, Fasanenstraße and

Hardenbergstraße, a building was eventually created for the chamber of industry and commerce, the stock exchange and Berlin businessmen and women, which was tamed by 19th century eaves height regulations and street planning specifications. The building had also been propped up at the head and tail end. The connection to the old building of the chamber of industry and commerce (Franz Heinrich Sobotka, Gustav Müller, 1954/55, no. 282) was hardly solved, and the public pergola facing towards Kantstraße was not realised. Set against this, the atriums of the building are impressive, which, covered in cut single glazing, unfold beneath the parabolic arches. More than 155 feet of room height unfold there whereby the suspending brackets upon which the storey ceilings are based form the element that characterises the rooms. The resplendent form consisting of its "structure, room and skin", which was intended for the building can be best recognised at its rear. There, you will indeed find an armadillo resting on gigantic metal paws.

Zentrum Hellersdorf (406)
Hellersdorf Centre
1997
Alice-Salomon-Platz, Stendaler Straße,
Hellersdorfer Straße
Andreas Brandt, Wolfgang Böttcher

The Plaza Mayor in the Spanish city of Salamanca served as a model example of the rectangular city square, which has an edge length of 400 feet. The core of the urban development design of the architects Brandt and Böttcher is flanked by a homogenous perimeter development, which for its part adapts Mediterranean square typologies. A university of applied science, a multiplex cinema as well as a town hall provide the quarter with its city function, which demands the large gesture of this urban development complex. Due to the fact that Hellersdorf still resembled a large building site during the phase of Germany's reunification and did not have any subsequent institutions bar the residential buildings, the last major housing estate of the GDR was provided with a market economy oriented city centre, which was not least reflected by the private property developers.

Invalidenpark (407)
Invaliden Park
1997
Scharnhorststraße, Invalidenstraße,
Schwarzer Weg
Christophe Girot

GARDEN In the "new city of Berlin", the structuring of open spaces was much more modest than the large numbers of buildings constructed to fill gaps, of which one is the Invalidenpark, now lined with ministries. In the 18th century, the invalids who lived here worked on the plot of land, before it was converted into a park in 1843 that was designed by Peter Joseph Lenné. The ruins of the Gnadenkirche that was devastated in the Second World War, and was later a border area, stood there until 1967. The rousing monument of the current park area is a narrow, granite ramp sculpture that people can walk on, which rises up out of a water basin. Interpreted by Girot as "showing the way into the future", the "sinking" piece of wall should be viewed

as a metaphor of reunification since it was officially inaugurated on 3rd October 1997. Strips of granite and grass are weaved into one another in the controversial design, which can hardly decide whether it should be a park or a monument. The Invalidenpark increasingly turns to stone facing the southern side whilst it increasingly becomes a green landscape with older trees towards the north. Therefore the park with the characteristics of a monument only has recreational value in the latter section.

Gemäldegalerie (408)
Painting Gallery
1997
Matthäikirchplatz 7
Christoph Sattler, Heinz Hilmer,
Thomas Albrecht

The plans for a new painting gallery at the Kulturforum had already been concluded when the wall fell. In an unparalleled act, the architect who had built the severely criticised neighbouring museums from the 1980s had previously been stripped of the right to carry out further planning work (see no. 311). The Stiftung Preußischer Kulturbesitz, the Prussian cultural heritage foundation, decided to stick with the planned new building at the Kulturforum although the unification of the city provided the option of now merging the long separated collections of paintings from East and West Berlin on the Museumsinsel (no. 50). The basement was converted into a study gallery because it had to accommodate more paintings than had originally been planned. The elongated, rectangular structure with a modern rusticated basement and terracotta facades has again adopted the eaves height and the build-

ing line of the historical buildings. In this process, the Villa Parey was integrated within the Sigismundstraße whilst the Villa Gontard was integrated with the Chief Management building of the state museums in the Stauffenbergstraße. The visitor enters a central pillared hall via a rotunda as a construction element connecting it to the buildings of the Kulturforum that were built earlier. The surrounding exhibition rooms are based on classical museums such as the Alte Pinakothek in Munich with their dark parquet floors, the colourful wall covering and the daylight ceilings.

Kontorhaus Mitte (409)
Kontorhaus Mitte
1997
Friedrichstraße 180–190,
Kronenstraße 60–65, Mohrenstraße 13–16
Josef Paul Kleihues, Klaus Theo Brenner,
Vittorio Magnago Lampugnani,
Marlene Dörrie, Walter Stepp

The ideally-situated block plot of land was divided up by Josef Paul Kleihues (no. 356) based on the module principle and then built with very sober new buildings, which pay homage to the beautiful simplicity of the rectangle, by him and four fellow architects. In this process virtually everything had been stipulated by "Master Kleihues", the number of storeys as well as the eaves height, the facade design and the way it was opened up. At the southern perimeter edge of Kronenstraße/Friedrich Straße Theo Brenner constructed a cuboid with a facade made of greyish green dolomite. Water Stepp's corner house at the Mohrenstraße is panelled with Red African granite, whilst the building made by Vittorio Lampugnani

and Marlene Dörrie has a facade made of bluish grey sandstone. However, the central element is Kleihues' office block in Friedrichstraße, which makes clear allusions to its creator by means of its notorious "Ship shape" optics – porthole windows in the entrance area and a front projection design in the shape of a ship's bow. The visitor is greeted by a spacious atrium with a glass roof in the block interior, which was designed by the architect himself.

Lindencorso (410)
Lindencorso Building
1997
Untern den Linden 21
Christoph Mäckler

The most powerful element of the building that reoccupies the corner block of Unter den Linden/Friedrichstraße boulevards, is the facade. The limestone in the lower three storeys is solid and built with self-supporting facing brick walls, the corner and edge stones are also solid special items. As is now customary, the natural stone facade is suspended in front of it in the upper storeys. All the stones are channelled horizontally and jointly pro-

duce a sculpture surface appearance together with the vertical joints. The building has the appearance of a bastion in accordance with all the rules of critical reconstruction and the appearance of depth of the external wall is further enhanced in the arcade area due to the fact that the sandstone coloured pillars stand out from the darkly designed entrance shop window zones. In the interior Mäckler has adopted a rather conventional approach with the office building and in some areas of the residential building. The ground floor zone is now used by a domestic car manufacturer as a showroom for the luxury brands. The building's special feature is its insistence upon "genuine" stone architecture. Up to now, it has the only contemporary solid facade on Friedrichstraße.

Max-Schmeling-Halle (411)
Max-Schmeling Hall
1997
Am Falkplatz 1
Jörg Joppien, Anett-Maud Joppien,
Albert Dietz

The Max-Schmeling Halle is the most -
positive upshot of Berlin's ultimately fu-

tile bid for the 2000 Olympic Games. The core idea of the young Frankfurt-based architects, who won an international competition in 1992, was a "green bridge" between the Jahn-Sportpark in the east and the former border sector in the west, which was transformed into a Mauerpark (no. 390) under the directorship of the garden designer Gustav Lange. Following on from this, a wall covered in grass was built, which continues the backfilling of the existing stadium and ends as a straight glass wall at Falkplatz. By looking through it, you can see both embankments in which three triple sports fields as well as the adjoining areas are located. The centre of the hill ranges above a fishbelly made of steel, which covers the largest multipurpose hall in Berlin which has up to 10,000 seats.

Verwaltungsgebäude KPMG (412)
KPMG Administration Building
1997
Taubenstraße 45
Christoph Mäckler

The administration building was built on a plot of land that was delimited by firewalls on three sides. The rear offices are accommodated in two narrow side wings

whilst the inner courtyard was sealed with a glass roof. The decoratively designed floor made of three different natural stones and the design of the rear firewall with open stairways are extraordinary. The facade also demonstrates a mixture of materials and designs that is typical of Mäckler's work. Whilst the major portion of the street facade creates a very compact impression due to a multilayered ashlar plaster the construction at the main entrance opens up in an ex-

pressive gesture with explicitly contemporary materials such as exposed concrete and metal. The main ledge with the window roofing that protrudes powerfully adopts a motif of the "Lindencorso", which Mäckler previously constructed along Unter den Linden (no. 410).

Niedrigenergiehaus Marzahn (413)
Marzahn Low Energy House
1997
Flämingstraße, Wittenberger Straße
Assmann, Salomon und Scheidt

The building, which seems to be a prototype, still stands as an "alien" in the much-maligned Marzahn district of prefabricated-slab buildings between the identical rows of apartment buildings from the GDR era. Its unconventional form is the result of the development of an apartment building where the power consumption levels do not exceed 40-kilowatt hours per square metre in the year. The building plate with its sloping sides curves convexly in a southerly direction. The northern facade has an almost dismissive appearance with its heat insulating uniformity, which is only interrupted by narrow window slits. The southern side reveals a horizontal structure facing towards the living spaces thanks to the continuous rows of balconies with transparent side rails in front of the warm glass fronts. The generous use of glass makes sure the house takes on a crystalline, dazzling appearance between the dominant grey of the WBS-70 standard panels. However, it will take some years before it can be established whether the lower power consumption levels will amortise the increased construction costs.

Grund- und Gesamtschule
Hohenschönhausen (414)
Hohenschönhausen Primary
and Secondary School
1997
Prendener Straße 29
Max Dudler, Betti Plog, Jörn Pötting

At a first, quick glace the new school building, constructed in the 1990s is more liable to conjure up images of school drills than of the reform projects of the century. Whilst the building is large and unambiguous, the gesture of this building at the cutting edge of the high-rise suburbia and the village like suburbs is equally unchildlike. A green, shimmering row of houses consisting of artificial stone runs some 1,000 feet along Prendener Straße in Hohenschönhausen. The intention of the planners in this process was to bring order to a disparate area of urban development and to still respect two existing development models at the same time. The long, slightly curved building tract corresponds to the scales of the major housing estate made of prefabricated slabs. The "stone houses2 which slide away towards the open countryside are reminiscent of the rural area of Wartenberg. All the classrooms have been built facing away from the roads and sound-insulated despite the giant shop window that was recessed within the long complex and which should signal openness. Max Dudler also

feels that this school building has a "wealth of asceticism" due to the very fact that the structure of the building does not impose any form of conduct upon the pupils but has the effect of stimulating their imagination.

Wohnhaus im Grunewald (415)
Apartment House in the Grunewald
1997
David Chipperfield

The three-storey mansion disconcerts the viewers due to its uniform facade facing the road. This dismissive gesture is not greatly diminished by the two large openings in the wall and the row of windows on the first floor that runs around the corner. The angular forms are vaguely reminiscent of the mansion architecture of classical modernism whereby the hulking form of the building's irregular brick panelling forms a peculiar contrast to the technical character of the surfaces made of glass and steel. The building is made up of cubes. They are set in front of a courtyard which opens up to the south facing the garden and which is also accessible via a stairway on the building's eastern wing. Their form and size is based on the intended respective uses of the interior rooms.

ARD-Hauptstadtstudio (416)
ARD's Capital City Studio
1998
Reichstagsufer 7-8
Ortner & Ortner

The ARD-Haupstadtstudio has positioned itself in a location where it cannot be overlooked in the centre of the government district. On a plot of land, which formerly belonged to the Humboldt university that is located in the vicinity, the architects constructed an independent building, which does not only accentuate the city area by means of its red facade, on which the broadcaster's logo is emblazoned, but also takes on a different type of public appeal due to its premises that are open to the public. The building is made accessible by an extensive foyer on the Wilhelmstraße and runs along the river Spree, with a sweeping form that reflects the bend of the riverbank. The side wings frame a glazed plaza that is located on the side of the river, which attracts employees and flaneurs with its restaurant and the beautiful view. The facade at the Wilhelmstraße closes around a room height glass opening in the centre, whilst the building's facade facing the river is accentuated by its reserved symmetry. The offset facade openings of the basement, the main storeys and the two top floors reinforce the calm impression – with the exception of the long corner window on the fourth storey, which makes it possible to catch a glimpse of the notorious news supplier, the Reichstag.

Potsdamer Platz: City Model of the Future? (417)

Potsdamer Platz is something like an urban development fulcrum between the east and the west. For decades, the Berlin wall (no. 301) ran straight across the square, where the first set of traffic lights in Europe was installed in the 1920s. The most recent history of the square, which has become a synonym of the "new city of Berlin", already started in the 1980s when plans were discussed for the "central area" under the urban development senator at that time Volker Hassemer. The basic idea at that time was to breathe new life into this peripheral inner city area, which then led to the Daimler-Benz automotive group purchasing a plot of land, running from the Landwehrkanal to the wall zone, immediately prior to the fall of the wall. The wall fell whilst the contractual negotiations were still progressing, and a peripheral city location became a top site in the centre of a European city with a population of several million people virtually overnight.

A mere six months after the reunification of Germany, the senate launched an urban development competition, which the Munich-based architects Heinz Hilmer and Christoph Sattler won in the autumn on 1991. The master plan envisaged once again providing the former wasteland with the appearance of a European metropolis. In specific terms, this meant that the basic urban development structure would adopt the block model of the Berlin city centre and was expected to emphasise the variety of uses of the city that is typical of Berlin by means of mixing residential, working, culture and shopping buildings.

The supposed recourse to an historical model of the city was not without its critics. Other architects who took part in the competition dreamt of the invention of a new type of cityscape that had never existed before or the implantation of an American city in the heart of Berlin. A passionate dispute between the architects involved ensued following this, which attracted the attention of the world's media. This is because the points were supposed to be set for Berlin's future development at Potsdamer Platz.

Renzo Piano (Genoa / Paris) and Helmut Jahn (Chicago) ideas for the specification of the master plan won through, who were commissioned by the large investors Daimler-Benz (now called: DaimlerChrysler) and SONY. Whilst Piano enlisted the services of several other architects and provided a certain level of architectural diversity on the part of the 19 buildings in total (see no. 403, 465, 472) Jahn provided a design forming "a united and integrated whole". Hence the two largest projects to the west of Potsdamer Platz could not be any more different. SONY presented a homogeneous glass-steel form of architecture, which permitted a Plaza to be constructed in its centre. DaimlerChrysler created a traditional European cityscape made of different individual buildings and narrow streets. The fact the area was constructed at the end of the 20th century despite having a city typology that had been developed in the 19th century, cannot be overlooked: An underground car park with direct access to the Tiergarten tunnel pays homage to the product, which provided the proceeds to make all this possible – the car.

An equally significant project has been built as the final module around Potsdamer Platz. The Lenné-Dreieck by the investor Beisheim.   meu

The new Potsdamer Platz with the Kollhoff high rise, Jahn Tower and Beisheim Center (l. to r.).

Birds eye view of the area around Potsdamer Platz

Bahnhof Alexanderplatz (Umbau) (418)
Alexanderplatz Station (conversion)
1998
between Dircksenstraße, Rathausstraße, Gontardstraße and Karl-Liebknecht-Straße
Rebecca Chestnut and Robert Niess

This station presently best demonstrates which urbane forces were unleashed by the double figure billion amounts, which the Deutsche Bahn spent in the 1990s. Hans-Joachim May and Günter Andrich converted the temple of transportation, which Johann Eduard Jacobstahl had built in 1882 into a vantage point with a crystalline platform hall on a basement resembling a barrier in 1964. In 1994, a project was commenced which was supposed to make the station more efficient than ever before in terms of both the transportation technology and the commercial side of matters. Chestnus/Niess cleaned up the old viaduct and supplemented it with a genuine basement as well as an attached facade that resembles a showcase. It exhibits the Fin-de-Siècle-Bijouterie and also the subsequent constructive acts of strength. The railway arches were opened for the first time for 50 new shops, which were expected to re-finance the investment. An open transit area was created in which old and new, passengers, flaneurs and consumers merge so seamlessly with one another and resembled the way in which Alfred Döblin once described Alexanderplatz in Berlin. In the near future the architects will set about designing the underground station.

Bezirksamt Mitte (419)
Mitte District Administration Centre
1998
Karl-Marx-Allee 31 at Schillingstraße
Johannis Heinrich in Bassenge, Puhan-Schulz, Heinrich, Schreiber

Captivating in terms of form, but dull in terms of functionality. By dint of this schizophrenic nature, the Bezirksamit Mitte is in fact very representative of Berlin following German reunification. It demonstrates in the same way as the three subsequent city hall projects, which the city council addressed since 1990, that the property developer by the name of 'democracy' did not act so eloquently as it did at a national level. Built as a seat of parliament from 1996 onwards, it was rendered virtually useless once again due to the merger of the district. It is all the more interesting that the design was also based on the styles used in the early 1960s. The Bezirksamt replaced the Hotel Berolina. But its cubic shape was retained to protect the collection of buildings. The storey ceilings do, of course, protrude between the facade tiles, which are for their part blue, which ensures the new skeleton structure has a

much more plastic appearance than Josef Kaiser's panelled complex. In addition, it is now really possible to walk through the building, which ensures that the idea behind the location has been accomplished. The metropolitan thoroughfare in the form of Karl-Marx-Allee (no. 289) and Schillingstraße which is a red light boulevard now really do cross one another.

Bundespräsidialamt   **(420)**
Office of the President of the Federal Republic of Germany
1998
Schloss Bellevue, Spreeweg 1
Martin Gruber, Helmut Kleine-Kraneburg

Pedestrians often only become aware of the elliptical diamond solitaire of the Bundespräsidialamt at a second glance because it so well concealed next to the Schloss Bellevue and at the same is embedded within the trees of the Tiergarten. The Bundespräsidialamit was the Federal Republic of Germany's first constitutional body to transfer its official residence from Bonn to Berlin back in 1994. The three-winged, classical palace complex (M.P.Boumann, 1785-90) consequently required an additional administrative building. The unconventional ellipse, where the external skin is completely covered with black glowing granite, is clearly based on the palace and its architectural scale in terms of its propor-

tions. The hermetic exterior of the building befits its lofty position as the office of the President of the Federal Republic of Germany. 124 offices that face towards the Tiergarten and the hall that is roofed over with glass have all been designed in white and are flooded with light. The dictate of the ellipse determines the entire room configuration and thus also stands for elegance and noblesse. The rejection of this building in urban development terms is perhaps the only possible stance at its location immediately next to a palace and within a park.

Boarding-House Behrenstraße   **(421)**
Behrenstraße Boarding House
1998
Rosmarinstraße, Behrenstraße
Petra and Paul Kahlfeldt

The nine-storey 100-feet high residential building belongs to the Rosmarin-Karree (no. 434) and has been jointly integrated within the depth of the block by the planners. Its facade is covered with bright coquina stone panels, which for their part ensure that the steely block construction of the centrally arranged winter gardens stand out. In this way the emphasis upon the vertical lines assumes a character resembling a relief. The 70 apartments, some of which are maisonette apartments, are a dutiful concession by the property developers of the Rosmarin-

Karree to the standard local 20 per cent residential accommodation quota that is stipulated for new buildings in Friedrichstraße.

Neuer Hackescher Markt (422)
New Hackescher Market
1998
Hackescher Markt
Bellmann & Böhm

This collection of buildings ranks amongst the most successful examples of

urban renewal in the 1990s. It was originally supposed to be called "Neue Hackesche Höfe" because it was based on the structure of the "Hackesche Höfe" (no.144) opposite that were built some one hundred years previously – but this name was forbidden due to the risk that people might mistake it for the original. The young architect duo Bellmann & Böhm who gained their first work experience in the latter phase of the GDR's - existence and built the "Quartier Schützenstraße" (no. 433) with Aldo Rossi, designed a collection of twelve individual houses, which are grouped around the quiet inner courtyards. In this way the historical perimeter block form of development will be restored at the same time. The mixed use of restaurants and bars, shops, offices and apartments ensure that there is a lively atmosphere at the popular Hackescher Markt. The traditional approach loses something due to the exaggerated colourfulness and the lack of consistency in terms of the details.

Kronenpalais (423)
Crown Palace
1998
Kronenstraße 10
Patzschke, Klotz & Partner

It is rare that an investor constructs a building that has room heights like those found in representative old buildings. Whilst normal new buildings accommodate six to seven storeys up to the eaves the "Kronenpalais" only has five storeys. In this way, it adopts the room heights of the neighbouring old building that is under a preservation order, with which it is not only connected internally, but with which it also forms a joint U-shaped inner courtyard. The facade that has been finely structured with ledges and pilasters adopts the typology of stores dating from the start of the 20th century. Three main storeys follow on top of round arches, which join together the lower storeys. The first attic is concealed by a balustrade, the second one is hidden underneath a copper ceiling with gable windows. The "Kronenpalais" is the most convincing building of the architects' of-

fice that had already become well known due to its external design of the Adlon Hotel (no. 401).

Grand Hyatt Berlin (424)
Hotel Grand Hyatt Berlin
1998
Marlene-Dietrich-Platz 2
José Rafael Moneo (architecture),
9D Design (interior design)

The five-star hotel with 345 rooms has a perforated facade made of red sandstone as well as white windows. Therefore, the first Grand Hyatt hotel in Europe is the most inconspicuous building of the DaimlerChrysler complex (no. 417). It is actually no wonder as it has been designed by Rafael Moneo, the sole architect. He designed it from the interior to the exterior in this case. His slightly deconstructed functionalism becomes most apparent on the roof. The swimming pool, sauna and the gym are accommodated in crystalline structures there, which stand as freely as you would expect

of a leisure area. The lobbies, lounges, restaurants, conference and ballrooms become wedged together to form the same "type of action". In none of the other many hotels, constructed in Germany since reunification, have the form and contents been implemented in a manner that is as consistent as the manner in which they have been constructed here.

DG Bank (425)
DG Bank
1998
Pariser Platz 3
Frank O. Gehry

Frank O. Gehry's only building could hardly have been located in a more prominent position. The Californian architect, who is famous for his spectacular designs, has built an office block for the DG Bank at Pariser Platz, one of the city's top addresses. However, the building complies with the strict building regulations that apply around the Brandenburg Gate in an almost disciplined manner in terms of the standard eaves height of the location and its regular perforated facade. But only at first sight. The glass surfaces, which are chamfered in some cases, of the almost rectangular rows of windows that are set deeper and the axes that have a bulky appearance may meet the facade design specifications, but imbue the building with the character of an Agent Provocateur. The architects allows this almost unbearable tension to be released in the building's interior. Surrounded by the offices that are distributed between four subterranean floors an atrium spreads itself out there, which gives the

appearance of being an amphibian between the strictly and soberly designed floors, by means of the unusually, expressively distorted roof constructions above the integrated auditorium. A genuine Gehry building without any doubt. The southern building section that is raised to a level of ten storeys with apartments behind a staggered facade on the plot of land that is 138 feet wide and 335 feet long is adjacent to Behrenstraße and allows the onlooker to forget the direct links of the building to the confusing front facade.

Dresdner Bank (426)
Dresdner Bank
1998
Pariser Platz 6
von Gerkan, Marg und Partner

The "design constitution" which should regulate the walls of the square of the inner city "salon" – Pariser Platz, provoked one of the most hotly disputed discussions relating to the reconstruction of the city. The modules of the Dresdner Bank, Liebermann and Sommer houses (Kleihues) as well as the Palais am Pariser Platz (Winking) are considered to be the most rigid results of this debate. The Dresdner Bank faces the square with a stone shadow mask, with a 49 percent proportion of windows in accordance with the constitution. The sandstone facade and the granite basement create the appearance of being a copy of previous works. However, this facade manages to break out of this strict corset by means of independent solar protection elements.

The actual bank building opens up behind the square's wall: The circular hall in steel and glass, roofed over with a lightweight design, is reminiscent of an amphitheatre. Meinhard von Gerkan solved the conflict resulting due to the rectangular cut of the plot of land the circular hall by placing the stairways within the spandrels. The ascent within the hall is made via a spiral that rises on its own within the rotunda. The fact that the building's exterior had to be held in check to accommodate the constitution and the spirit of consensus, which had been achieved with difficulty at times, was compensated for by the investment in careful details in the building's interior.

Estradenhaus (427)
Estraden House
1998
Choriner Straße 56
Wolfram Popp and Gregor Siber

The residential building with ten apartments, two offices and a shop on the ground floor does not differ greatly from the standard municipal blocks of apartments on the Prenzlauer Berg. It is also not exceptional that there are two apartments per floor of differing sizes of 860 or 1,160 square feet in the seven-storey building. It only stands out in terms of its

exterior by means of its balcony railings that appear to be transparent made of fine-meshed steel fabric and horizontal rows of windows. The apartments themselves have a "loft-type" open ground plan without room partition walls. An additional special feature is the mobile collapsible wall that can be pulled out throughout the entire length of the apartment, and stands at a slight angle in the rooms, which can be pushed together like a curtain to a compact length of 6.5 feet. It conceals or reveals the open kitchen and bathroom areas. The majority of the residents opt not to use the additional turning/sliding wall variants to divide up rooms that were also developed by the architect. The building was given its name due to the Estrade, a height projection along the window facades of 1.2 feet and almost 6.5 feet in depth at the ceiling and the floors.

Jüdisches Museum (428)
Jewish Museum
1998
Lindenstraße 13
Daniel Libeskind

The building of the Jewish Museum (extension of the Berlin Museum, Ph. Ger-

lach, 1735, no. 24) strikes into the city like a bolt of lightning. On the one hand, it has its special formal position, and on the other hand, it formulates the fault line of Jewish history. Libeskind created a very intellectually and structurally challenging work of architecture by means of the large-scale form of a Star of David that has been folded upwards. This demanding concept was also continued with in terms of the implementation details and in the process also made impossible constructions possible, such as wall pieces that "float" freely in glass surfaces. The construction follows an abstract network of reference points of Jewish culture and history in Berlin. Diffraction and confusion are stylistic tools. So-called "voids", areas that people cannot go through, were an option to implement the unspeakable for Libeskind – the destruction of Jewish life. However, the building was also subjected to some modifications of its basic design (competition 1989). It was thus impossible to implement the sloped position of the external walls. However, the building's forceful impact remains unaffected by this. Even when empty, i.e. without the actual exhibition, visitors were attracted to the building in their droves and it thus exhibited itself.

Krematorium Baumschulenweg (429)
Baumschulenweg Crematorium
1998
Kiefholzstraße 221
Axel Schultes, Charlotte Frank

The unconventional new building was constructed in the middle of the cemetery site and embodies an intriguing sense of interplay between its presence and a due level of reservation. The simplicity of the bare longitudinal facades made of exposed concrete is dispensed with to its front side by means of its generous openings and glass surfaces leading to the atriums and the ceremonial halls. The condolence hall that extends throughout three storeys of the building is located in the core of the cube. At the same time it is the most prominent room of the complex. "Distancing rooms" are extracted from this huge hall by means of 29 exposed concrete columns, in which individual groups of mourners are separated from one another, but can still remain united in their mourning. Light descends into the room from above through glass-covered openings of the roof construction. A large and two small ceremonial halls are located to the side of the atriums, which can be accessed from both the main hall and also from the atrium.

Wohn- und Verwaltungsbau
Mehrower Allee (430)
Residential and Administrative Building on Mehrower Allee
1998
Mehrower Allee 53 A
Walter von Lom & Partner

Council housing coupled with an administrative building of the WBG Marzahn, provides an unusual sensation of space within the area that used to be the largest new housing development area in Germany. The Marzahn major housing estate was created between 1977 and 1987 (see no. 374). It stood for an East German innovation in the field of housing construction, however, in this case the standardised panels were grouped together to form city figures covering large areas. The ratio of open spaces vis-à-vis the structures ultimately continued to be "inhumanely" overstretched in this process. More recently improvements in the living environments, refurbishment programmes and, as in this case, the closure of gaps and supplementary buildings, have been used to add other urban spatial

qualities to the former "elite district2. Walter von Lom designed a band shaped development to subsequently consolidate the estate. The administrative building pulls the living cubes together with it like a locomotive. Steel pergolas, shaped as covered walks, connected the individual structures. The ground floor zones are reserved for small trades. The courtyard, lane and the square form new configurations, which have to contend with the surrounding multi-storey buildings. The use of brick for the facade is also as alien as the basic shape of the collection of buildings; however, in overall terms the attempt to integrate two city models has been successful.

Oberstufenzentrum für
Sozialversicherungen (431)
Centre for Advanced Social Security Studies
1998
Nalepastr. 201–209, Helmholtzstr. 37
Léon, Wohlhage, Wernik

The new building in the Schöneweide district, which was formerly one of the largest industrial areas in Berlin, supplements the existing vocational college built in 1912 that is under a preservation order. Its rugged location in urban development terms ensured that the new building would have to be able to assert itself. The smoothly plastered brick of the building with a sports hall located on the second and third floor, a cafeteria, school administration rooms and the teachers' rooms was positioned on the plot of land in such a way that another street corner was created once again. The simply designed building is connected with the classrooms of the old building via a glass wing. The entire school complex is made accessible from the entrance that is divided into three sections and is deeply recessed. And the school building has also succeeded in setting a new trend in other respects. The orange red bricks of the old building enter into an almost cheerful union with the pale smoothly plastered facade of the younger building that has been varnished in a pale orange colour.

Photonikzentrum
Berlin-Adlershof (432)
Berlin-Adlershof Photonics centre
1998
Carl-Scheele-Straße 16
Sauerbruch, Hutton

Although the two structures of the Innovationszentrum für Optik, Optoelektronik and Lasertechnik, the innovation centre for optics, optoelectronics and laser technology, may appear to be very amoebic and the scope for new designs was ex-

ploited to the full, the buildings have still actually been created in line with the building's use requirements. In the case of this research institution, it was important to keep the development expenditure to a minimum whilst exploiting the available area to the maximum extent by means of large office spaces that can be darkened. The building formations (they reveal themselves as "outstanding colourful characters" within the academic site of Adlershof) were additionally built whilst taking account of the trees. In the three-storey laboratory and office wing the internal structure of the building is arranged around a central axis made of "use strips" of a width of 23 feet and a

depth of 23 to 66 feet. The swaying facade area consists of a double glass skin. The architects selected a simple steel construction with glass external walls for the smaller, single storey hall building, which is used for major experiments. The colouring of both structures is actually their most attractive feature. Alternating colour spectrums were used for the mounting of the concrete parts. The buildings really start to shimmer when the colourful Venetian blinds are lowered as the sun shines.

Quartier Schützenstraße (433)
Schützenstraße Quarter
1998
Schützenstraße, Markgrafenstraße,
Zimmerstraße, Charlottenstraße
Aldo Rossi, Götz Bellmann & Walter Böhm

You can no longer tell that there used to be wasteland right up to the 1990s at the point where the colourful square building now stands. At first sight, the collec-

tion of buildings conceals the fact that it was built as "a united and integrated whole". This historical parcelling out of the block's interior, which was supposed to serve as a basic prototype for the new plans, is also revealed in the external design. The distinct facade design that excels with bright colours skilfully represents the small-scale nature and the juxtaposition of the historical and functional mix, albeit commercial and office rooms, a residential building as well as a hotel, are concealed behind it in the main. The collage of six different, historicizing facade designs characterises the appearance of the perimeter blocks: The cute copy of the courtyard facade of the Palazzo Farnese in Rome is the most striking feature of the Schützenstraße. The roof design is intentionally reminiscent of the Paris Mansard roofs. The inner courtyards, which are entirely on a par with the interior in terms of their wealth of details and their design, are also well worth seeing.

Rosmarin Karree   **(434)**
Rosmarin Square
1998
Friedrichstraße 83
Jürgen Böge, Ingeborg Lindner-Böge

The Rosmarin Karre forms one of the last modules in the reconstruction of Friedrichstraße. In this case, it combines the differing architectural approaches – the glass facade of the Quartier 207 (no. 397) in the south suggests transparency set against the solid stone facade of the Lindencorso (no 410) in the north – to form its own expressive style. The new building is indeed based on the historical

block structure but waives the complete development of the plot of land at Rosmarinstraße and instead adopts the line of the existing older buildings that is 13 feet narrower of the former Commerz bank at the corners facing the Charlottenstraße. The apartments on the roofs were designed by the architects Petra and Paul Kahlfeldt, who were also responsible for the neighbouring Boarding-House (no. 421).

Innovationszentrum für
Umwelttechnologie (UTZ)   **(435)**
Innovation Centre for
Environmental Technology
1998
Volmerstraße 9
Eisele+Fritz, Bott, Hilka, Begemann

In the science campus of Adlershof (see no. 432) that is still heterogeneous and characterised by monuments and barracks in equal measure the extension of the UTZ that is 660 feet in length seems to be out of scale. In terms of its ground plan, the building has been planned in a meandering shape with two four-storey wings. The architects still succeeded in shaping the facade sections in very different ways despite the longitudinal extension. Protruding and recessed sections interrupt its monumental style. The wooden panels have a pleasant appearance as the external claddings, the positioning of the columns provides the street facade with depth and a special sun screening system consisting of vertically arranged solar protection slats is the structuring element on the courtyard facade. The basement and the roof zone are continuously linked in their design and

hold the building together. An innovation centre for environmental technology must also stand out itself by saving energy. In this sense, five pillars help to ensure that the building is environmentally friendly: building air conditioning via the cavity ceiling, a sun screening system to prevent the facades getting too hot, optimised daylight incidence, the photovoltaic facade of the entrance hall and the rainwater management system.

Auswärtiges Amt (Erweiterung) (436)
German Ministery of Foreign Affairs
(Extension)
1999
Werderscher Markt 1
Thomas Müller, Ivan Reimann

A series of variants that were discussed for the accommodation of the Auswärtiges Amt led to a decision being made in favour of the former Reichsbank, or rather the former East German parliament building at the Werderscher Markt

(no.455). The existing building was adapted by Kollhoff and Timmermann, whilst a new building was added to it by Müller and Reimann. This extension has to fulfil two main functions in urban development terms. It must cover up the front facade of the old building without losing the perceived link, and it must redefine the urbane space around the Werderscher Markt. The cube of the new building, which is continued with throughout the width of the old building, is broken down by means of three bulky recesses. Two courtyards and a city loggia provide an insight into the functional, but high quality, administrative building. The reception courtyard opposite the old building serves as the main entrance; it was issued with an elegant column design in correspondence with the existing building. This newly created external area serves as an access point for official visitors. In functional terms the new building accommodates dual rows of offices and a comprehensive library with a reading room. The fact that the suggested structural transparency is not just for the sake of appearances is proved by a visitors' centre that is open to the public.

Grundschule und Kindertagesstätte
Curtiusstraße   (437)
Primary School and Day-Care Centre
at Curtiusstraße
1999
Curtiusstraße 39-41
Andrew Alberts, Tim Heide,
Peter Sassenroth

Years, or as in this case, even a decade can lie between the decision of the tender and the completion of a building. The decision in favour of the tender for the unusual school and nursery school complex was made back in the period of the red-green coalition, which had set itself the objective of achieving the "ecological reconstruction of the city" by which it also meant the conservation of small, ecologically important green spaces. Therefore, on the school plot of land, a comprehensive room allocation plan of almost 100,000 square feet was to be accommodated on the one hand, and on the other hand, the existing trees on the rear section of the plot of land were to be preserved. The playground and the external sports area were transferred to the enormous roof platform so the trees could be saved. This extends across the whole length of the building of 584 feet. The roof structure rests on V-shaped columns and is secured in place by lattice steel side parapets. Beneath it, there is a united, three-storey building complex parallel to the road, which is rhythmically separated in spatial terms by means of building sections that swing outwards, and it is interrupted by a gymnasium.

GSW-Hauptverwaltung (438)
GSW Headquarters
1999
Kochstraße 22
Sauerbruch, Hutton

The block structure of Friedrichstadt, which was created in the Baroque period, was extended in the 'Gründerzeit', and

reconstructed in the present, has been provided with a dazzling skyscraper in the form the GSW building. The height of the building and its colours obviously break the rules of the immediate neighbourhood, but the high-rise building also alludes to the nearby towers of the Axel-Springer publishing house and the giant buildings on Leipziger Straße. During the age when the wall still stood, the two latter buildings had been built as ideological fence posts on either side of the border. In 1961, the architects Paul Schwebes and Hans Schoszberger built a high-rise building here in the former press district, which the GSW used. The new building is based on it as an elegantly curved plate, makes use of old and new spout heights and precisely copies the building lines despite all its dynamic features. The architects developed a ventilated skin for the slim disk structure, the solar protection elements of which provide it with changing appearances, which are visible from a distance, ranging from soft pink to Bordeaux. The uniform Friedrichstadt road copes easily with this eccentric building colouring, but if such buildings became the rule then they would probably lose a lot of their impact.

Bundesministerium für Verkehr, Bau und Wohnungswesen (ehem. Geologische Landesanstalt) (439)
Federal Ministry of Transport, Building and Housing (former Geological Research Institution)
1999
Invalidenstraße 44
Max Dudler (extension building)

The Federal Ministry of Transport forms part of an impressive complex with historical allusions in the Berlin city centre. August Tied constructed the Museum für Naturkunde, the natural history museum, that was completed in 1889, flanked by a twin building. The western subsection of this overall complex (the former Geologische Landesanstalt and later the GDR Ministry for Geology, see no. 101) was comprehensively restored for its new function, the atrium was kept clear of walling and its iron roofing was reconstructed. On the western facade, the Panke river has been opened and passes by the ministry as a moat. An adjoining building and a separate extension building designed by Max Dudler were built as the old building could not meet the space

requirements of the Ministry – there is only sufficient space for the management sector here. The new buildings make use of a strictly cubic architectural language. They are based on the scale of the old building, and imitate its block structure but not its facade design with decorative

elements and structural members. The new buildings have a strictly regular degree of windowing throughout with a generous ratio of glass in relation to the stone curtain wall. The new building sections that were created in this way can be described in typological terms as a variation within a certain tradition of administrative buildings.

Hallen am Borsigturm (440)
Halls at the Borsig Tower
1999
Berliner Straße 27
Claude Vasconi

Berlin had more than a dozen shopping malls built in the city to rectify the lack of shopping attractions following the reunification of Germany. However, this was the only project to be accommodated within older buildings. Claude Vasconi is the person to thank for the fact that the architecture from the Gründerzeit was not demolished but reused. Promoted to the position of master planner for the industrial sector by means of this concept in 1994, he supplemented the brick stone facades and steel supporting frameworks to make them appear like they once used to: He implanted shops and offices with lots of glass, a great deal of aluminium, some stainless steel and also by means of the use of black paint.

New Suburbs: Apartments for Citizens who aren't coming after all (441)

When the first prognoses for the reunified capital city were created from 1990, the demographics surpassed themselves with audacious reflections. Up to 2010, it was estimated that Berlin would house up to five million people. It had already experienced such a boom before, at the end of the 19th century: within a short number of decades, the population at that time doubled. In 1939, the city already had five million inhabitants. No wonder then, if the city's development politics created space for the prognosed "New Berliners" with huge investment housing programmes. A city concept from the 19th century was revived: the suburb. At the same time, the decision for such city expansions was a refusal of the current trends in city development in other European metropolises, whose borders are not characterised through urban structures but through "wild growth". All the projects were carried out in this sense, which were developed under the names of Neu-Karow, Französisch Buchholz, Rudower Felder etc.

Without a doubt, the most famous project is Neu-Karow – a suburb for about 5,000 inhabitants in North East Berlin. On the basis of a traditional city layout with streets, squares and parks (Design: Moore, Ruble, Yudell), within few years, multi-storey apartment blocks, apartment houses and terraces as well as schools, childcare facilities and shopping centres developed. Even if Neu-Karow was something of an experimental field for lots of young architects, the result is still sobering. Only a few buildings stand out from the masses because of their quality. The reason for this could be the rapid planning and construction time, through which otherwise consecutive planning stages were connected in parallel and implementation plans were drawn up without any binding development plan. Nevertheless, the suburb projects deserve recognition: In Neu-Karow, authorities and investors entered into a

Public-Private-Partnership, in which reduced development areas were sold to private project developers, who were then obligated on their side to create public infrastructures. The experiences with this well received concept introduced a new regulation of the so-called town-planning contract, which has been anchored in the German Federal Building Code since 1998.   meu

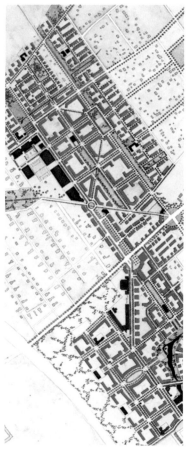

Master plan for the suburb Neu-Karow; proposal: Moore, Ruble, Yudell.

New suburb in Neu-Karow.

Bundesschlange (442)
The Federal Snake
1999
*Between Stadtbahn, Ingeborg-Drewitz-
Allee and Joachim-Karnatz-Allee*
Georg Bumiller (town planning)

FLOP Among the approximately
12,000 apartments, which the federal
government built for its public service
employees who migrated to Berlin, these
718 are the most central: they anchor the
political project corporately into the
curve in the River Spree known as the
"Spreebogen": Four cubes and a 1,640
feet long "serpent" were designed in such
a way that they give the ribbon of governmental buildings known in Germany
as the "Band des Bundes" a dignified closure and combine it to the petit bourgeois
quarter on the other side of the Stadtbahn
(No. 98). The large format, with which the
Berlin youngster, Bumiller, blew away the
competition for the Moabiter Werder in
1993, was berated shortly after completion as "the largest disaster of the Berlin
rebuild". The yellow brick fronts, which
remained inflexible despite the involvement of three design offices, and apartments without balconies, which did not
surpass the standard of council housing,
provoked a building vacancy of around
70 percent at the beginning. In the meantime, the settlement has now been pass-
ably revived.

Haus der Deutschen Wirtschaft (443)
The House of German Economy
1999
Breite Straße 20–21/Gertraudenstraße
Schweger + Partner

In the building for three associations –
BDI, DIHT and BDA – the important economic lobbists settled near the governing

Berlin on the Spree Island. The building
adheres to nuances which characterise
Friedrichstadt in general: stone cladding
and a eaves height of 72 feet. The newly
created, no longer divided building
blocks blur the preceding structures,
which were defined through small-scale
designs and the contours of the Baroque
period. The headquarters of the three associations in the communal block is reflected in the discreet differences in the
grey of the sandstone cladding. The infrastructure of the building, like the conference tower, is communally used. This
is also the case for the inner courtyard,
which is covered in a glass structure and
serves as an internal communication
zone. The development pulsates with the
shoreline towards the River Spree. The
building edge to Gertraudenstrasse follows the former alignment of the street
and, in doing so, cements the multiple
tracks of the East-West connection. What

are noteworthy are the different modu-
lated noise protection window variations,
which also show the three users. In total,
there is more reason than emotion in the
shape of this Berlin block. The "voice of
the economy" sounds very unobtrusive
here.

Bürohaus Hohenzollerndamm 183
(444)
Office block on Hohenzollerndamm 183
1999
Hohenzollerndamm 183
Jürgen Böge, Ingeborg Lindner-Böge

The facade of the office building on Hohenzollerndamm was meant as a subtle
answer to what was known as the Berlin
architecture dispute of the time (see No.
375): the glass facade was perfectly re-

alised next to stone-perforated facade. The design is characterised by a structure of the office building's main structural body in Hohenzollerndamm and two lateral building wings on Sächsische Straße and Gieselerstraße, which are orientated in dimension and material to the adjacent residential buildings dating from the "Gründerzeit", a period of industrial expansion starting around 1871. The natural stone facades made from light limestone conserve their elegance and power through a minimization of detail, whereby the window frames are covered by stone and the railings are drained inwardly. The facade on Hohenzollerndamm is orientated towards the street's metropolitan character and is completely glazed and combined with adjacently flush natural stone supports made from gneiss.

Katholische Akademie Berlin, Deutsche Bischofskonferenz (445)
Catholic Academy in Berlin, German Conference of Catholic Bishops
1999
Chausseestraße 12/Hannoversche Straße 5
Höger Hare Architects

The building complex of the Katholische Akademie contains a new church construction, among other functions, which has developed into a unique, publicly accessible fallback location in the middle of the city. The entire structure was added as a succession of courtyards and building structures on a shabby block boundary south of the Dorotheenstädtische Friedhof. Here, the old building of the Academy was joined by a representation building of the Deutsche Bischofskonferenz, a conference hotel and an office

building, which all surround a small ceremony room like a core building. In terms of town planning, the architectures relate to the idea of a "monastery in the city" and allow physical space to work together in interplay with the buildings. The St.-Thomas-Kirche is surrounded by a reinforced concrete pergola, a type of reverse cloister with connected garden courtyard. In design and consequence, the church building clearly sets itself apart from the other sub-buildings. Its space

enclosing walls are covered in 2,000 granite sheets, which are interspersed upwards with glass building blocks. This simplicity is even more impressive in the surrounding city fuss.

Konrad-Adenauer-Stiftung (446)
Konrad-Adenauer Foundation
1999
Tiergartenstraße 35
Thomas van den Valentyn

Since the middle of the 1970s, the Konrad-Adenauer-Stiftung has been represented with a branch in Berlin. Of all the partisan foundations, it is the only one up to today which only has a branch with about 30 employees based in Berlin.

However, the construction of the CDU-associated organisation counts among the most exclusive of its time. With the design, Thomas van den Valentyn drew, as he did a few years previously with a music school in Weimar, from deep within the richness of quotations of the classical modern era. Freely suspended landings in the outer area, a roof garden as a detached high space, which is available using an expansive ramp – these details appear like quotations from architecture history through to the 20th century. The spatial organisation of the building conceals a concrete cylinder, 66 feet in diameter, behind the hermetic, right-angled cubature. This concrete cylinder, in turn, is located over a two-storey "wooden" events room. Van den Valentyn himself called the building a "delicate box", his concept of a modern facade expresses itself in the travertine-clad box which oscillates between "meaningful architecture" and "strict silence".

Leibniz-Kolonnaden (447)
Leibniz Colonnades
1999
Leibnizstraße 49–53,
Wielandstraße 19–22
Hans Kollhoff and Helga Timmermann

The first impression from the Leibniz-Kolonnaden is the beautiful city square, which stretched between the two building rows. That this open space with trees and fountains does not belong to the surrounding development but rather simply develops through it, can be seen in its paving, which even continues under the bordering rows of columns. The building with small green rear court yards has different usages: office and business spaces, a hotel and apartments. In the upper floor of the Southern part of the house, there is also a kindergarten which has small pavilions on the roof. The varying facade design fits visibly to the use behind it: this means that the higher office spaces are distributed on less storeys than the apartments. The simple, dark stone facade, heavy brass and solid wood verify the elective affinity, which has dealt with the shape and material.

Lustgarten (448)
Pleasure Garden
1999
Karl-Liebknecht-Straße
Hans Loidl

GARDEN The Lustgarten, the front garden between the Alte Museum (No. 62),

Dom (No. 136) and the former Palast der Republik (Nr. 337), stands representationally for garden art of the 1990s. It is characterised by an intensive dispute with its own tradition, a rediscovery of the historical layout and the creation of places, which should, on the one hand, represent and, on the other, should invite you to linger. In the 1930s, the Lustgarten was altered with a pavement covering. This needed to be reacted to with contemporary means in the middle of the 1990. So, in 1994, Gerhard Merz tried to seal off the Lustgarten with a bus stop backed up against Karl-Liebknecht-Straße for this reason and in 1996, in a renewed expert proceedings, Gustav Lange suggested terracotta-potted box trees, which were unsuitable to the Berlin climate. However, Hans Loidl, who had occupied second place in both of these proceedings and was now directly commissioned, was the first to succeed in realising a modern interpretation of the Lustgarten. For the layout, he orientated himself on the historical design of Karl Friedrich Schinkel (No. 44). This was aligned with his central axiality to the preceding construction of the Dom. However, Loidl alluded to the modern Dom in his conception.

Landesvertretung der Freien und Hansestadt Bremen (449)
State Representative for the Free and Hanseatic City of Bremen
1999
Hiroshimastraße 22–26
Léon, Wohlhage, Wernik

The representative of the Hanseatic city consists of two building parts, which act at the same time as the relay between the close city density on the Reichpietschufer in the South and the residential character of the adjacent embassy quarter found in the North. The eight-storey guest house on the lively street is designed in the style of the urban perimeter block development, while the slightly separated representative office which is set back from the edge of the road with its four storeys and more generous facade design searches for its design contacts in

the neighbouring embassy residencies. The sober overall impression is thwarted by the irregularity of the deeply incised openings for windows and doors. The red plaster is reminiscent of North German

brick, the simplicity of the Hanseatic commercial reasoning. Even the garden, only visible with difficulty from the outside, is, with its shell-covered ways and waterway, a sentimental souvenir from the cool North.

Messe-Erweiterung Süd (450)
Southern Extension of the Exhibition hall
1999
between S-Bahnhof Eichkamp and Marshall-Haus
Oswald Mathias Ungers with Walter A. Noebel

In terms of investment, the exhibition hall was the most expensive building site in the country in the 1990s. In order to hold the large events of Green Week, Bautec, the International Consumer Electronics exhibition and the Tourism Exchange in Berlin, the covered surface was increased by a storey from 1 million to 1.7 million square feet at a cost of 1.8 billion Deutschmark. After the competition of

1990, the two-storey hall wings of Marshall-Haus (No. 269) had grown towards the South, where a second main entrance was built on Jafféstraße. A system of tunnels, ramps and connecting bridges, stretching miles, allows vehicles to be able to drive right to the exhibition stand. All hardware is subordinated to a square grid, which appears to the outside as terracotta-filled steel lattices. Whether the trademark of the old architect master, Ungers, who had already erected the Frankfurt Exhibition hall, inspired the Berlin trading centre is however questionable: its purely rational black boxes are considered "out of style", since the industry leader, Hanover, built glass meeting points for the Expo exhibition.

Nordische Botschaften (451)
Nordic Embassies
1999
Rauchstraße 1
Berger + Parkkinen (overall concept)

This noteworthy joint project of the Nordic countries of Denmark, Finland, Iceland, Norway and Sweden developed in the old Diplomatenviertel, the Diplomat's Quarter, on the Southern edge of the Tiergarten. The association-rich building provoked a clear enclosure of the building area using a 50-feet high border made from about 4,000 prepatinated copper plates. Inside, the open styles of Rauchstraße are taken up and converted into themes such as the courtyard, square and block. The contours of the six different individual buildings, five embassies and a communal house, resulted from the building lines, the tree population and the incisions of the passages as well as the Southern opening of the plot

of land. National architects realised the individual embassies on the basis of the overall concept by Berger + Parkkinen, the public communal house "Felleshus" contains a lobby, auditorium, exhibition surface and conference rooms. The Nordic embassies are not just outstanding for the reason of their architectonic expression but also because of the economical cooperation solution and the legal conception from special and communal property.

Reichstag (Umbau zum Plenarbereich des Deutschen Bundestags) (452)
German Seat of Parliamentary Government (Conversion of the Plenary Area of the German Parliament)
1999
Platz der Republik 1
Lord Norman Foster & Partners

That the representation of the people had already attracted 180,000 visitors one week after their move, was the seal of approval of the entire capital project. Yet, at the same time as, the new parliament headquarters until that date had been main point of contention, the Reichstag (no. 106) represented the heightening and deepening of the German history. Even the Briton (!) Foster – entrusted with the conversion after the international competition in 1992 – needed three specialist colloquiums and the ceremony of Christo's unveiling to get used to the building. After he wanted to put it under quarantine at the beginning with a giant roof, he only picked up Paul Baumgarten's conversion from the 1960s in the end. Anything which then re-revealed itself to be war ruins, he supplemented generously and simply with steel and glass. In the retreaded plenary room, which is the largest in the Western world with 17,216 square feet, the visitor tribunes are pushed so closely to the parliament members' places, that the guests can read their files. What is unique is the fact that the people can practically "raise the rafters" on their representatives: After a long argument, a modern replacement was found for the dome which exploded in the 1950s. As well as a mirrored cone for lighting and ventilating the plenary room, the oval high-tech construction contains two counter-rotating platforms, which allow you to look out on both the representatives and, predominantly, the city.

Stilwerk Design Center (453)
Stilwerk Design Centre
1999
Kantstraße 17-20 / Uhlandstraße 9–11
Novotny, Mähner & Associates,
Studio + Partners (interior)

What took the place of a sober bank house from the 1950s was meant to become a tasteful embassy. However, in the end, some shop interiors can, at best, impress, which were designed by differing architects. As a whole, the building is rather reminiscent of European city buildings of the worst possible kind. The interior of the five-story vertical mall are generous and nicely simple; however details, such as the ceiling lights or the fixing of the shell plates on the tower of the lift are of a sloppiness, which doesn't let itself be confused with style. At least, Kantstraße has gained profile with other design settlements.

Schaltanlage in Friedrichshain (454)
Sub-Station in Friedrichshain
1999
Thaerstraße 26
Frank Assmann, Peter Salomon

The 110-kilowatt substation from the Bewag power supplier takes its place in the tradition of the municipal technical buildings of the architect Hans Heinrich Müller, who realised a series of landmark buildings in the 1920s. However invisible and dematerialised the function of the building presents itself, it is nevertheless present and solid in the city space. In the immediate proximity, which is characterised by the wasteland of the former abattoir, the grey monolith looks like an unscalable fortress. The facade made from basalt lava loses its exclusive character as you approach and develops almost haptic qualities.

Auswärtiges Amt
(ehem. Reichsbank) (455)
Ministry of Foreign Affairs
(former Central Federal Bank)
1940 (old building), 2000 (conversion)
Am Werderschen Markt, Kurstraße 36–40,
Unterwasserstraße 9–10
Heinrich Wolff, Hans Kollhoff

The new official residence of the Auswärtiges Amt developed in one of the oldest parts of Berlin. The core building of what later became the Reichsbank stemmed back to 1690; over the coming centuries, numerous conversions and additional building took place. There were already plans to expand the Reichsbank back in the time of the Weimar Republic. The architect, Heinrich Wolff's first sketches wanted to replay to the inflation with a symbol of stability. This plan was taken up under the National Socialist rule.

Adolf Hitler himself decided the competition of 1933, into which Gropius, Mies van der Rohe, Poelzif and Tessenow had

entered themselves among others. When the official residence for over 4,000 bank employees was ready, its safes also accepted the stolen gold from Hitler's campaign of destruction. The cubic capacity seems to take hold like a casting of the terrain; a representation facade shows itself towards Wederschen Markt. The block is interspersed with several courtyards. The GDR, which used the treasury from 1959 for the central committee of the SED, symbolically denazified the "Nibelungen refuge" by removing Nazi reliefs and the light banking hall was replaced by a "black box" for conferences. This refusal, typical for the division time, of historical continuity was continued by the Auswärtiges Amt on the one hand, when they allowed the building to be supplemented though a newly built cube (see No. 436). The old building on the other hand was transformed by Hans Kollhoff in 1995. This allowed everything to survive which was good in terms of trade, and supplemented the rest in an equally solid way. Colour surfaces by the artist Gerhard Merz connect the layers to an overall piece of art work, which represents the united Germany excellently.

Bundesministerium für Bildung und Forschung (ehem. Ständige Vertretung der BRD bei der DDR) (456)
Federal Ministry for Education and Research (former Diplomatic Representation of West-Germany in East Berlin) 2000
Hannoversche Straße 28–30
Jochem Jourdan & Bernhard Müller

The building, which was selected by the Ministry for Education as a second office residence, is a defining point of German-German history. Nowadays, long since re-included in a perimeter block development, it now accepts any institution, responsible for questions of the future. The building's career began as a barracks wing under Friedrich II. During the Weimar Republic, it was used as a police school and shortly after the Second World War as the Institute for Civil Engineering. After the foundation of the GDR, it housed a part of the building academy and served later as the diplomatic presentation for the Federal Republic of Germany in the GDR, the quasi embassy. The sober master building and the attic studio (Hans Scharound (no. 281) planned the reconstruction of Berlin here) was restored and renovated after the wall came

down and was supplemented by a laterally starting timber frame. Here, at the new construction, the shape infringes on the otherwise clearly necessary restraint. The upper storey overhangs, touches on few supports and, as a metaphor for the department for research and innovations, has a somewhat over-orchestrated effect. However, it risks at least moulding the street front. In the re-closed inner courtyard, there is still a relict from the Permanent Representation of the Federal Republic in the GDR, a bright garden pavilion, which had been build originally as an event building but also had to receive all the many GDR citizens who wanted to leave the country.

Botschaft von Großbritannien (457)
British Embassy
2000
Wilhelmstraße 70–71
Michael Wilford

The new embassy of the United Kingdom has been built in exactly the same position, which was the diplomatic representation of her Majesty before the war as well. For the new building, which is connected directly on the Hotel Adlon (no. 401), an additional piece of land was purchased, to be able to come to grips with the spatial demands of a modern embassy. For the time being, the building is easy to spot due to the strict building regulations which apply around the Brandenburg Gate (no. 40). Nevertheless, Wilford's building comes up to standard in all points to subversively slip in the British eccentric character. From the brusquely cracked, sandstone facade, which is structured in line with the guidelines, two brightly coloured structures peak cheekily from the top of the first storey, where the visitor centre and the auditorium are located. Many things on this building are subtle. Surprisingly the light inner courtyard with a high English oak tree, which is situated just behind the entrance onto Wilhelmstraße. It forms the beginning of the change between open and closed spaces. A step leads into the winter garden, which serves as the reception room. The office floors surround the courtyards in a U-shape and, with their balconies, allow insight and outlook onto events. Even the would-be mansard roof with its prepatinated copper glaze turns out to be a curtain-like concession to the building regulations: it conceals a simple flat roof. The architects succeeded in the feat of submitting the editions flawlessly and creating a building whose demonstrative external strength behind the inaccessible facade is ironically interrupted.

Botschaft der Vereinigten Staaten von Mexiko (458)
Embassy of the United States of Mexico
2000
Klingelhöferstraße 3/Rauchstraße 27
Teodoro Gonzáles de León,
Francisco Serrano

International trends and pre-Columbian motives characterize the Mexican modern building, which has been represented in Berlin since 2000 with an impressive example. The Mexican Embassy marks the Tiergarten triangle as the Northern equivalent to the CDU central (no. 460). Vertical, inwardly inclining concrete supports made of white concrete form a narrow triangular forecourt, which leads to the minute entrance of the building. In close intervals, these surface-dressed prefabricated supports stand, like a curtain before a uniformly, glazed facade. Gonzáles de León, one time colleague of Le Corbusier, continues the game of large shapes under the light on small building surfaces inside the building. A very high cylinder set into the building clock forms a foyer with countless windows, which all the rooms in the house open out onto.

New Old Capital: Novelty on the one Hand, Continuity on the Other (459)

The 20th June 1991 can be entered into the most significant dates in the youngest history of Berlin, after 3rd October 1990: with a tight majority, the Deutsche Bundestag voted in favour of transferring the seat of the government from Bonn to Berlin. Since the foundation of the Deutsches Reich, Berlin has administered uninterrupted capital and governmental functions. The city has a large spectrum of political buildings due to these functions. In addition, every era on the Spree has written new architectural history. This is because with every new political system, the requirements on the city's representation have changed. In this way, the Reichstag (no. 106) did not just embody the Kaiserzeit. It also formed a town planning counterweight to the Stadtschloss der Hohenzollern (no. 7) due to its monumentality. Even when the Volksvertreter (people's representative) in the Reichstag still did not have the political power of a parliament in today's sense of the word, the growing democracy manifested itself with a powerful building in the cityscape.

The political architecture of the Weimar Republic on the other hand did not reach beyond the planning for the capital due to its frequent government changes. For the square in front of the Reichstag, after unsuccessful participation in the competition to expand the Reichstag, Hugo Häring put forward designs for a "Democratic Forum" in 1929. On a semi-circular rostrum opening out towards the Reichstag, the people would be able to "take a seat" in the truest sense of the word and be able to enter into a symbolic interplay between parliament and public. Over sixty years later, the winners of the Spreebogen competition of 1993, Axel Schultes and Charlotte Frank took up this idea of a place for citizens again with the Bundesforum.

The cautious attempt in the Weimar Republic to formulate an architectonic expression for a democratic system, was initially ended with the assumption of power by the National Socialists. From 1993, numerous governmental buildings developed in Berlin, which were characterised by a clear tectonic organisation and stone solidity. On Wilhelmstraße, for example, between the years of 1934 and 1936, the Reichsluftfahrtministerium (no. 229) was erected in accordance with plans by Ernst Sagebiel. With the new construction on the corner of Leipziger Straße, the Third Reich continued a tradition of governmental buildings, which had begun in the middle of the 19th century in Prussia: the extension of Wilhelmstraße to a governmental axis. After demolishing the Reichskanzlei and the Reichspräsidentenpalais, the over-dimensioned Neue Reichskanzlei (no. 248) developed there between 1937 and 1939 from a plan made by Albert Speer (no. 225). The Neue Reichskanzlei's gallery of mirrors had gigantic dimensions of almost 500 feet.

A transfer of political power from Wilhelmstraße began with the division of Berlin. The GDR had their most important political buildings constructed in the area of the Spree Island, among which the Staatsratsgebäude (No. 308) and the Palast der Republik (No. 337). Not far away, the central committee of the SED took up residence in the former Reichsbank (No. 455), which is used today as the official residence of the Auswärtiges Amt and has come to stand exemplarily for a new self-image of the Federal Republic of Germany: the political and structural legacy of governmental buildings of past – mostly undemocratic – systems is not covered up. Instead, it is put into a new context with the help of conversions or new buildings. The numerous governmental and parliamentary locations from the different eras contribute therefore to the fact that the Berlin cityscape has become a type of open-air museum of the political architecture in Germany.   meu

285

The demands placed on state representation changed with each new political system.

Bundesgeschäftsstelle der CDU (460)
Federal Office of the CDU
2000
Klingelhöferstraße 8
Karl-Heinz Petzinka, Thomas Pink

According to the words of their former treasurer, Matthias Wissmann, in 1999, the CDU wanted the new building of their Berlin Bundeszentrale to stand out "pleasantly from the batch productions" which otherwise characterise Berlin. The office of Petzinka, Pink und Partner who was commissioned with the difficult task, planned a four-story, glazed winter garden over a stone foundation, which completely traced the rhombus-shaped corner plot. In this clad construction, so developed for the purpose of ecologically correct ventilation, a six-storey ellipsis-like structure was erected like an inverted stranded ship hull. This structure opens out onto an atrium open on all levels, which tapers towards the ceiling. On the ground floor, there is a bistro, main and sub-foyers and conference room, which can be joined together with the main foyer to form an events room for up to 300 people. The upper levels, which must do without the natural ventilation effect of the winter garden, are reserved for the party leadership. Parts of the surface should be rented out.

Bundespressekonferenz (461)
Federal Press Conference Building
2000
Reinhardtstraße 53–59,
corner Schiffbauerdamm
Johanne and Gernot Nalbach

Once again, no German institution has local politics so directly in view as the Bundespressekonferenz. The journalism association, which could see across the Rhine Republic with its "Haus am Tulpenfeld", was at the point of being in danger of actually losing its dominant position, because numerous news producers found their own respectable market places in Berlin (see No. 161, 416). This was compensated through a construction vis-à-vis from the "Band des Bundes", which concentrates completely on its core task. From 1998, a typical Berlin block developed, above which the conference room alone rises. Placed on its South side in the Piano Nobile, 16 feet high and completely glazed, the greyish marbled frames represent an absolute visual shaft, which is directed towards the Chancellor and the members of parliament. On the other hand, the 600 offices look completely neutral: their facades resemble a test card thanks to the lightly crazy staccato pattern made of black basalt and the luminous fields.

Friedrich-Ebert-Stiftung (462)
Friedrich-Ebert Foundation
2000
Hiroshimastr. 17–25
Fritz Novotny, Arthur Mähner,
Volkhard Weber

The design for the new building of the Berlin headquarters of the SPD-associated Friedrich-Ebert-Stiftung stemmed from the architecture office which had planned the Bundeszentrale of the SPD in the 1970s in Bonn among other things. The new building in the Botschaftsviertel – from the outside towards the street a U-shaped three-winged complex – is characterised by a dark, solid clinker facade. The strong four-storey perimeter block development surrounds a circular, completely glazed lecture hall, which breaks through facade with a two-storey glazed circular segment on the west side. 14,000 square feet of office space is placed in stone wings. The uppermost storey is provided with a glazed relaxation mezzanine, as is sufficiently well known from numerous bank and management buildings. The room can be expanded using mobile partition walls to a 32,000 square feet large "conference landscape" on the entire ground floor. The transparent side of the building, opening out onto the Landwehrkanal, will pick up the theme of the open forum from the 1970s in the garden design as well.

Villa Gerl (463)
Gerl Mansion
2000
Im Schwarzen Grund
Hans Kollhoff

The private villa in the periphery city idyll of South West Berlin refers, over all criticism, to the grand basic vocabulary of the Italian country estate. A classically structured Palladio with four towers, which nevertheless has the effect as if they had been plugged into a solid cube during their growth, rises out of the long rectangle of the ground plan. The overall stocky impression does not reduce the timelessness of the design in any case. All details substantiate a tasteful planning and design. Without taxing the pretentious ornamentation of the contemporary luxury palaces, the villa uses classic proportions, avoids decorations on the facades and does not make it look ridiculous with its determination to be present. The double brickwork is triple plastered; a 23 feet high hall has an almost atrium-like effect, which is also visible from the outside.

Berliner Wasser Holding AG (464)
Haus III
Berliner Wasser Holding AG
Building III
2000
Stralauer Str. 32-41
Christoph Langhof

The Haus III of the company central of the Berlin water companies pushes itself capriciously into the picture of the Molkenmarkt, which is badly dissected with traffic. The five-storey closed reinforced concrete building is clad in a strange glittering outer shell made from diamond-patterned titan zinc and slopes from below upwards. The metal facades, above which will-o'-the-wispish reflections flicker, is only interrupted by tiny arrow-slit like holes. The immense four-axis projection, which marks the entrance area, is in curious contrast to the clumsiness of the cubature. With its prism-like, fractured window openings in the expressionistically folded front made from granite-coloured cast stone, the building seems to be trying to be more than just an office building.

Hochhaus Potsdamer Platz 1 (465)
High-Rise building at Potsdamer Platz 1
2000
Potsdamer Platz 1
Hans Kollhoff, Helga Timmermann

With the red clinker-clad building on Potsdamer Platz (no. 417), the architects Kollhoff/Timmermann have succeed with their modern interpretation of the multi-storey tradition, which dated back to the first half of the 20th century and whose models are predominantly in the USA. Together with the glazed Sony-en-ter (no. 472) it forms a new gate position between the once-divided city halves and connects the newly created Leipziger Platz with the Kulturforum (no. 311). On the triangular ground plan, the twenty-story building steps down to the roof height of the neighbouring buildings and blends itself harmoniously into its surroundings. Inside, a triangular atrium which is raised one storey serves as a distributor room. The solid tower vanishes as it rises upwards like a gothic cathedral and is crowned with golden keystones.

Kapelle der Versöhnung (466)
Chapel of Reconciliation
2000
Bernauer Straße/Hussitenstraße
Rudolf Reitermann, Peter Sassenroth

In 1961, with the building of the Berlin Wall (no. 301), the new-Gothic evangelist Chapel of Reconciliation in Bernauer Straße (built 1892–94 by Gotthilf Ludwig Möckel) became the middle of the fronts of the Cold War. While the parish lived predominantly on the West side of the wall in Wedding, the building itself stood in the East sector and was sealed off by the border guards. In 1985, the church, which had become run-down in the meantime, was demolished to "increase security, order and cleanliness on the city border to Berlin-West". In 1995, the parish received the plot of land with the condition of building a chapel in its place. The architect team of Reitermann and Sassenroth emerged from the public competition as the victors. Off-centre between the foundations of the old church, a two-layer, 30-feet high building developed with an irregularly rounded outer layer made from vertical wooden disks.

The outer casing surrounds a circular vestry, designed as a supporting rammed clay construction, expanding outwardly to the organ loft and the altar.

Kindertagesstätte in Neu-Karow (467)
Day Nursery in Neu-Karow
2000
Münchenhagener Str. 43
Höhne & Rapp

The large windows with their white frames and the red-brown brick of the facades is vaguely reminiscent of the philanthropist architecture of the Dutch provenance. A stroke of luck for the kindergarten. Despite the sober and unornamental design of the building, a friendly place has emerged here. The building has a simple street front and is staggered towards the garden. The terraces which develop from this, with

wood-planked floor and circular railing play with the associations to arks and sea. The building fronts to the garden are completely glazed and the lightness of the lounge areas is strengthened more by the beech parquetry. Doors, lighting and ceiling coverings connect themselves in an alliance to peace and discreet reservation. In comparison to the normal kindergarten storms made from violently strong colours and plastics, everything here is limited to white and natural tones as well as the green of the plants and trees in the garden which penetrate from outside.

Landesvertretung von Rheinland-Pfalz (468)
State Representative for Rhineland-Palatinate
2000
In den Ministergärten 6
Heinle, Wischer und Partner

The Landesvertretung for Rhineland-Palatinate, which opened at the end of 2000, is situated between the neighbouring representatives of the Saarland (no. 487) and the states of Lower Saxony/Schleswig Holstein (no. 476). With these, it forms the northern row of what is known as the "Föderations-Viertel", the "Federation Quarter". Originally, the town-planning department envisaged the construction of new State Agencies to be on the plot of the former Auswärtiges Amt (no. 455) and the Reichskanzlei of Hitler (no. 248) between Voßstraße and Wilhelmstraße. However, due to the plans for the Holocaust memorial, only five lots could be zoned in. With the pavilion-like, open constructions of the individual state agencies, the federal self-image of the states was supposed to be taken into ac-

count and the transition between the heavily built-up Friedrichstadt and the Tiergarten meant to be overcome. The four-storey U-shaped body with horizontally structured natural stone facades surrounds a generous central foyer. The extension of a guest wing expands the eastern building wing. A green roof terrace can be reached via a free-standing lift in the hall; on the roof level, there are conference and breakfast rooms.

Landesvertretung von Baden-Württemberg (469)
State Representative of Baden-Württemberg
Tiergartenstr. 15
Dietrich Bangert

The design, awarded first prize in a competition in 1997, stands in Tiergartenstraße in immediate proximity to the embassies of Austria, India (see no. 475, 479) and Egypt. The plot is clearer larger than the neighbouring plots, the building of the Landesvertretung stands in the middle of the building site and makes the most of it. The access to the monolith

building block is through an entrance cone, set back behind the passenger drop-off area, which is trapezium-shaped and three storeys high. This entrance cone stretches from the fourth storey to the Tiergartenstraße. Inside, the architects have created a refined series of rooms which are lit indirectly from above. The room series is made up of foyer, skylight room, loggia and terrace leading to a garden courtyard, which opens out there with the same large gestures as on the entrance side. In the first and second storeys, the prosaic management and office spaces are situated, arranged in a U-shape towards the narrow garden side. The view of the Tiergarten (no. 60) is reserved solely for the management levels. In the ground floor, the simple white building is clad with a high granite foundation.

Paul-Löbe-Haus (470)
Paul-Löbe Building
2000
Konrad-Adenauer-Straße, Otto-von-Bismarck-Allee
Stephan Braunfels

As a part of the "Band des Bundes", the town planning concept developed by Axel Schultes and Charlotte Frank for the Spreebogen development, the Paul-Löbe-Haus and the Marie-Elisabeth-Lüders-Haus (No. 505) represent, on the other shore of the Spree, the east located heavy weight to the Bundeskanzleramt (No. 482). In 1994, Stephan Braunfels won the competition for the realisation of both the office buildings of the German Bundestag approaching the Reichstags building (no. 106). The buildings, named after the old term of Alsenblock and Luisenblock, form the partitioned edges to the Spree shore using prominent structural parts like canopies and rotundas. The Paul-

Löbe-Haus, measuring 656 by 328 feet, forms a symmetrical double ridge. This ridge, in turn, holds eight courtyards, surrounded on three-sides. In the west, a giant canopy towers in the direction of a planned citizen forum as a city-spatial, public buffer zone between executive and legislative. The building will traverse from a light hall from West to East, which holds it together like a backbone. The ridge structure enlarges the facade surfaces and offers a multitude of well-lit work spaces.

Presse- und Informationsamt der
Bundesregierung (471)
Press and Information Bureau
of the Federal Government
2000
Reichstagufer 12/14,
Dorotheenstraße 80–84
KSP Engel und Zimmermann

The press and visitor centre, which went into operation as the first building block of the "Berlin Republic", stands for Germany's change to media democracy. With it, for the first time, the Federal Government created a unit for its own advertising, after it was almost always the guest of the Bundespressekonferenz on the Rhine (No. 461). At first sight, the complex, which measured in terms of new building was the most expensive project of the move, is reminiscent of the journalists' "Haus am Tulpenfeld" in Bonn: the podium is situated here, as it was

there, in an small exposed, open cuboid, which, in turn, stands in front of a bar, behind which the organisation runs. However, its completely glazed longitudinal sides in Berlin contain a black box, in which itself, the palest appearance can be shifted in the right light. Anyway, the free-standing pavilion has a much more exclusive effect than the Bonn counterpart in front of the background of the compacted Friedrichstadt. Moreover, the stage possesses a proper curtain in the form of a 394-feet long pane (printed black instead of transparent).

SONY-Center (472)
SONY Centre
2000
Potsdamer Straße 4, Kemperplatz
Helmut Jahn

On the 285,140 square feet large area on Potsdamer Platz (no. 417), the Japanese SONY Group built their European central. The electronics giant would not have been able to use any better competition design: the glass building ensemble

plays with the technical calling of the head of its house in shape, colours and material and is both opaque management outposts and public-open plaza. The forum, spectacularly covered by a complicated canvas construction, with shops, cinemas and restaurants is not just the heart of the building; it also combines the individual parts of the building. The office tower, which towers over everything, with its 26 floors behind a unique sweeping facade crowns the east summit of the SONY Center. The Deutsche Bahn AG moved in here. In the office wing along Potsdamer Straße and Bellevuestraße, there are other users of economy and culture residing together with the building owner. The mandatory residential section is located in the Esplanade Residence on the North wing over the protected remains of the former Grand Hotel Esplanade, which was integrated into the modern complex in a type of In-Vitro architecture and now supported the wondering strollers as a preserved showcase piece.

Velodrom/Schwimmsporthalle (473)
Velodrom/Swimming Hall
2000
Paul-Heyse-Straße 26
Dominique Perrault

The extensive complex of bicycle hall and swimming pool on the est end of "Grün-derzeit" Berlin is characterised initially by its invisibility. Sports halls are normally an architectural and town development problem case; however, the facilities are able to successfully reconcile their function with the already difficult, incomplete city space between the existence of old buildings and record sized settlements. The actual sports halls, planned from the occasion of the (failed) Olympic bid in Berlin in 1993, were immersed onto a green hill, covered in blooming apple trees and are, from a distance, as good as invisible. Only a walk in this open city landscape allows a glimpse of the sports halls. The Velodrom building, which is underground, with its circular shimmering roof made from filigree steel webbing as well as the similarly-covered swimming hall are embedded into the new cityscape like metal lakes. Unfortunately, the design is not as strong in detail in the overall concept as the facilities turned out.

Wohnhaus Corneliusstraße (474)
Residential Building on Corneliusstraße
2000
Corneliusstraße 3
Heinz Hilmer, Christoph Sattler

"High quality living" in individual "residences": this is what the residential building built in the Tiergarten triangle behind the CDU central (no. 460) prom-

ises. In block 6, users with safety requirements find a hybrid made from compacted Berlin residential block and free-standing city house, 60 flats of up-market design with sizes between 861-2,700 square feet. In the centre of the entire complex of the Tiergarten triangle, there is a "pocket park", which is available to the inhabitants as well using narrow alleyways between the blocks. The houses carry the trademarks of different architects, in order to guarantee an individual design to the individual houses. Block 6a and 6b are connected with two other blocks using a "cloisters"-termed development corridor. The design for blocks 6a and 6b came from the Hilmer and Sattler office. Secured around the clock by a porter, the main entrance to the entire complex is located in block 6b. Depending on the size and type of the apartment, they are each attached to a loggia or winter garden. In particular, the residential and dining areas are generously designed and exposed to light on all sides.

Botschaft Indiens (475)
Indian Embassy
2000
Tiergartenstr. 16-17
Léon, Wohlhage, Wernik

India, independent since 1947, is, in terms of the number of inhabitants, the second largest country on earth today. The new embassy building in the Southern Tiergarten (no. 60) should, on the one hand, give a picture of the modern India, and on the other hand, it should express in its building the multitude of the subcontinent with its many cultures, languages and religions. The design from the Berlin office of Léon, Wohlhage, Wernik, which emerged victorious from a restricted competition in 1998, tries a contemporary interpretation of the historical Indian construction art. The deep, but narrow plot was largely built over. Inside, a cubature, joined to inner courtyards is staggered, strictly arranged behind itself. In this, a circular entrance atrium is cut in as a prelude, which breaks though the facade to the Tiergarten. In the garden courtyard, which is

characterised by water surfaces, a cylinder is fitted which houses the bureaus of the ambassadors. Behind that, the residential wing closes the introverted unit. A large outdoor staircase on the east side of the building, which is clad with crudely broken rough sandstone from Rajasthan, leads to the roof garden.

Landesvertretung von Niedersachsen
und Schleswig-Holstein   (476)
State Representative for the States of
Lower Saxony and Schleswig Holstein
2001
In den Ministergärten 8 and 10
Birgit Cornelsen, Caspar Seelinger, Martin
Seelinger, Maximilian Vogels

The Landesvertretungs of Lower Saxony
and Schleswig Holstein, which are located in one building due to reasons of costs,
form the northwest conclusion of the five
state buildings on the newly constructed
street "In den Ministergärten". The land
belonged to the no man's land of the
Berlin Wall (no. 301) up until 1989. Beforehand, the Garten der Reichskanzlei
(no. 248) and the former Außenminis-
terium were located here. The concept of
the young joint venture by Cornelsen +
Seelinger, which emerged successful
from a competition and a further revision
phase, includes two compact six-storey
timber-framed buildings with subtle facades made from grey Italian sandstone
and dressed with larch wood. The two
buildings are connected by a glazed entrance hall. In the hall, there is (like a
house in a house) a lounge and cafeteria
construction which extends towards the
park. In the almost identical building
timber frames, which are clad in a horizontal natural stone facade, the ground
floor houses the traditional Frisian
"Friesenstube" and its Lower Saxonion
counterpart. Above this, there are offices
as well as in the uppermost floors, the
workspace and residential quarters for
the states' Prime ministers with a view
out on the Brandenburg Gate (no. 40) and
the planned Holocaust memorial.

Botschaft der Schweizerischen
Eidgenossenschaft   (477)
Embassy of the Swiss Confederation
2001
Otto-von-Bismarck-Allee 4
Diener & Diener

The autonomy of Switzerland seems to
have been converted into an accurate
structural emblem in Berlin. Since 1919,
the Confederation has been using a former city palace in the Spreebogen (Friedrich Hitzig, 1875) as its consulate. It re-
sisted both the megalomaniac conversion
plans of the Nazis as well as the bom-
bardment in the Second World War. Today, laying parallel to the "Band des Bundes", the embassy building is a relict of
the old vacated district known as the
"Alsenviertel". The Basel-based architects Diener & Diener constructed an extension building which was the same
height but somewhat deeper, immediately next to the east side of the old building
with its vast representation and residential rooms. Instead of the generous three
storeys of the old building, the new building has to accommodate the diplomatic
and consular duties on five storeys. It
breaks away from the existing building
less through the cubature and more
through its own language of materials
and the changing windows throughout

the building and gives a self-confidence
counterweight to the palace in perfect exposed concrete architecture. The artist
Helmut Federle designed a wall layer
with blind windows from the western
compartment wall.

Jakob-Kaiser-Haus (478)
Jakob-Kaiser Building
2001
Dorotheenstraße/Wilhelmstraße
Busmann und Haberer, de Architekten Cie.,
von Gerkan, Marg & Partner, Schweger und
Partners, Thomas van den Valentyn

Before the three large newly built complexes of the Deutscher Bundestag were named after important representatives of the parliamentarianism in the Weimar Republic, they were named after the locations, in which they perform extensive city repairs. The Jakob-Kaiser-Haus occupied an area of Dorotheenstadt, a baroque city expansion area once characterised by residential and trade houses and later by institutional buildings. With the two-part building formation, above all, the Reichstagsgebäude (see no. 106) retrieved its urban facade. On both sides of Dorotheenstraße, two thirds of the representatives' offices, the meeting rooms of the party members and other functions of the Federal Government and the Bundestag are situated. Five architect offices came to a solution which differs from the old plot structure. Towards the River Spree, open courtyards and main buildings arise. The entire ensemble has an effect like a versatile but not irregular puzzle. The Berlin ruling on building heights earmarked a height scope of six complete storeys and a penthouse level. In addition, three listed and renovated original buildings are integrated: the Reichspräsidentenpalais by Paul Wallot, the Kammer der Technik and the Haus Sommer.

Botschaft der Republik Österreich
(479)
Embassy of the Republic of Austria
2001
Stauffenbergstr. 1–4/Tiergartenstr. 12–14
Hans Hollein

The one-time Austrian embassy was located in a city palace in the same street, somewhat further south than today's location, up until the so-called "Anschluss" of Austria by the Nazis in 1938. This building was destroyed in the Second World War. For the 1996 prize competition, the corner plot at the entrance of the new diplomatic quarter in the Tiergarten was selected. The European open architecture competition made the decision for Hans Hollein, who was able to build his first building in Berlin since the construction of a city villa on Rauchstraße. On the corner between Stauffenbergstraße and Tiergartenstraße, an ellipse-like entrance building with an attached U-shaped cubic building part is located

between the solitary buildings of the Diplomatenviertel and the neighbouring Kulturforum (no. 311). The festival and representation areas of the ambassador are located in a striking copper-clad head structure, which is available with a multi-storey foyer near the passenger drop-off area. The four-storey flat-roofed building part in U-shape includes the consulate department towards Stauffenbergstraße. In the rear part of this building, reminiscent of a city villa, there are flats. While the multitude of inner rooms have their appeal, the heterogeneous exterior comes across as an "architectural goulash".

Botschaft der Republik Ungarn (480)
Embassy of the Republic of Hungary
2001
Unter den Linden 76
Adam Sylvester

Despite entrance into the list of historic monuments, the 1965/66 built embassy of the former People's Republic of Hungary (by Karl-Ernst Swora and Rainer Hanslik in cooperation with Endre Koltai and Laszlo Kovácy) was demolished in 1999. This building with its aluminium glass facades and circular glazed ground floor zone no longer corresponded to the "Spirit of Hungarian Architecture", as

was emphasized by the embassy. In addition, the building had become too large. On the reduced corner plot (the neighbouring house was sold), a building emerged, whose architects see themselves in the succession of "pre-modern" Berlin architecture. On the same site, the Haus Schulte by Alfred Messel once stood. The new six-storey building was erected according to plans of the Budapest architect Adam Sylvester, who emerged from a national competition as the winner. Particular characteristics of the building are the hand-finished ornamental ceramic plates on the facades which have been structured in accordance with "classic" proportion regulations. Also the almost completely glazed building corner is unusual for the boulevard Unter den Linden. The combination of yellow-grey sandstone and ceramic is meant to be reminiscent of the secession architecture by Vienna and Budapest.

Botschaft der Republik Usbekistan (481)
Embassy of the Republic of Uzbekistan
2001 (conversion)
Perleberger Straße 62
André Janka, Azamat Tokhtaev

The central-Asian CIS state of Uzbekistan has based its new embassy in Stephankiez, an old working-class Berlin quarter. The building, which had been erected in 1880 as the officers' mess, served as a restaurant in the post-war period and then became a brothel. Through its changes in use, an important example of Berlin military architecture could be maintained. What has developed from this is a curious blend of Prussian building tradition and oriental decorative art. What's predominantly worth seeing is the typical Uzbekistan plaster carvings in the ballroom, which is also open for cultural events.

Bundeskanzleramt (482)
Federal Chancellery
2001
Willy-Brandt-Straße 1
Axel Schultes, Charlotte Frank

The Bundeskanzleramt forms the western conclusion to the so-called "Band des Bundes", which is meant to connect the once separated city halves physically, mentally and symbolically. The building complex, whose garden facilities extend over the Spree, has a clearly East-West orientation. This is emphasised through the different designs of the facades, which seem to melt into both the garden and the Ehrenhof (courtyard of honour). In the management buildings, the architects have succeeded in creating noteworthy rooms. On the other hand, north-

bound and southbound, the building has a rather abrupt and abrasive effect, which is also not compensated by the large semi-circular formed openings in the middle management building ascending from the complex. Even the sandstone claddings along the longitudinal axis are proof of the misdirected cost savings: neither the building owner nor the contractors wanted to take the responsibility for the original idea to build the entire building out of white concrete.

Cubix Kino (483)
Cubix Cinema
2001
Rathausstraße 1
nps Sergei Tchoban

The first construction after the collapse of the wall in the Socialist city centre (no. 309) took the ground plot of the "Alextreff", which stood here between 1968 and 1995. The Russian scene designer, Sergei Tchoban, who also added his touch to the Palasthotel and the Haus der Elektroindustrie which are nearby, erected the robust floor design from the TV tower up to the nine new cinema screens. The balustrades of the neighbouring buildings barely reach the foyer, which is the size of a house. His facades made from giant showcases and black glossy granite inflate the cinema palaces from the 1920s just like the modernistic aesthetic, which dominate the site. This allowed Berlin's first metropolitan multiplex (2,600 seats) to become almost as urban as its best Modernistic cinemas (no. 305, 316).

Deutsches Technikmuseum (484)
German Museum of Technology
2001
Trebbiner Straße 7
Helge Pitz, Ulrich Wolff

Styled in the middle of the 1980s, but first completely accessible in 2005, the postmodern extension has an "out of style" effect today. This is thoroughly as the inventor intended; it was – differently to the sheet constructions, which harbour the largest part of the museum – styled

from the very first as a museum in its own right. Open installation cables, visible support structures, bare steel as well as many ecological accessories should have saved around two thirds of the costs and made the building into the exhibit for structural engineering. In addition, the series of closed clinker walls intimate at the library laying behind them. The vast glass corner guides the view to the historical vessels, and the candy bomber hanging over it doesn't just arouse interest for the four dozen further aircrafts inside. That the visitors here, in comparison to many modern-day museums, remember the exhibition rather than the building speaks ultimately for it.

Landesvertretung von Brandenburg und Mecklenburg-Vorpommern (485)
State Representative for the States of Brandenburg and Mecklenburg-Western Pomerania
2001
In den Ministergärten 1 and 3
von Gerkan, Marg and Partner

The competition in 1998 initially awarded first prize to the Lübeck-based office of

Mai, Zill und Kuhsen. For reasons of functional fitness, the second-place design from the office of von Gerkan, Marg und Partner was awarded preference to be realised. As well as the Federal states of Lower Saxony and Schleswig-Holstein (No. 476), Brandenburg and Mecklenburg-Western Pomerania also combine their state agencies into one building. The independency of both the Federal states was to find its expression in the material selection of the facades and in the communal garden complex. Dominated in external areas by a strong Prussian screened slate facade, the northern character of Mecklenburg-Western Pomerania was meant to emerge in an interior facade clad in pinewood. The garden complex unites pines, originating near Brandenburg, with water surfaces. Together, both the L-shaped and different height building angles separate a multi-storey hall. From here, an event area is developed in the ground floor; in the upper storeys there are management and representation areas.

Landesvertretung von Hessen (486)
State Representative for the State of Hesse
2001
In den Ministergärten 5
Michael Christl, Joachim Bruchhäuser

The Federal state of Hesse purchased a 32,280 square feet large plot of land in the area known as "In den Ministergärten" in 1997, after the initially planned location for the state representative had

been abandoned on the Klingelhöfer triangle of the Tiergarten. From an architecture competition advertised throughout Europe in 1998, the office of Michael Christl and Joachim Bruchhäuser from Frankfurt am Main emerged as the victor. The competition jury felt reminded of Frank Lloyd Wright by the overhanging function storeys of the cubic-orthogonal composition of several building structures around a central two-story foyer. A similarly overhanging canopy forms the entrance to a five-storey, Hesse-sandstone clad building, which shows the ground floor as far as possible as an open space in comparison to the neighbouring Landesvertretungs. Here, a public bistro and spaces for exhibitions and events should be located, while the offices for the management do not start until the second floor of the building. In the striking uppermost cantilever storey towards the street, the residential and representational areas of the Landesvertretung are housed.

Landesvertretung des Saarlandes (487)
State Representative of the State of Saarland
2001
In den Ministergärten 4
Peter Alt, Thomas Britz

The representation of the second-smallest Federal state shares underground garages, garden and domestic services with the neighbouring state agencies of Rheinland-Pfalz (No. 468) and Lower Saxony/Schleswig-Holstein (No. 476). From a competition limited solely to the Saarland, the design from the office of Peter Alt and Thomas Britz from Saarbrücken emerged as the victor. The architects designed a positive-negative game in the duplication of a cube with a 66-feet edge length, as it was planned as the ideal measurement for the city mansions designed in the development plan. On the avenue side, a glazed atrium area as high as the building is cut out of the cube, which was added in the rear part as a connected mass. This positive mass is, in turn, surrounded by a stone walkway construction formed from an ideal dimension. On the ground floor, a large reception area with adjoining rooms is structured towards the park in extension of the entrance hall, while the dining areas are housed in the first floor. Guest rooms and the apartment of the state's Prime minister are situated in the penthouse storey.

Neues Kranzler Eck (488)
New Kranzler Corner
2001
Kurfürstendamm/Kantstraße/
Joachimstaler Straße
Helmut Jahn

FLOP The new development of the Victoria Area combines the Kurfürstendamm boulevard with Kantstraße and supplements the existing building complex from the 1950s, in which a Berlin institution, the "Café Kranzler", was situated (see No. 290). With the canopy-surrounded cosiness from the post-war prosperity, the new sharp-edged glass block no longer has anything in common. The multi-part building had to incorporate the listed low buildings and the former Bilka department store, however this forced association has a rather tolerated effect. Like a giant, the multiply folded building ensemble provided with inner courtyards with its pinnacle on Kantstraße kneels over the lower Bilka roof

and greets the Kurfürstendamm with the dominant gesture of technocracy. The cool building accommodates businesses, offices and an aviary.

Neues Tempodrom (489)
New Tempodrom
2001
Anhalter Bahnhof
gmp

In 1980, the squatter Irene Moessiner, who had millions in legacy, bought a circus tent and pleased, from then onwards, the alternative scene with free world mu-

sic concerts, first at Potsdamer Platz, then next to the Kongresshalle (no. 285). As the capital city project (no. 459) expanded there, the next move was meant to be the last. At the beginning, politics only supplied the stand at Anhalter Bahnhof. Finally, though, they provided the bulk of the construction costs. Against real tent or eco-designs by Frei Otto and Jutta Kalepky, a huge steel construction established itself, which only came close to the old appearance in form. The jagged, white tent was enthroned on an exposed concrete foundation, in which precious wood meets with asphalt. Next to the central arena, an improvisation stage is housed as well as a musical thermal baths called Liquidrom. The programme ranges from mass spectacles to exclusive ceremonies. The Ballhaus of the Berlin Republic developed from the anarchical corral.

Tierheim Berlin (490)
Berlin Animal Shelter
2001
Hausvaterweg 39
Dietrich Bangert

In the uppermost North east of Berlin, where each year as many four-legged housemates become abandoned as people live in the Mitte part of Berlin, the largest and most architecturally ambitious animal shelter in the world developed from 1993. On 20 hectares, the ex-partner of the Kanzleramt architect Axel Schultes (no. 482) designed a one-storey "social centre" for man and animal. The central exercise arena is surrounded by

15 rotundas (a total of 24 are planned) with twelve kennels for 640 dogs. Beyond the meditative-minimalist green, gravel and water surfaces, there is a wing as long as an inter-city train, in which visitors can come fact to face with 700 cats at eye level. At right angles to this, cages for 300 small animals, offices, bungalows for the directors of the home, side rooms as well as a meeting place, clinic and a conference room stretch out. Giant glass discs display the outcast creatures as if they were models, while naked exposed concrete walls hide all these people who carry the responsibility for the asylum.

Universal Studios and Spreespeicher (491)
Universal Studios and Spree Warehouse
2001
Stralauer Allee 1-2
Reinhard Müller (conversion)

In immediate proximity to the Oberbaumbrücke, the former cold store is situated directly on the River Spree. After it was used as a warehouse up to the 1990s, it has been renovated and is now the headquarters of the global music concern, Universal. Whose logo adorns the newly inserted glass facade, without which the building would not have any windows. The opening of the wall during the renovation led to violent discussion because it meant a clear incision into the listed mass of the building which had been windowless until that point. In contrast to the Universal building, the neighbouring Spreespeicher (built between 1907–1913) has been clearly more cautiously renovated, as modern elements fit almost seamlessly into the historic building. New windows appear as natural components in the old building mass.

Berlin's Inner-city Plan:
Strategy for the Coming Decades (492)

In November 1996, the senate of Berlin presented an extensive plan for the centre of Berlin under the title "Planwerk Innenstadt Berlln", Berlin's inner-city plan. Deliberately, the first presentation was made in the framework of the Stadtforum as a prelude for a "dialogic" urban renewal. In open discussion, the preliminary plans for both the teams of Manfred Ortner/Fritz Neumeyer (City West) and Bernd Albers/Dieter Hoffmann-Axthelm (historical centre) were debated in more than 30 planning workshops and 20 public Stadtforum discussions until May 1999, when the senate's plans were agreed as the binding central theme for the coming 30 years, and the requirements were adapted to the people concerned. Hans Stimmann (no. 400) is the spiritual father of the Planwerk Innenstadt. At this time, he was acting in the function as state secretary for urban development management.

The Berlin Planwerk Innenstadt can claim to be the first Berlin inner-city plans, which went through with declared urban economic objectives. The fundamental suggestion of the Planwerk was: inner development precedes external development; that means development of a functioning inner-city core instead of sprawling across the surrounding countryside. This approach demands breaking with the planning objective of the modern age, to dismember the city into mono-functional large areas. Instead of this, the approach intends the creation of smaller units of social and function mixing and co-determination of the plots to the point of the city quarter. The Planwerk Innenstadt led to a passionate argument between partisans and critics of the modern style in the specialist community, which also brought itself to international attention.

Particularly innovative is the conversion of the abstract planning objectives. In this way, senate-owned plots in the inner-city were to be sold off at a cheap price to allow the building of residential buildings in immediate city locations. The background for such considerations are the comprehensive calculations, according to which every new apartment on the periphery of the city would result in investments in the public infrastructure.

Three-dimensional representation of the plans for the inner-city, dated May 18, 1999.

With the attempt to develop the inner-city more strongly than before as a residential area as well, the senate would like to counteract the persistent exodus from the city centre. As one of the first large projects, which would not have been possible at all without the debates, almost 50 town houses on plots with a width of over 200 feet will be developed in the Friedrichswerder quarter by the end of 2006. On filet plots between the Auswärtiges Amt and Gendarmenmarkt, 50 private landowners are reconstructing a piece of the civilian settlement – the heart of every traditional European city. The architects are subject to a strong set of design regulations, which solely allow facades made from brick, plaster or natural stone. meu

Plans envisioned for Fisher Island.

Botschaft des Königreichs Spanien (493)
Spanish Embassy
2002 (old building: 1943)
Lichtensteinallee 1
Jesús Velasco Ruiz, José Luis Iñiguez de Onzoño; old building: Walter and Johannes Krüger, Pedro Muguruza Otano

Between 1938 and 1943, the Franco Regime built an embassy building on the edge of the Tiergarten (no.60) in the newly developing Diplomatenviertel. Spain received the plot from the Reich's government within the scope of the megalomaniac Berlin plans by Albert Speer (no. 225) as a declaration of support for the Allies. The same applied to the Italian and Japanese embassies nearby. On the trapezium-shaped plot, an acute-angled two-winged building developed from the plans by architects Walter and Johannes Krüger with Pedro Muguruza Otano on the corner between Thomas-Dehler-Straße and Lichtensteinallee. The building was partially destroyed in the war; the only thing remaining was the office wing which was repaired in the 1950s, while the representative main building with its porticus on the corner and the residence

wing both deteriorated. After Spain's decision to move back into the old embassy, the TYPSIA (Madrid) office made extensive clearing-outs of the historic building. The office wing was completely removed and in its place a new office part with a foyer formed. In the representation wing, only the facade was kept. The main building was restored, by replacing the profiles from the period of origin of the house with equally sized, square stone sheets.

Institut für Chemie der Humboldt-Universität (494)
The Institute for Chemistry at the Humboldt University
2002
Newtonstraße 14
Volker Staab

When Volker Staab won the competition for the Institut für Chemie in the middle of the 1990s, the first big holes appeared in Berlin's state budget. The resulting rounds of belt-tightening have predominantly brought more users into the building: from the outside, it is only strange large yellow plaster surfaces which catch the eye, which suppress the red, unevenly expensive cast stone. The urbanite structure remains completely preserved: the L-type basic shape of the building forms a place, on which the large-scale test buildings from the 1930s (see 230) stand as if on show. At the same time, the comb structure makes sure that hundreds of inquisitive people, which frequently come and go from here give the maximum life to the memorial field.

THE NEW BERLIN

Schule für geistig
Behinderte am Mummelsoll (495)
School for Mentally
Handicapped at Mummelsoll
2002
Eilenburger Straße 4
Grüntuch Ernst

In view of the location immediately on the North East city border, one likes to suppose that problem children should be shunted off to here. However, the school at Mummelsoll is only the best example of an entire series of educational buildings for disabled people, which developed in the East of Berlin after the wall came down. The glazed auditorium foyer which is head and shoulders above the street, does not hide the students at all. The wavy section, due to which the Berlin avant-garde architects Grüntuch Ernst received the bid in the middle of the 1990s, labels the house as exceedingly ambitious, whose classrooms even have galleries. In addition, the compact complex (maximum depth of 85 feet) excels itself through a very simple orientation and low building costs.

Landesvertretung
Nordrhein-Westfalen (496)
State Representative for
North Rhine-Westphalia
2002
Hiroshimastraße 22-26
Petzinka, Pink und Partner

The Southern Tiergartenviertel was considered, during the existence of the Ber-

lin wall, as a refuge between the park and the city. Many plots of land laid idle, as the owners – in most cases foreign embassies – had their headquarters in Bonn and East Berlin. After the fall of the wall and the German reunification, the contemplative quarter awakened from its politic-induced numbness. The former Diplomatenviertel with the kudos of a residential suburb was meant to become the address of the embassies and state agencies once more. The architecture competition for the state representative of North Rhine-Westphalia plumped for the Düsseldorf-based office of Petzinka, Pink und Partner in 1999. Crucial for the decision of the jury was the innovative construction of the building, which was exemplary in terms of ecology but fitted explicitly modern into the upmarket development of the Tiergartenviertel. The load-bearing structure consists of ten parallel-structured, multi-hipped steel frames, which are connected to each other through slabs and edge beams laying in between them. The facade design followed the main idea of a glass, open house. The installation of an air conditioning unit could be avoided as the concept allowed for natural ventilation. On the roof, a photo voltaic system was installed, which creates a part of the energy which is required for the operation of the building.

Botschaft des
Königreiches der Niederlande (497)
Embassy of the
Kingdom of the Netherlands
2001
Klosterstraße 49–50
Office for Metropolitan Architecture (OMA),
Rem Koolhaas

You'd never believe the little Netherlands to be capable of so much extravagance. Off the Diplomatenviertel in the Tiergarten, the embassy of the neighbouring country resides near to the water in Rolandufer in Mitte. The building fits externally into the local block development; however, it breaks with all other conventions. A narrow strip, in which the apartments of the embassy members are located, borders on to the compartment walls of the neighbouring buildings and is separated from the actual residence through a courtyard. This transparent building part accommodates the representation and studies of the ambassador and is accessible in an unusual way. Instead of storeys, which are one on top of the other and reachable by stairways and lifts, the folded split-levels are reached

through a passageway which runs through all eight floors to the roof terraces. This serves as air circulation at the same time. The study of the Netherlands ambassador overhangs like a gazebo: with a free look across the quiet water of the River Spree.

Deutsches Historisches Museum
Erweiterungsbau (498)
German Historical Museum
Extension building
2003
Hinter dem Gießhaus/ Unter den Linden 2
Ieoh Ming Pei

The museum was so close to the heart of the former chancellor, Helmut Kohl, that he immediately commissioned the architects with the extension building himself without any prior competition. The two-part new building with its triangular ground plan, located in Am Festungsgraben, supplements the baroque arsenal (no. 16), in which the museum had been housed to date. A glazed round tower building crowns the new part of the building, which serves to develop the subsequent exhibition wing, with its entrance, rotunda and stairway and corresponds to the conventional museum typology. While the entrance area with its glassy transparency articulates an invitation to the public, the facade of the exhibition area is clad in natural stone. A tunnel combines the new building with the historical arsenal, whose beautiful

Schlüter courtyard, named after the architect of the Baroque period, is covered by a glass roof again as it was before.

**Institut für Physik
der Humboldt-Universität** (499)
*The Institute for Physics
at the Humboldt University*
2003
Newtonstraße 15
Augustin & Frank

The Institut für Physik is the most prominent project of the ambitious architects Augustin und Frank. The Berlin architects, who were still really young, interpreted the building, which was almost a hectare, made up of special laboratories, lecture rooms, study rooms and offices, which the competition from 1998 demanded, as a labyrinth. However, from the outside, the building shows an elaborate transparency: the view breaks through distorted ornamental supports made from wood, bamboo plants, wicker boxes, servicing bridges and room-sized glazing, in order to remain clinging to sloping neon lights and indirectly lit coloured walls. Instinctively, the visitor remains standing, looks, is amazed and is barely cleverer than before at the end: as the actual experiments, which take place in the North of the complex, remain hidden behind frosted glass.

**Kommunikationszentrum
der Humboldt-Universität** (500)
*Communication Centre at the
Humboldt University*
2003
Rudower Chaussee 26
Daniel Gössler

Residing in the midst of the science city of Adlershof, the accommodation of the

HU computer pool and their library grew to the Kommunikationszentrum. To house this, there was initially only the former energy central from the times of the Deutsche Versuchsanstalt für Luftfahrt (no. 230) on the plot of land. The Hamburg architect Daniel Gössler received the commission because he preserved the long scales according to a type of basilica and interlocked it closely with the new L-shaped strip made from charcoal grey zinc plates. Before the ambulatory-like diagonal wing, there is room for a light-grey auditorium cube as well as a veritable reception area. At the rear, the central square of the lowered reading room is included. In the rear part of the red-painted old building, the study areas of the library are situated today, in front, the cafeteria for the entire campus.

Haus Knauthe (501)
Knauthe House
2000
Leipziger Platz 10
Axel Schultes Architekten

The Haus Knauthe is the only building on Leipziger Platz which has a private owner – a fact which is reflected in the architecture. Since where with economically surface-optimised office buildings, every visitor finds it hard to catch their breath as soon as they enter, the house no. 10 is presented in a more generous flair. The entrance area receives visitors with a bistro and leads to a rear part of the building, whose glass surfaces themselves provide the daylight in the depth of the plot. Circular segment and curves are the basic forms, which have been set on all storeys against the strongly, orthogonal

cubature of the building. That the house carries the trademark of the Kanzleramt architects is possible to recognize in details such as the three-dimensional cut-out window hinges.

Geschäftshaus
Leipziger Platz 14 (502)
Commercial Building
at Leipziger Platz 14
2001
Leipziger Platz 14
Jan Kleihues

With the office premises on Leipziger Platz, Jan Kleihues has created a masterpiece of contemporary architecture: clear facade, unspectacular appearance, and carried out in precise detail. The basic design principle delivered the fortunate circumstance of a prescribed building height of 72 feet, which corresponds exactly to the width of the plot of land: the square is the characteristic of the building. The fundamental order, which is characterised through this, is determined by the symmetry of the diagonal and allows neither vertical nor horizontal emphasis. Instead of that, the direction neutral principle of the network results, which also allows for the connection of the stone and glass strips between the first and fifth upper floors on the square side. The facade is clad in smooth, yellow Roman travertine. The opening of the building occurs through the main entrance on Pariser Platz. A two-storey foyer, which embodies the cubic conversion

of the facade's geometry and corresponds to a cube in its volume, is lined with dark-grey serpentine stone and has a connection to the significantly more intimate, wood-clad entrance on Voßstraße.

Wohn- und Geschäftshaus
Leipziger Platz 7
(503)
Residential and Commercial Building
at Leipziger Platz 7
2003
Leipziger Platz 7
KSP Engel und Zimmermann

The building lives from the passageway which leads through it diagonally from Leipziger Platz to the new street in the south. A side wing serving as a glass bridge connects both main buildings. The complex leaves a narrow, brightly illuminated light court open over the passageway. The building is accessed through entries which are encased in natural stone and lie deep in the building. In the residential and shops area three fields of more deeply lying windows alternative with a massive limestone pillar. The office area stands out with its equal alternation of fields of stone and glass which form a grid in front of which glass parapets have been laid. The most striking feature of the facade is the horizontally protruding concrete swords which optically interrupt the verticals. All in all, this building has been worked out quite well; however, it is not one of the masterpieces from this office with three letters.

Geschäftshaus Leipziger Platz 9 (504)
Commercial Building at Leipziger Platz 9
2003
Leipziger Platz 9
Christoph Langhof

This building for business and commerce by Christoph Langhof stands directly next to the old East German watchtower at the former border (wall) with its ornaments and decorations, trying to "seduce humanity into feeling good". Large sized window surfaces of wooden and aluminium constructions have been placed over a two-story pedestal with roughly hewn elements of natural stone. Elaborately designed roofs form the conclusion of the characteristic horizontal tri-partite division which links this building to the structure of its neighbours. The plastic geometric facade with decorative elements, which ensures a clear architectural form, gives the building an exterior appropriate to its location while distinguishing it from the otherwise repetitive facades at Leipziger Platz.

Marie-Elisabeth-Lüders-Haus (505)
Marie-Elisabeth-Lüders Building
2003
Schiffbauerdamm
Stephan Braunfels

In keeping with the requirements of a "working parliament", in which short walking distances are important, the Jakob-Kaiser-Haus and Paul-Löbe-Haus (nos. 470, 478) as well as the old Reichstag building (no. 106), which houses the Bundestag, are connected with one an-

other by subterranean corridors. The Marie-Elisabeth-Lüders-Haus stands somewhat off to the side of these buildings on the other side of the Spree River. However, the Alsenblock and Luisenblock greet each other with their cantilevered, majestic canopies; the impressive, massive constructions are also connected with an arched footbridge. This "hop over the Spree", the long formal gesture of the "Band des Bundes", appears to overcome the river with no effort at all. The Marie-Elisabeth-Lüders-Haus is home to the functional areas of the Bundestag which have to manage without being quite so close to its plenary chamber: the Library of the Bundestag, with catalogue room and reading room, the scientific services of the Bundestag, press documentation and archives. The employees of the Bundestag have a total of about 731,700 square feet of usable space in 600 rooms at their disposal. The three-storey round library tower is the heart of this system, which is closed off to the city on three sides but then opens to the Spree. This area, the Spreeplatz, has remains of the Berlin Wall (compare no. 301), an outdoor staircase and a terrace of sculptures.

St.-Canisius-Kirche (506)
St. Canisius Church
2002
Witzlebenstraße 30
Büttner/Neumann/Braun

The first new Roman Catholic church building was erected in the new Berlin after the fire of 1995. Initially, Heike Büttner's plans were in just third place, be-

cause of his innovation with space. It divided the area crosswise: at the intersection lies St. Mary's chapel, a wooden cavity with keyhole floor plan. The part toward the street stayed open except for the entrance in the middle. The rear is covered by a 66-feet high concrete cube, whereby only its left half is used by the parish: huge wooded gates are followed by a democratic room with hidden confession cabinet, chairs and plaster, raised

only a little, running through it, around the altar. It is hardly possible to marry, pray or come together in a more lovely, inspired, casual setting. The right half of the cube is an empty, inaccessible tunnel into the void. It reminds even the most hardened of unbelievers of phenomena which can only be coped with through faith. No other church has ever collected atheists where they are more forceful.

Sehitlik-Moschee   (507)
Sehitlik Mosque
2003
Columbiadamm
Hilmi San

The new building for the largest mosque in Berlin is a political issue. It got into the headlines when it became known that both minarets, each 28 feet in height, and the dome of the mosque 15 feet higher than indicated in the construction plans. On top of that, three wooden doors ornamented with ivory and tortoise shell had been added. The use of such materials is forbidden in Germany as well as in Turkey, from where the doors had been delivered. After a long dispute between

the building authorities and the owners, an administrative fine of 80,000 euros was imposed. The highly traditional architecture of this mosque, with its elaborate details, is remarkable. The attention getters are the two 94 feet tall minarets. The facades are covered with marble and light natural stone and the pitched roofs of the minarets and dome are coated with zinc. Underneath them there is room on two storeys for as many as 2,000 worshipers.

Bertelsmann-Stiftung   (508)
Bertelsmann Foundation
2004
Unter den Linden 1
Thomas van den Valentyn; Rupert and York Stuhlemmer (reconstruction)

The dress rehearsal for reconstruction of the palace has taken place: the first reconstruction in new Berlin as decided on in 2001. Thomas van den Valentyn of Cologne (nos. 446, 478) was awarded the commission because the copy of the Commandantenhaus which he promised was the truest to the original and, at the same time, it was a classically modern exclamation mark. Thanks to the traditional art of laying bricks and state of the art photogrammetry, Stuhlemmer & Stuhlemmer's have been able to execute a brilliant recover of the facade of the Prussian Palazzo Pitti. Piled up on the inside are a

blatant mass of media on the ground floor, the genuine representation in piano Nobile and a sky chapel with computer screen roof over the winter garden. Compared with the consistent exterior appearance, there is a break, as is generally to be feared with a castle.

Botschaft der Vereinigten Arabischen Emirate (509)
Embassy of the United Arab Emirates
2004
Hiroshimastraße 16-20

This new embassy building has an exceptional position in the embassy district of Berlin. While most countries decline to borrow directly from their own architecture, this building draws on the fount of Arabian building tradition for its form and ornamentation. The heart of the building is the so-called oasis, a recep-

tion hall under a glass dome of which the walls and floor are covered with blue marble. At many places the Arabian seems to be very superficial, yet in view of the many interchangeable, purely functional buildings of other countries, the effect of this local colour on the beholder can hardly be said to be unappealing.

Ritz-Carlton Hotel (510)
Ritz Carlton Hotel
2004
Potsdamer Platz
Heinz Hilmer, Christoph Sattler

The hotel is one of the two twin towers which the master planners Hilmer & Sattler have proposed for the north side of Potsdamer Platz in their master plan. Besides that, the hotel forms the prelude to the Beisheim Center, to which four further buildings in the rear belong. The design by the Munich-based architects was inspired by the Chicago high rises of the 1930s. The finely profiled facade is accentuated vertically; the conclusion of the tower is stepped. At the request of the investor, it bears a marker with his name. As the architect Christoph Sattler has acknowledged in the meantime, all the towers at Potsdamer Platz could just as well have been somewhat taller.

Parkside Apartments (511)
Parkside Apartments
2004
Henriette-Hertz-Park/Lennéstraße
David Chipperfield

This building clothed in mussel limestone is undoubtedly one of the most important new residential buildings which
has been completed in Berlin since 2000.
David Chipperfield knew how to endow
the 390 to 3,800 square feet flats with a
plastic hull that looks like a polished jew-

el case because of its rounded corners.
The irregular distribution of its windows,
balconies and loggias first creates an impression of an erratic design, but on a
second look they fit in nicely with a vertically oriented structure. The foyer and
lobby likewise breathe the spirit of a matter of fact modernity. Upon leaving the
foyer with polished black granite floor
and light mussel limestone one reaches
the lobby, where a lounge suite special-
ly designed for the house invites one to
stay for a while. The new building's capri-
cious exterior notwithstanding, its flats
fulfil all generally accepted requirements
placed on a premium inner city residence
and thanks to its open floor plans allow
individual configurations.

Akademie der Künste (512)
Academy of Arts
2005
Pariser Platz 4
Günter Behnisch with Werner Durth

Germany's largest academy of fine arts
longs to return from the idyllic seclusion
of Tiergarten (compare no. 295) to its

erstwhile location at Pariser Platz. Admittedly, the only remains of this seat,
which is incomparably more appealing
to the public, were Ernst von Ihne's exhibition hall, in which Albert Speer modelled Germania and later the east German
border police enforced a regimen of terror. In 1993, after this address had become available once again, the "cultural
signboard of the nation" selected Günter
Behnisch, the old master of West German
architecture, as their draughtsman. His
fully transparent work of passageways
puts the Artists Association and its relics
on display to the greatest possible extent,
opens up to everyone the best view of
the Brandenburger Gate and the Reichstag (nos. 40, 106) and at that time set off
the so called Berlin architecture dispute
"stone or glass" (compare no. 375). In the
sequel, the Academy had to give up on a
march through to Behrenstraße and en-
trench themselves four storeys deep in
the ground.

Mahnmal für die
ermordeten Juden Europas (513)
Holocaust Memorial
2005
Ebertstraße at Behrenstraße
Peter Eisenman

The idea of a central memorial place for
the victims of Nazi terror goes back to
the 1980's. Debates about its location,
contents, dedication, size, form and developers, as well as the general meaning
of historic monuments, eventually led to
a holocaust memorial. Just two design
competitions were needed for the current
worldwide trick in dealing with the in-
comprehensible to take hold, namely de-

constructivism. Peter Eisenman, a theoretician of this style, placed about 2,700 slanted concrete steles ranging from virtually zero to overwhelming height on a property of almost two hectares in such a way that two people anywhere in it are scarcely able to pass by each other. There is also a subterranean hall which informs the visitor by remembering many Jewish victims by name and relating a sample of family histories about them. One can only wonder whether this artistically finished cemetery will be misunderstood as the last resting place for the confrontation with the Nazi past.

**Philologische Bibliothek
der Freien Universität** (514)
*Philological Library
of the Free University*
2005
Habelschwerter Allee 45
Norman Foster

Today, the Free University has the reputation of being a faceless, mass produced university. This view is reflected architecturally by the so-called rusty bucket (1972, Candilis/Josic/Woods): this top address for formation of the front city is an icon of structuralism, which wanted to populate the world with equal modules. It was no less a figure than Norman Fos-

ter (no. 452) who planted his opposing concept directly between its two main axes. A bubble of light metal appears in the place of the corten steel grid; the eternal extendibility redeems a limitation of capacity to 25,000 of the 62,000 students of former times. While this super brain, which does not even measure 190 feet, is being celebrated by the Free University as the crystallization core of a "German Oxford", Berlin's Humboldt and Technical universities have recently acquired much more spacious quarters for their books (compare no. 500).

Botschaft der USA (515)
United States Embassy
started 2004
Pariser Platz
Moore Ruble Yudell

Like France and Great Britain, the United States of America are also returning with a new building to the historic site of their embassy in Berlin. The start of construction was delayed many times because the Americans and the Berlin Senate were unable to agree on a security concept. The United States insisted on barriers which, among other things, would have made it necessary to relocate a street, whereas the State of Berlin did not wish to make more concessions than were being made to other embassies too. A compromise was finally agreed: the facades at the southwest corner of the embassy were moved to behind the property boundary. Moore Ruble Yudell, the architects and planners from California, have reworked their classical victory design to give it a more modern form in its details. The facade facing Pariser Platz will have a slit that marks the entrance and extends to the top of the building.

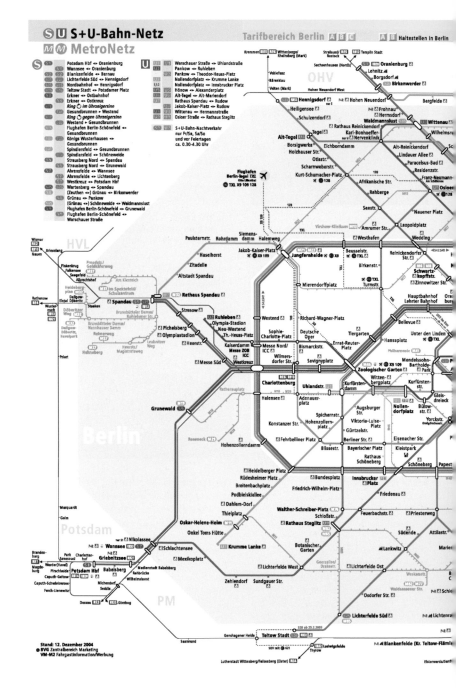

Fahrscheine bitte vor Fahrtantritt entwerten.
Tickets must be validated before use.

Legende

S+U-Bahn-Linie mit Umsteigemöglichkeit
MetroTram-Linie
MetroBus-Linie
► Halt nur in Pfeilrichtung
Behindertengerechter Zugang
Behindertenfreundlicher Zugang
Bus-Anbindung zum Flughafen
Fernbahnhof
ZOB Zentraler Omnibusbahnhof
Parkplatz
BVG-Fundbüro

Baumaßnahmen

Lichterfelde Süd ↔ Hennigsdorf
verkehrt bis 24.2.2005
Nordbahnhof ↔ Hennigsdorf
verkehrt ab 25.2.2005

Teltow Stadt ↔ Potsdamer Platz
verkehrt ab 25.2.2005
Bezeichnung der Bahnhöfe
unter Fortlassung der Tarif-
bezeichnung Berlin bzw. Potsdam

Service

Berliner Verkehrsbetriebe (BVG)
10773 Berlin
www.bvg.de - Info@bvg.de
imode.bvg.de - wap.bvg.de

BVG Call Center: (030) 19 44 9
Tag und Nacht. Rund um die Uhr.
Auch am Wochenende.

BVG Fahrinfo SMS
Standort-Nr. senden an 77 3 77

BVG Fundbüro
am U-Bhf Kleistpark/U-Bhf Bülowstr.
Potsdamer Str. 182 (nahe Pallasstraße)
10783 Berlin (Schöneberg)
(030) 19 44 9

Bahn Berlin

S-Bahn Berlin GmbH
(030) 29 74 33 33
www.s-bahn-berlin.de
kundenbetreuung@s-bahn-berlin.de
DB-FundService Hotline 01805/99 05 99

S-Bahn-Kundenbüro
Am S-Bahnhof Nordbahnhof
Invalidenstr. 19
10115 Berlin (Mitte)

Die Bahn
www.bahn.de
11 8 61 gebührenpflichtig

Die Haltestellen im Bereich der Gemeinde Schönefeld
(Landkreis LDS, Wabe 5/B/7) gehören sowohl zum
Tarifbereich Berlin, Teilbereich B als auch zum
Landkreis Dahme-Spreewald.

Flughafen
Berlin-Schönefeld SXF
162 171

BVG Berliner Verkehrsbetriebe

S Bahn Berlin Deutsche Bahn Gruppe

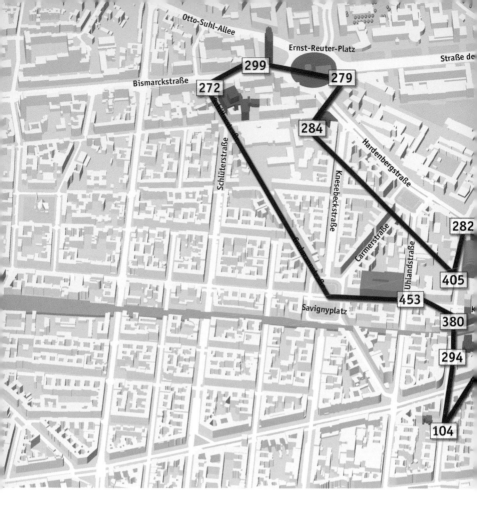

1. West Berlin

Duration: 60 min.

Tips for a break!
Café im Literaturhaus
Paris-Bar
Café Hardenberg

This is the part of the city where the centre of West Berlin arose out of the ruins of World War II. The few older constructs still here are easy to recognize along this route. We leave the train station at *Zoologischer Garten* (228) and head toward the east. We cross *Hardenbergplatz*, go past the *Kaiser-Wilhelm Memorial Church*

(107, 302) and cross *Budapester Straße* to reach the *Europe Centre* (314). The *Peek & Cloppenburg department store* (389) and *Salamander House* (378) are located in *Tauentzienstraße* on successive corners of ensembles.

Returning, we go past the *Kaiser-Wilhelm Memorial Church* (107, 302) again. Here our street bends toward the left and its name changes to *Kurfürstendamm*. We continue on to the *Kranzler Corner* (290, 490). Just a slight excursion into *Fasanenstraße* to the left is required to reach the *Winter garden ensemble* (104), where it pays to take a break in the *Café im*

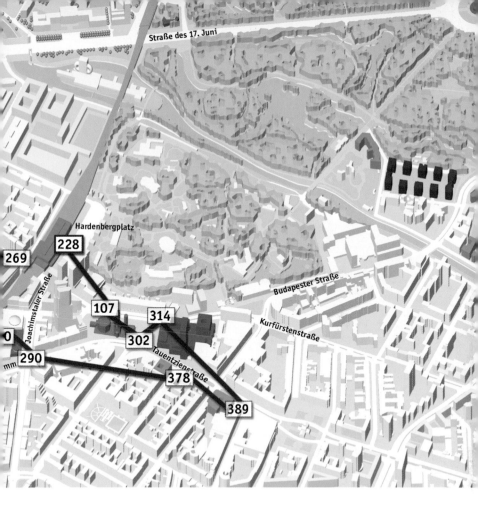

Literaturhaus. Returning, we come to the *House of the Jewish Community* (294), which stands out on the left before the railroad overpass. We reach *Kantstraße* at the *Kant-Dreieck* (380). We can already see the *Ludwig-Erhard House* (405) from its south side and will come closer to it later on. First we turn left into *Kantstraße* (tip for a break: Restaurant Paris Bar, *Kantstraße 152*).

Reaching the *Stilwerk design centre* (453), we walk through a section of Charlottenburg to the *Schiller Theatre* (272). From here one can hardly miss the *Telefunken high rise* (299) as well as *Ernst-Reuter*

Place (279), named after one of the most famous mayors of Berlin. Leaving this circle, we go into *Hardenbergstraße* on its right hand side and pass *Hardenberg House* (284) (tip for a break: Cafe Hardenberg, *Hardenbergstraße 10*). We come to *Fasanenstraße* again, where we can see the *Ludwig-Erhard House* (405) from its north side. We pass by the *Chamber of Industry and Commerce* (282) and *Amerikahaus* to return to our starting point.

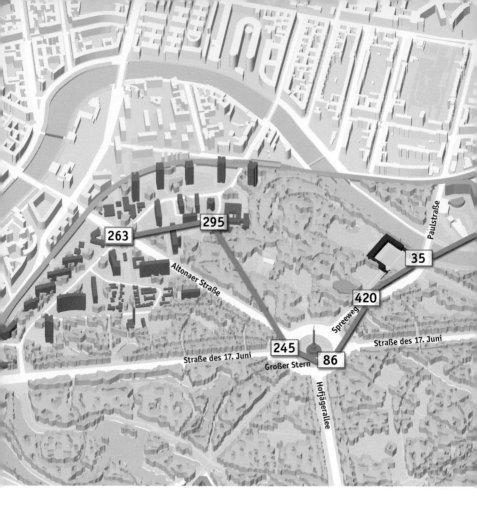

2. A walk through the Tiergarten

Duration: 60 min.

Tips for a break!
Café of the Academy of Arts
Beer Garden House of the Cultures of the World
Starbucks Coffee House at Pariser Platz

Our walk through the "green lung" of Berlin starts at U-Bahn station *Hansaplatz*. We go into *Bartningallee* and then turn right into *Hanseatenweg*, reaching the *Academy of the Arts* (295) after a curve to the left (tip for a break: the café in the Academy). Following paths toward the east through the woods, we soon see the *Victory Column* (86) towering over the *Great Star* (245). The *Office of the President of the Federal Republic of Germany* (420) seems to be trying to hide in the Tiergarten like some futuristic ferry with its smooth surface and ergonomic form. Less than 100 metres later we take a leap back into the past: the official seat of Germany's president, *Bellevue Castle* (35). Turning right into the *John-Foster-Dulles-Allee*, we see the *"Federal Snake"* (442) on the opposite bank of the *Spree River*, winding along toward the east. With the Spree on our left, we continue to the *House of the Cultures of the World* (285)

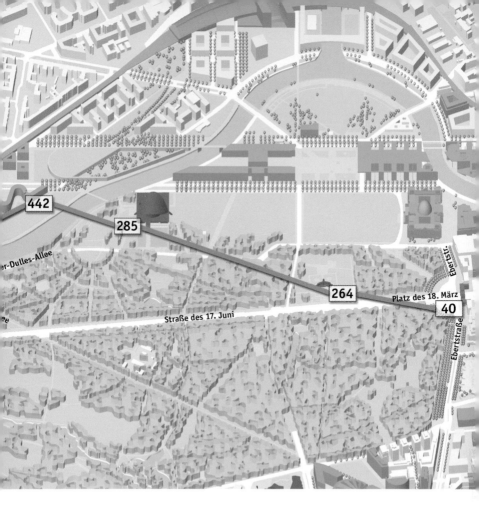

442

285

er-Dulles-Allee

264

Platz des 18. März

40

Ebertstr.

Ebertstraße

Straße des 17. Juni

°e

(tip for a break: beer garden facing the water). The impressively formed "pregnant oyster" can be seen once more from a distance while our route leads us diagonally through the Tiergarten to the *Soviet Cenotaph* (264). It is worthwhile to take the steps to visit the structure in the rear. Following the majestic aisle formed by the *Straße des 17. Juni* we finally reach the *Brandenburg Gate* (40).

Optionally, one can go up into the dome over the *Reichstag* on the left – it might be necessary to wait – and then take a break in Starbucks Coffee House at *Pariser Platz* after having passed the Bran-

denburg Gate. Alternatively, one can continue directly with Tour 6 to stroll down Berlin's grand promenade *Unter den Linden*.

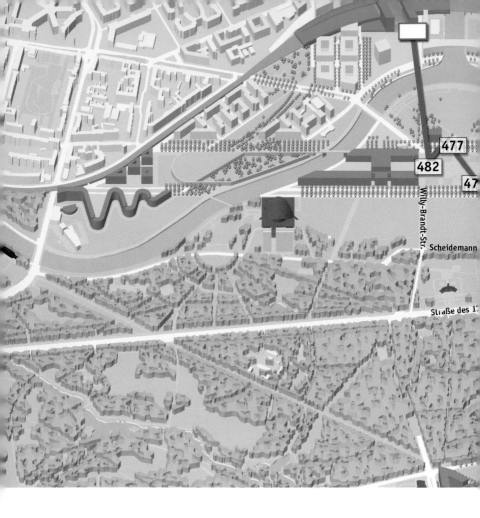

Witty-Brandt-Str.

477
482
47

Scheidemann

Straße des 17

3. Through Berlin's Government District

Duration: 90 min.

Tips for a break!
Café Käfer in the Reichstag
Habel Weinkultur, Luisenstraße
Café Einstein, Unter den Linden

From the upstairs platforms of Berlin's *Hauptbahnhof* (central train station), formerly *Lehrter Bahnhof*, one has a view of Berlin's government district with its historic and modern buildings. Having arrived with the S-Bahn, we take the exit "*Moltkebrücke*" toward *Reichstag* and *Brandenburger Tor* and follow the *Ella-*

Trebe-Straße to take the bridge toward the *Embassy of the Swiss Confederation* (477) and the *Federal Chancellery* (482). The *Paul-Löbe House* (470, also known as Alsen block) stands across from the Chancellery. From the *Crown Prince Bridge* we can also see its counterpart, the *Marie-Elisabeth-Lüders House* (505).

On the city side of the bridge we pass the *Federal Press Conference Building* (461) and go right alongside the overpass until we can go left into *Luisenstraße* to reach the *State Representative for Saxony-Anhalt* (88) directly on our left (tip for a break: Habel Weinkultur/ Brasserie).

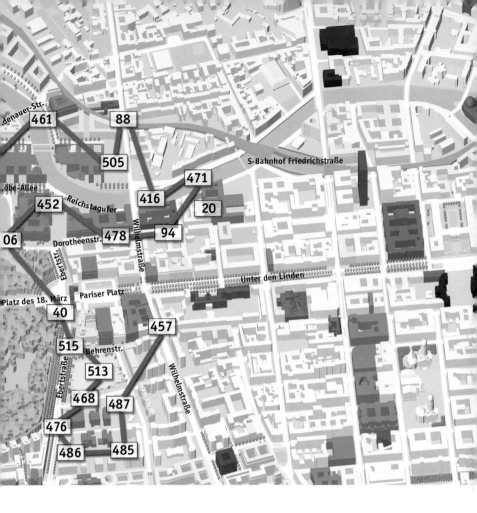

We then go back under the railroad bridge and straight on, passing by the rear of the *Luisenblock*, on our way to the *ARD Capital City Studio* (416) on the *Reichtagsufer*. Our walk continues around the *Press and Information Bureau of the Federal Government* (471, 20) and into *Dorotheenstraße*. We come to the former *Institute Building* (94) on our right. Crossing *Wilhelmstraße*, we go through the *Jakob-Kaiser House* (478). Further on to the west we are soon greeted with an appearance by one of Berlin's most famous buildings, the *German Parliament Building* (106, 452 - *Reichstag*), where we can take a break inside at the Café Käfer.

Either at this or some later time it would be well worth the while to go up into the dome, keeping in mind that it will probably be necessary to wait in line. A short path through a green area leads to the *Brandenburg Gate* (40). Passing it, we go by the new *United States Embassy* (515) and then *Holocaust Memorial* (513). Shortly thereafter, we go left into the street *In den Ministergärten* to see the buildings of various German federal states (476, 468, 486, 485, 487). We go left into *Wilhelmstraße*, passing the *British Embassy* (457) and continue to Berlin's grand promenade *Unter den Linden* at the end of this tour.

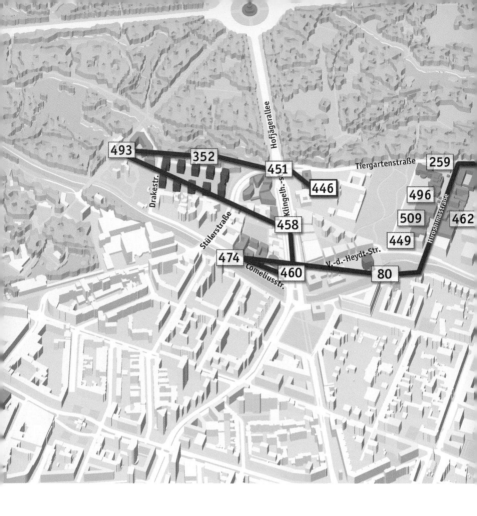

4. Diplomatic Berlin

Duration: 60 min.

Tips for a break!
Café am Neuen See
Café in the Art Gallery (Gemäldegalerie)

We take a bus to the seat of the *Konrad-Adenauer Foundation* (446); the bus stops have the same name. On our right we see the *Victory Column* (86) in the distance through the Tiergarten. We go west into *Stülerstraße* around the *Nordic Embassies* (451) for just a few metres until *Thomas-Dehler-Straße*, which we turn into on our right. With the *City Mansions* (352) to our

left we follow this street to its end and go to the right around the *Spanish Embassy* (493), which is located deep within the Tiergarten. Tip for a break: *Café am Neuen See.*

Next we go back via *Drakestraße*, left into *Rauchstraße* and right into *Klingelhöferstraße* to the *Embassy of the United States of Mexico* (458). *The Federal Office of the CDU* (460) and the *Residential Building Corneliusstraße* (474) are located at the canal (*Landwehrkanal*).

We cross *Klingelhöferstraße* and come to the *Villa von der Heydt* (80). The diploma-

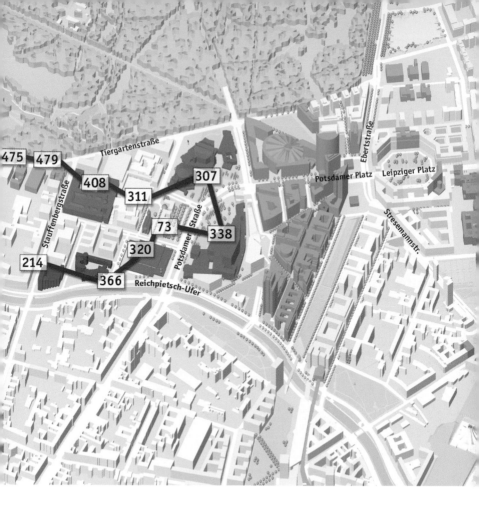

tic quarter continues with *Hiroshimastraße*. Next we see the *German State Representative for the Free and Hanseatic City of Bremen* (449), followed by the *Embassy of the United Arab Emirates* (509). Next comes the *State Representative for North Rhine-Westphalia* (496) with the *Friedrich-Ebert Foundation* (462) opposite it across the street and then the *Japanese and the Italian Embassy* (259, 258) on our left and right. Turning right into *Tiergartenstraße*, we come to the *Embassy of the Republic of South Africa*, an then, in immediate succession, the *Indian Embassy* (475), the *German State Representative of Baden-Württemberg* (469) and

the *Embassy of the Republic of Austria* (479). The *Embassy of the Arab Republic of Egypt* is located in *Staufenbergstraße*.

Now we are approaching a centre of cultural Berlin. The *Art Gallery* (408) (tip for a break: cafeteria in the gallery) and the *New National Gallery* (320) are at the *Culture Forum* (311), near Potsdamer Platz. From their somewhat elevated locations we can easily see *St. Matthew's Church* (73), the *State Library Building 2* (338), and *Philharmonic Hall* (307) too. We find the *Berlin Scientific Centre* (366) and the *Shell House* (214) at the *Reichpietschufer*.

5. Potsdamer Platz and Leipziger Platz: The New Centre

Duration: 60 min.

Tips for a break!
Huth Wine Tavern, Alte Potsdamer
Straße 5
Billy Wilders in the SONY Center

This tour through Berlin's new centre starts at its train station *S-Bahnhof Potsdamer Platz* (253). In our immediate vicinity the striking *high rise at Potsdamer Platz 1* of small red bricks (465) stretches toward the sky and to the north of us stands the cream coloured *Ritz Carlton Hotel* (510). The *SONY Centre* (472), of

such dimensions that it cannot be overlooked, forms the heart of the new *Potsdamer Platz* (tip for a break: Café/Bar Billy Wilders, Potsdamer Straße 2). We go through the *SONY Centre* and arrive directly at the complex comprising *Philharmonic Hall*, the *Musical Instruments Museum* and the *Chamber Music Hall* (307).

Now we cross *Potsdamer Straße* and walk into narrow *Eichhornstraße*. We come to the *Grand Hyatt Berlin* (424) on the left, where we walk into the lobby just to take a look. We cross *Marlene-Dietrich-Platz* keeping to our right, where we turn into *Theaterufer*. This brings us to the *Debis-*

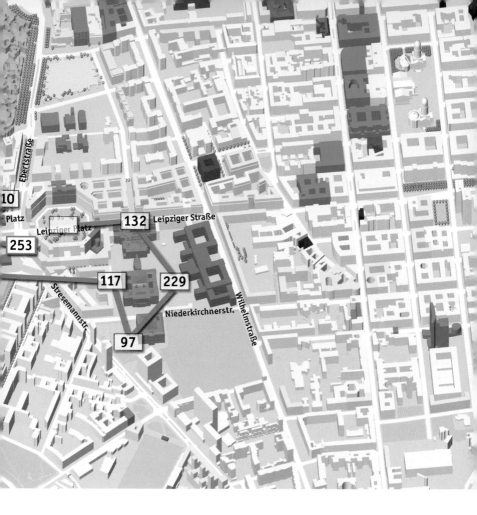

Ebertstraße

10

Platz

Leipziger Platz

253

132 Leipziger Straße

Stresemannstr.

117 **229**

Niederkirchnerstr.

Wilhelmstraße

97

House at Potsdamer Platz (403). It marks the highest, southernmost point of the modern business and shopping district. Its architecture is embedded in a waterscape at the foot of the building. Returning, we keep to our right until *Alte Potsdamer Straße*, which we turn into. *Huth Wine Tavern* (163) forms a structural counterpoint to the modern design of Potsdamer Platz and shows how diverse Berlin's architecture can be (tip for a break: Huth Wine Tavern). Continuing, we cross *Stresemannstraße* and go right. After a while we come to *Niederkirchnerstraße*. The modern office building "Stresemann 111" stands across the street to

our right. Going left here, we see the *Berlin Parliament* (117), once home to the *Prussian Legislative Assembly*, and the *Martin-Gropius Building* (97), which testify of yet different eras.

Passing by a stretch of the old Berlin Wall, we go left into *Wilhelmstraße* and walk along the front of the *Federal Ministry of Finance*, which used to be the *Reich Aviation Ministry* (229). We turn left at *Leipziger Straße* and go by the *Federal Council of Germany* (132, "*Bundesrat*") about 200 metres later on our left. *Leipziger Platz* opens up to us in the west (compare with 1, 157, 220, 375, 501–504).

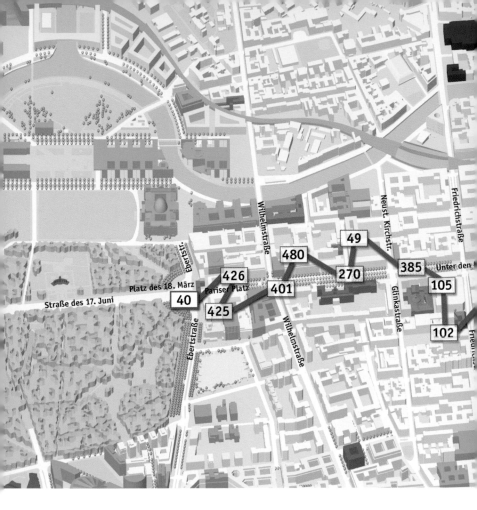

6. Unter den Linden

Duration: 45 min.

Tips for a break!
Café Einstein, Unter den Linden 42
Opernpalais, next to the Staatsoper
Unter den Linden

This tour through Berlin's old city centre along the grand promenade *Unter den Linden* starts at the *Brandenburg Gate* (40), one of the most famous landmarks of Berlin and the Federal Republic of Germany. Historic Pariser Platz is home to a fair number of interesting buildings of recent times, including the *Dresdner Bank*

(426), the *DG Bank* (425), the *United States Embassy* (515) and the *French Embassy*, to name just a few. As we leave the square going east, we first look at the *Hotel Adlon* (401), which has been reconstructed. The *Embassy of the Republic of Hungary* (480) on the left is followed by the *Embassy of the Russian Federation* (270) on our right.

Going left here into *Schadowstraße*, we come to the *Schadow House* (49). We turn into *Mittelstraße* and then right again into *Neustädtische Kirchstraße* to go back to *Unter den Linden*. *Pietsch House* (385) is at the corner. Here, we can stop for a

break at Café Einstein. We cross *Unter den Linden* and go left into *Behrenstraße* past the *Comic Opera* (105) to the *German Civil Servants Association* (102).We cross *Friedrichstraße* to reach the *Behrenstraße Boarding House* (421) and *Rosmarin Square* (434) in the block on our left. We take *Charlottenstraße* to return to *Unter den Linden*.

At the corner, we have a good view of the old building of the *State Library* (171) across the street. With the *Old Palace* (66) on the right we go through the *Forum Fridericianum* (32). From there we pass by the *State Opera* Unter den Linden (27)

on our way to *St. Hedwig's Cathedral* (33) and the *Administration Building of the State Opera House* (280). Then we return to *Unter den Linden* via *Oberwallstraße*. The formerly *Princesses' Palace* (22) is located at the corner on our left. Named *Opera Palace*, it now houses an "opera café", where we can take a nice break.

Going toward the Spree, we reach the former *Arsenal* (16) and the new building of the *German Historical Museum* (498) before the reconstructed *Commander's House* (87) and the *Castle Bridge* (56) mark the end of this tour.

7. Friedrichstraße –
The New Old Shopping Boulevard

Duration: 45 min.

Tips for a break!
Starbucks Coffee House at the
International Trade Centre
Sale et Tabacchi, taz Building at
Kochstraße 18

We begin our walk at the U-Bahn Station
Oranienburger Tor. First we walk to the
Federal Ministry for Education and Research (456) by going away from the city
centre on Friedrichstraße, turning left
into *Hessische Straße*, going left into *Hannoversche Straße* three streets later and
then on to the Ministry.

Back in *Friedrichstraße* again, we see the
overpass in the distance and walk toward
it. First we pass *Friedrichstadt Palace*
(350) on our left and then the *Spree Terraces* (363). We go under the overpass
and come to the *International Trade Centre* (344), also on the left. Tip for a break:
Starbucks Coffee House, on the right.

We continue to the south, crossing *Unter
den Linden*, to go by the *Gardens at Gendarmenmarkt* (392), on the left behind
the intersection with *Behrenstraße* and

the site of the former *Friedrichstadt Passages* (372) from *Französische Straße* to
Mohrenstraße. Today, these are the modern city *Quarter 207* (397), *Quarter 206*
(396) and *Quarter 205* (395). Now we go
left into *Mohrenstraße* for a short distance
and arrive at the *House of German Crafts*
(276). We go over part of *Friedrichstraße*
and on to *Kronenstraße*, turning right, to
reach the *Crown Palace* (423). In this area
we have also seen parts of the *Kontorhaus
Mitte* (409).

After a short swing to the north we come
to the *U-Bahn Station at Mohrenstraße*
(271), which lies next to the *Embassy of
the Czech Republic in Berlin* (343). Going
south in a semicircle toward *Friedrichstraße* again, we pass by the *Step-Down
Station at Buchhändlerhof* (199) in the
back yard of Mauerstraße 78–80.

The *Residential and Commercial Building*
(367) in *Friedrichstraße* 56 is not very far
away from that famous, historically significant terminus of our tour: *House at
Checkpoint Charlie* (376), also in *Friedrichstraße*. Tip for a break: Sale et Tabacchi, farther on at Kochstraße 18.

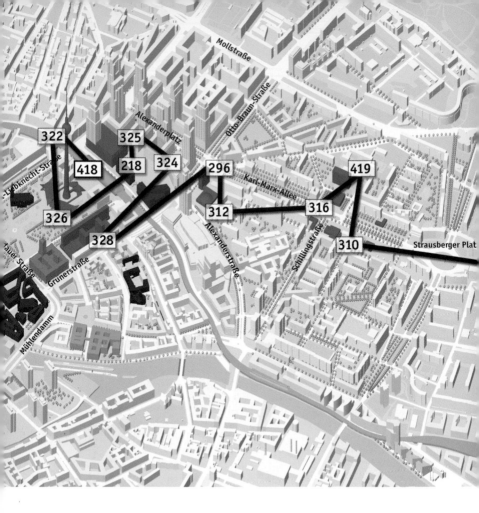

8. "Socialistic" Berlin
Karl-Marx-Allee and East City

Duration: 50 min
This route all the way to Frankfurt Gate, when taken by foot, can only be recommended to experienced hikers; however, it is ideal for bicycle riders.

Tips for a break!
Restaurant at the top of the Television Tower
Café Alberts at Frankfurt Gate

With this tour from west to east we go back in time to the beginnings of the socialist German Democratic Republic (DDR) and the architecture dictated to it

from communist Moscow. We start at *Alexanderplatz Station* (418). The *Television Tower* (322, 326), by far the tallest structure of Berlin, is a symbol of the progressive thinking of the DDR. It can be seen from all parts of the city.

We go under the train tracks through to the *Berolina House* (218) and continue to *Kaufhof*, formerly the *Centrum Department Store* (325). Both buildings are directly at the border of *Alexander Place* (324). From there we advance to the *Town Hall Passages* (328). Returning along the main thoroughfare at our right, *Grünerstraße*, we pass under the tracks again

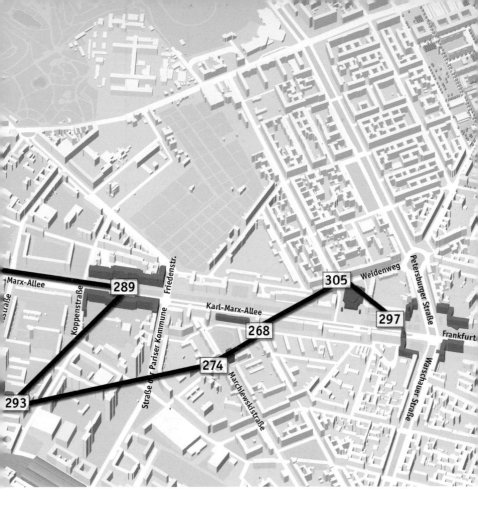

Marx-Allee

Koppenstraße

289

Friedenstr.

305

Weidenweg

Petersburger Straße

Karl-Marx-Allee

297

268

Frankfurt

Straße der Pariser Kommune

274

Warschauer Straße

Marchlewskistraße

293

and continue to the intersection with *Alexanderstraße*, the location of the *Haus des Lehrers* and the striking dome of the former *Kongresshalle* (312), now the Berlin Conference Center (bcc). We continue along Grünerstraße to *Karl-Marx-Allee*, formerly the mighty east west axis *Stalinallee* (263, 268, 274, 289, 296, 297, 305, 306, 315, 331), where we turn right and go east.

The District Office of *Berlin-Mitte* (419) stands behind the *International Cinema* (316). Directly opposite at the corner to Schillingstraße lies the building of the famous former *Moscow Restaurant* (310).

After passing through *Strausbergerplatz*, we can take a right into *Andreasstraße* and proceed about 450 metres to take a look at the *Helmut Lehmann "closing time home"* (293) for retired persons in house no. 21. We continue on *Karl-Marx-Allee* to *Block C* (289). Here the tour passes through a classical example of socialistic urban planning.

Passing over the *Weberwiese* ("Weber meadow") we reach a high rise with the same name (274). The *Access Balcony Houses* (268) point the way to the *Kosmos Film Theatre* (305) and finally to the *Frankfurt Gate* (297), the end of the tour.

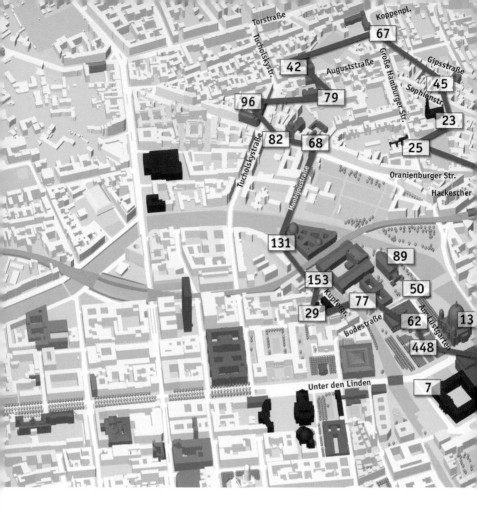

9. Through Historic Berlin

Dauer: 105 min

Duration: 105 min

Tips for a break!
There are numerous restaurants and cafés at *Hackescher Markt* and in the *Nikolaiviertel.*

The tour starts from the north side of S-Bahn station *Hackescher Markt* (99). We proceed deeper into this quarter, past the *Old Berlin Craftsmen's Yard* (25) to the *Sophia Church* (23). Going around it to *Gipsstraße* we come upon a remarkable

residential building (45). We go to the *Hollmannsche Wilhelmine Amalie Foundation* (67) at *Koppenplatz*, which we leave again the same way we came. Two buildings in *Auguststraße* are of special interest: a *residential building* (42) from the 17th century and a *former Jewish* hospital (79). The former *Postal Service Authority* (96) and the *New Synagogue* (82) are best viewed from the opposite side of the street. For the *Artist's Courtyard* (68), however, one ought to cross the street.

We continue to *Museum Island* (50). We first see the *Bode Museum* (131) from the west before the *Pergamon Museum* (153)

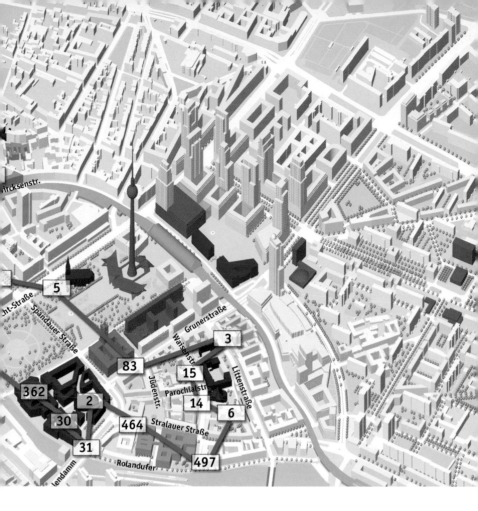

ircksenstr.

5

ht-Straße

Spandauer Straße

Grunerstraße

3

83

Watsenstr

15

Jüdenstr.

Parochialstr

14

Littenstraße

362

2

464

30

Stralauer Straße

6

31

Rolandufer

endamm

497

can be seen along *Am Kupfergraben*. The old *Magnus House* (29) is on this side of the "moat". Now we experience the powerful museum architecture. We first stroll past the *Old Museum* (62) and the *New Museum* (77). Leaving the *Old National Gallery* (89) behind us, we reach the *Pleasure Garden* (448), with the *Berlin Cathedral* (136) on the left. The *Berlin Castle* (7) was once situated here, almost on the same spot where the *Palace of the Republic* still stands today (337).

We go to the southwest a short distance to reach the *Nikolai Quarter* (362). From the *Berlin Wasser Holding AG* (464) and

the *Embassy of the Kingdom of the Netherlands* (497) we reach the oldest remaining part of Berlin: To the *City Wall* (6). Northward, we find the *Parochial Church* (14), *Podewil Palace* (15) and the *Franciscan Cloistser Church* (3). Proceeding along the *Berlin City Hall* (83) toward the west, we come to *St. Mary's Church* (5), to the former *Holy Ghost Chapel* (4) and finally to the starting point of our tour.

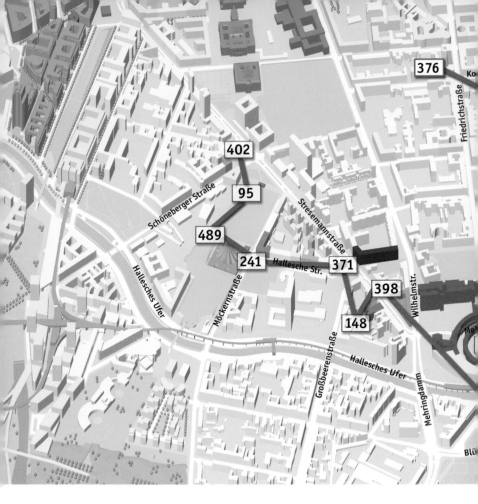

10. From Mitte to Kreuzberg

Duration: 75 min.

Tips for a break!
Sale et Tabacchi in the taz House,
Kochstraße 18.

This tour starts at the *House at Check-point Charlie* (376). We walk into *Koch-straße* toward the east, pass the *taz House* (377), where we can take refreshments at Sale et Tabacchi, and the *GSW Headquarters* (438), go past the building of the *Axel Springer Publishing House* (318) and continue until the accommodations of the former *German Debt Administration* (184)

in *Oranienstraße*. The residential development in *Ritterstraße Housing Construction* (349) can be reached through a small inner courtyard. The *Berlin Museum*, formerly the *Superior Court of Justice* (24), stands next to the new *Jewish Museum* (428). The former building of the *German Metalworkers' Union* (207) forms the corner development of *Alte Jacobstraße* and *Lindenstraße*.

We follow the *Landwehrkanal* ("militia canal") and the railroad line over it to *Mehring Place* (333). The *American Memorial Library* (275) is located directly to the south on the other side of the canal.

Further to the north at the entrance to *Stresemannstraße*, which leads directly to *Potsdamer Platz*, we reach the *Willy-Brandt-House* (398), which is the party headquarters of the SPD. The *Hebbel Theatre* (148) is on the left. At the corner of the *Stresemann Mews* (371) we go diagonally to the left and then around the *Letter Distribution Office* SW 11 (241) northward to the *New Tempodrom* (489) and *Anhalter Railway Station* (95). Our tour ends at the office and residential building at *Askanischer Platz* (402).

APPENDIX

Index of objects

The black numbers listed in the index refer to the property numbers. In the property index, you will find additional coloured numbers behind the property number. These refer to the property drawings corresponding to the different eras in the *Architecture City Plan of Berlin*, also published by the Verlagshaus Braun.

INDEX OF OBJECTS

INDEX OF OBJECTS

APPENDIX

INDEX OF OBJECTS

INDEX OF OBJECTS

INDEX OF OBJECTS

APPENDIX

INDEX OF OBJECTS

APPENDIX

INDEX OF OBJECTS

INDEX OF OBJECTS

APPENDIX

INDEX OF STREETS

APPENDIX

INDEX OF ARCHITECTS

Index of architects

APPENDIX

APPENDIX

INDEX OF ARCHITECTS

INDEX OF ARCHITECTS

THE AUTHORS | PICTURE CREDITS

The authors

Markus Sebastian Braun (editor), born in 1966. Mr. Braun studied history, German language and literature, and economics. From 1993 to 1995 he was editor of Copernicus, a popular scientific magazine. Today he is a publisher and lives in Berlin.

Rainer Haubrich, born in 1965. Mr. Haubrich is a reviewer of architecture and heads the feuilleton department of DIE WELT, a German daily. He studied history as well as the history of art and political sciences, he has written three books about Berlin architecture and sat on the state monument council of Berlin. In 1996 he was awarded the German-French journalist prize.

Hans Wolfgang Hoffmann, born in 1970. Mr. Hoffmann studied architecture and since 1995 has been a freelance author on construction policy, urban development and design, especially for the Frankfurter Rundschau, the Berliner Zeitung and taz. He has been executive manager of a mediation project in Berlin since 1997.

Philipp Meuser, born in 1969. Mr. Meuser lives and works in Berlin as an architect (BDA) and is also author and editor of numerous publications on urban development and architecture in international contexts.

Picture credits

All pictures, which are not separately listed in the following, stem from Andreas Muhs. If not otherwise indicated, reference is made to the consecutive numbers of the properties.

Alte Nationalgalerie (SMPK) © Christian Gahl, Berlin: 50 re. / Archiv der Akademie der Künste: 185 li., 331 li. & re. / Archiv der Botschaft des Königreichs Spanien, Büro TYPSIA: 480 / Archiv für Kunst und Geschichte, Berlin: 74 li., 281, 347 re., Architektengalerie/Libeskind, Daniel / Archiv Wolfgang Schäche: 225 / Bauhaus-Archiv, Berlin: 179 o. / BASD Westphal+Schlotter Architekten: 128 / Berliner Architekturwelt, Sonderheft 13, 1913, S. 118: 90, S. 118: 157 / Berliner Verkehrsbetriebe (BVG): Seite 314 / Berlinische Galerie. Landesmuseum für Moderne Kunst, Fotografie und Architektur. Architektursammlung © VG Bild-Kunst, Bonn 2001: 265 / Bosch-Archiv: 177 / Bildarchiv Preußischer Kulturbesitz (BPK): 7 li., 11, 18 li., 44 li., 107, 137, 141 li., 198, 220, 224, 235 li. & re., 248, 263 re. & li., 300 li. & re. / © by ,Windtunnel', New York, für I. M. Pei Architect: 484 / HdK-Archiv: 21 / IBA-Archiv, Berlin: 356 / König, Wilmar: 221 / Kreuzberg Museum, Archiv Südost-Express: 347 li. / Ladendorf, Heinz: Andreas Schlüter. Baumeister und Bildhauer des preußischen Barock. Leipzig 1997, S. 127: 17 / Lauer, Udo: 351 / Meuser, Philipp: 5, 7 re., 13 li. & re., 32 li., 50 li., 102, 113, 123, 135, 147, 169, 179 u., 185 re., 194 re., 210 li. & re., 267, 303, 333, 344, 356 li., 374 li. & re., 400 li., 415, 417 li. & re., 429, 441 li. & re., 451, 454, 459, 463, 492, Architektengalerie außer Daniel Libeskind / Office for Metropolitan Architecture Rotterdam: 489 / Moore, Ruble Yudell Architects: 515 / Ribbe, Wolfgang/Schäche, Wolfgang (Hrsg.): Baumeister, Architekten, Stadtplaner. Biographien zur baulichen Entwicklung Berlins. Berlin 1987, S. 67: 18 re., S. 229: 74 re. / Sammlung Museen Preußischer Kulturbesitz (SMPK) Kupferstichkabinett: 38, 44 re. / Senatsverwaltung für Stadtentwicklung: 400 re., Seite 316-334 / Stephan Braunfels Architekten, Fotograf: Jens Weber, München: 488 / Stiftung Preußische Schlösser und Gärten Berlin-Brandenburg, Bildarchiv: 1 / Storch, Kaspar: 202 / Technische Universität Berlin, Plansammlung: 141 re. / Wolters, Rudolf: Albert Speer. Oldenburg 1943, Frontispiz: 225 li. / Verlagshaus Braun Archiv: 506, 514

Titelfotos: W. Gerling: Reichstagskuppel

NOTES

NOTES